NARRATIVES OF ATTACHMENT, DANGER AND SURVIVAL

NARRATIVES OF ATTACHMENT, DANGER AND SURVIVAL

Edited by

Linda Cundy

KARNAC

firing the mind

First published in 2026 by
Karnac Books Limited
62 Bucknell Road
Bicester
Oxfordshire OX26 2DS

British Library Cataloguing in Publication Data

A C.I.P. for this book is available from the British Library

ISBN: 978-1-80013-459-1 (paperback)
ISBN: 978-1-80013-464-5 (e-book)
ISBN: 978-1-80013-463-8 (PDF)

Typeset by vPrompt eServices Pvt Ltd, India

www.firingthemind.com

FSC www.fsc.org
MIX
Paper | Supporting responsible forestry
FSC® C011748

Karnac Books is committed to a sustainable future for our business, our readers, and our planet. This book is made from Forest Stewardship Council® certified paper.

Contents

Acknowledgements

Following the initial enthusiasm shown by many colleagues keen to contribute to *Narratives of Attachment, Danger and Survival*, this project has had a challenging journey that in some respects mirrors the experiences of those who struggle to start a new life. Sadly, some authors needed to withdraw for various reasons and there have been numerous delays. However, this has created opportunities to bring in new material that was not originally planned but that has added further depth to the content. Even so, it has also delayed completion. I would like to thank my author colleagues for their contributions, their support, and their patience.

Graeme Galton's expertise was invaluable in helping devise a contract that was sensitive to the complexities involved for Cora Hart, co-author with Nancy Borrett of a chapter about dissociative identity disorder, where it was essential for each alter to be committed to writing and publishing their experiences.

Struggling with my own difficulties in writing anything relevant and coping with the frustrations of numerous setbacks has been challenging. I have found motivation and inspiration through my conversations in particular with Annie Power, Maggie Turp, Charlotte Hastings,

Judy Davies, and Ruthie Smith. I am also grateful to my sister-in-law, Karen, who allowed me to stay in her summer house on the beautiful Danish island of Samsø for a writing retreat.

Thanks, too, to Kate Pearce at Karnac Books for her forbearance while we navigated the many complexities involved in completing this book.

About the editor and contributors

Nancy Borrett is an experienced psychotherapist, music therapist, and supervisor who has worked at the Clinic for Dissociative Studies (CDS UK) in London since 2011. She had previous experience in a variety of NHS settings and has a small private practice. Nancy also develops and delivers training about understanding and working with dissociative disorders to therapists, NHS teams, and other professionals. Based on collaboration with people who have lived experience, she hopes to promote ethical therapeutic practice, accurate understanding, and compassion for people with dissociative disorders. Nancy had a first career as a violinist and continues to find inspiration in music.

Charles Brown is a UKCP fellow, a member of the College of Psychoanalysts and Jungian Analysts (CPJA), and a member of the Arbours Association and an associate member of the Association of Group and Individual Psychotherapists. He is a member of the International Network of Democratic Therapeutic Communities (INDTC). He is an honorary Fellow at the British Association for Psychoanalytic and Psychodynamic Supervisors (BAPPS). Charles is an addictions therapist, qualified psychoanalytic supervisor and group facilitator, and a training therapist, trainer, and training supervisor.

He also maintains a small private practice in South London. He has a long-standing interest in identity and meaning.

Linda Cundy (editor) is a UKCP-registered, attachment-based psychoanalytic psychotherapist and clinical supervisor with a private practice in North London. Trained as a counsellor in the 1980s, Linda worked for a number of years for mental health services until retraining at The Bowlby Centre in the 1990s. She is also an independent trainer and conference speaker, nationally and internationally, specialising in attachment, human development, and clinical practice. Linda has curated, edited, and contributed to six books to date and is series editor for the Psychotherapy Matters books published by Karnac in association with UKCP.

Judy Davies graduated in communication studies and then worked in a variety of media-related jobs before training as a psychotherapist. Alongside her private practice she worked for a number of organisations including the Tavistock Clinic, ChildLine, and SANEline, and also as a school counsellor. Following this she joined an NHS mental health service, where she specialised in EMDR treatment for post-traumatic stress.

Cora Hart is a survivor of extreme abuse from a multi-generational organised criminal network within which she was born and raised. She has dissociative identity disorder, also known as DID. Long-term psychotherapy enabled her to escape. No longer being abused and controlled, she is discovering the joys and challenges of life with freedom and choice. Despite experiencing extreme trauma until midlife, Cora and her alters have achieved academically to a high level. They are strong defenders of human rights and dream of an inclusive world without violence or injustice. They draw strength from newly found close friendships, music, nature, and art.

Mary Kelly is an expert by experience. She comes from an army family, born in Athlone and educated in Cork, Ireland. A former nurse, carer, mother and grandmother, and law graduate, she works in a criminal law firm in London, and volunteers in the London refugee community kitchen and as an end of life doula. Gardening, along with political and social activism, saved her from total mental breakdown post cult. She worked as a nurse in occupied Palestine and helped set up a women's peace camp at Shannon airport prior to the invasion of Iraq in 2003. She is a member of the Family Survival Trust which supports people affected by cults, and campaigns for the law on coercive control to be amended so leaders of cults can be prosecuted for crimes against members.

Hyun Suk Lee (이현석) has worked as a psychotherapist and counsellor with a diverse range of people from primary school children to older people, in various organisational settings for the last fourteen years. He is also a specialist mental health mentor working with university students, and an integrative supervisor, facilitating a reflective space for the groups of trainee counsellors and student advisors. He holds an MA in analytical psychology, PgDip in psychodynamic therapy, and a diploma in integrative supervision. He is an accredited member of BACP, and a registered member of UKCP and FPC. Hyun is involved in organising and engaging with physical and creative therapeutic projects such as table tennis sessions and a singing group for the North Korean refugee community in London.

Zibiah Alfred Loakthar is a senior lecturer at the University of Essex where she co-directs the Centre for Trauma, Asylum and Refugees (CTAR). Zibiah is a course director for MA Refugee Care and supervises doctoral students in this field. She is Director of Equality Diversity and Inclusivity and Co-Director of graduate studies for the Department of Psychosocial and Psychoanalytic Studies, and sits on the University of Sanctuary committee and the Eastern Arc of Sanctuary Steering Group. Zibiah enjoys interdisciplinary research and fostering cross-sectoral and cross-cultural collaboration. As an oral historian, Zibiah has edited the journal *Oral History* and worked on life story projects in partnership with museums, libraries, charities, and community organisations. Her interviews with talking therapists are archived within the British Library's National Life Story Collection. Zibiah has many years of practical experience working within social justice and equality sectors with mainstream charities and with diverse minoritised communities, leading advocacy, arts, community development, disability, education, health, heritage, human rights, memory, oral history, and volunteering projects in London and in Ghana. She chairs front line charity Community Language Support Services, and also volunteers as a trustee for North London Deaf Children's Society and for the British Schools Museum.

Jacqueline Samuel is a therapist with nearly thirty years of experience, specialising in helping individuals navigate the complex impacts of leaving religions or faith groups. Based in Hertfordshire, she also supports clients dealing with addictions, depression, and anxiety. Her work is informed by her international experience, including time spent abroad and working with clients who have relocated to new countries. Jacqueline's deep understanding of attachment and trauma enriches her practice and her contributions to this compilation, including a chapter that explores the challenges and healing processes involved in leaving communities of faith.

Joe Secrett is a freelance youth worker with more than twenty-two years' experience supporting young people from inner city environments. For the past ten years, his focus has turned to serious youth violence and child criminal exploitation and he delivers specialist mentoring, group workshops, and professional training in this area, among others. He has seen, first hand, the impact of serious youth violence in his community and is passionate about making a positive impact on this in any way he can.

Ruthie Smith is a psychoanalytic psychotherapist (The Bowlby Centre), energy psychotherapist, and teacher, who is keen to integrate a spiritual perspective into her work. She has taught on psychotherapy training and supervision programmes and lectures at events and conferences in the UK and abroad. After ten years as a principal individual psychotherapist in the NHS supervising work with complex trauma, she established The Flame Centre in London specialising in trauma, and devised a post-qualification clinical training in energy psychotherapy, which she currently co-directs under the auspices of Energy Psychotherapy Training Ltd. Her book, *Energy, Soul Connecting and Awakening Consciousness: Psychotherapy in a New Paradigm* (2024) is published by Karnac.

Maggie Turp is a psychotherapist whose work draws on psychodynamic, attachment, and narrative perspectives. Her publications include *Psychosomatic Health: The Body and the Word* (2002), *Hidden Self-Harm: Narratives from Psychotherapy* (2004), and a number of journal papers. She is an active member of the Climate Psychology Alliance and contributes to the CPA therapeutic support service. She co-edits the climate psychology journal *Explorations*, and is sole editor of the "Cli-Fi Corner" section, which reflects her special interest in the ways in which fiction and autobiographical narratives help us to imagine and think through both current threats and losses and possible future scenarios.

Foreword

Maggie Turp

The first time I met Linda Cundy, we were speaking at the same conference—from an attachment-informed and object relations point of view respectively. Linda's warmth and enthusiasm for her subject shone through. Her firm grounding in attachment theory was evident and at the same time lightly worn: there was nothing doctrinaire about her presentation. On the contrary, her patients and their dilemmas came to life in the room as she spoke about them. I felt immediately that this was someone with whom I could have any number of conversations and come away each time feeling both that I had been heard and that my own understanding had been enriched. Over the fifteen or so intervening years, this has indeed turned out to be the case.

Linda's publications have the same qualities of liveliness, warmth, and quietly held erudition as were apparent to me when I first heard her speak. We read them for enjoyment and enlightenment rather than simply as essential items on a reading list—although they are that too. Linda and I share an understanding that it is primarily through the telling and retelling of self-narratives that new meanings and new possibilities come into view. Our training and experience as psychotherapists have acquainted us with the general shape of the terrain to be traversed, but the emphasis remains on the individual nature of each life trajectory.

In making sense of their experience and negotiating change, each patient must find their own way, negotiating dense thickets and steep upland paths, retracing their steps when resources are exhausted or obstacles become overwhelming, tracking back and starting over, often only to find themselves in an old familiar impasse, and nevertheless—with the therapist as support and guide—finding the courage to try again.

Nowhere are the vicissitudes of this journey clearer than in the carefully gathered and curated set of individual self-narratives that make up *Narratives of Attachment, Danger and Survival*. Many of the authors writing here are recounting their experience publicly for the first time. We are alongside them in the horrendous, sometimes life-threatening, situations in which they find themselves. We share with them the pain of their disillusion. We follow them in their efforts to extract themselves and embark on a journey of recovery. We celebrate their hard-won gains. We mourn with them that which is irretrievably lost—a familiar and loved environment, a close community, the never-to-be-recovered years without the children who had to be left behind.

Among the myriad examples of contested leave-taking that make up the book are some that will be relatively familiar—such as the difficulty of leaving a violent relationship, or the losses and gains associated with seeking refuge from one's country of birth—and others that we are less likely to have encountered—for instance, one woman's internal struggle with the dilemma of whether or not to leave a religious community, not because the good object has turned bad but because her sexuality would have to be suppressed in order to continue to belong. A common theme running through the diverse individual accounts is the speed and ease with which one can fall into a situation that subsequently reveals itself as restrictive and in some cases toxic and, by contrast, the painful and exhausting struggle involved in extracting oneself, the setbacks along the way, and the losses that are the price of regaining a measure of control over one's life.

The range of situations and the diversity of cultural backgrounds and ethnicities represented by the writers add further value to this highly readable book. In a world of psychotherapy still dominated by white, middle class European or US therapists, Linda has done us a great service in bringing a rich diversity of voices—Black British, Korean, Jewish, Irish—to the table. The chapters that make up the volume vary widely in both content and emphasis and yet perfectly complement one another. Where one includes a checklist of resources for those seeking to leave a toxic situation, another lists danger signals that might alert a potential victim in time for the situation to be avoided. Where one is focused on the ongoing process of recovery in the present and future, another looks back to early experiences and attachment patterns as the author searches for the roots of his or her vulnerability. Where one reflects on naivety and youthful idealism, another underlines the reality of the genuinely good things initially on offer, with the shadow side only becoming apparent, the trap only closing, when the individual has been drawn in.

The individual authors and the ways in which the narratives are presented are likewise varied and break new ground. (There are parallels here with Linda's previous edited book *Attachment, Relationships and Food: From Cradle to Kitchen*.) Some chapters take the form of an individual telling his or her own story. Others take an alternative form—a chapter co-written by psychotherapist and patient; a chapter on gangs presented as a dialogue between a psychotherapist and a youth worker; an account by a South Korean psychotherapist of his work with a North Korean person whose journey to seek refuge brought her to Britain, involving a thoughtful consideration of how social mores and politics find their way into the quasi-sacred space of the consulting room. Having to leave one's homeland—whether on account of persecution, war, climate heating, or environmental degredation—is a topic of ever-increasing relevance. "Large populations will need to migrate, and not simply to the nearest city, but also across continents" (Vince, 2022, p. 11). A moving and poetic chapter highlights the "philosophical existential discomfort about where 'there' and 'here' may be", adding further to our understanding of the challenge faced by persons seeking refuge far from home.

The myriad voices and ways of approaching the topic of contested leavings add up to a book that is—to borrow a phrase from Gestalt—much more than the sum of its parts. After the variety, the drawing together of the themes is deftly achieved by Linda in the final chapter, "Dangerous liaisons: Picking up the pieces". Here again, Linda's deep grounding in attachment theory shines through, yet her analysis is never doctrinaire. She invites the reader to explore with her, to think together with her, and always to hear the unique voice and experience of every individual.

This excellent and groundbreaking book—I can think of nothing quite like it in the library of either attachment theory or psychoanalysis—is erudite and moving. It is highly accessible, both to those of us working in the field of psychotherapy and to lay readers. I myself have learned a great deal from it and am delighted to have been invited to contribute a personal appreciation of its many merits.

References

Cundy, L. (Ed.) (2022). *Attachment, Relationships and Food: From Cradle to Kitchen*. London: Routledge.

Vince, G. (2022). *Nomad Century: How to Survive the Climate Upheaval.* London: Allen Lane.

Preface

Linda Cundy

Stories of defiance against oppressive regimes create a community of opponents who share the same abhorrence of stifling authoritarianism. In this sense, one may speak of a "storied community" which is the group of people who are joined together by certain shared narratives. A storied community provides the coherent narratives which are essential ingredients of resilience and offers a transitional space which can act as a secure base.

—Renos Papadopoulos, 1999, p. 332

It is around 10.30 p.m. one winter evening in 1992 and I've been working a late shift as a counselling supervisor at ChildLine, back then a twenty-four-hour telephone counselling service for young people in crisis or distress. I'm heading to the bus stop to go home, my ID lanyard still around my neck. There is a woman waiting for the bus with several young children; the eldest is a boy of maybe seven or eight. They are not adequately dressed for the time of year and look dishevelled. The mother seems intoxicated, or perhaps suffering from a mental health condition. She is shouting, swearing at her children, and threatening to hit them. As a ChildLine employee, whose job is to provide support to young people experiencing abuse, I cannot stand by and see her lash out at these youngsters. I speak up, expecting to elicit her rage. As tactfully as I can, I suggest that maybe the children are tired and becoming a handful, but that hitting them is not the best way to manage their behaviour.

As anticipated, the woman starts to scream at me, telling me to mind my own f***ing business, that she's well known to social services and the police—"They all know me!" But what takes me by surprise is the reaction of the eldest boy who steps in between his mother and me. "DON'T YOU SPEAK TO MY MUM LIKE THAT! IT'S NOTHING TO DO WITH YOU, YOU INTERFERING ****!"

This was the moment I fully understood the strong bond between a child and his or her parent, even an abusive one—or, perhaps, *especially* an abusive one—the complex cocktail of feelings aroused that might include fear of being hurt, fear of being abandoned and left alone in the world, but also love, protectiveness—and shame; Fairbairn's (1952) notion of the moral defence: "They would love me and care for me if I was not such a demanding, unlovable monster." This is "attachment to bad objects". With decades of clinical experience since that encounter, I now recognise that feeling ashamed of the caregiver is also often thrown in for good measure,

Attachment is a fundamental survival strategy. Most people survive infancy but many do not thrive; insecure attachment is adaptive but sets limits on flourishing. However, this is a book about attachment to bad, or suffocating, or dangerous "objects" in various guises that threaten thriving and even survival.

So how was it conceived? In the intervening years since those ChildLine days, following my training in attachment-based psychoanalytic psychotherapy, I have published several books, all multi-authored but curated and edited by me. I enjoy working with others on writing projects and have also supported authors as they prepared their own publications. So, when I was asked to meet with a woman who wanted advice about writing a piece for a psychotherapy readership, I agreed. That is how I came to meet Mary Kelly, expert by experience of being drawn into, living in, and eventually escaping, a cult. As I listened to her story and registered her desire to make her experience meaningful through educating others, I could sense my own engagement stirring and a conversation start up in my head: "This is so interesting.

What if I were to offer this …?" "Don't be crazy! You have so many other commitments! Don't you dare!" I remember the fateful moment that I explained to Mary which journals she might approach, and the advantages and disadvantages of each. Then, ignoring my own warning, I suggested another option; "Or you could write a chapter for a book." Mary's immediate response; "I'll write something for a book."

I have no personal or professional experience of cults but I was deeply impressed by Mary and an idea had been taking shape during that conversation: a collection of chapters about different kinds of danger and the challenges of leaving them behind. I immediately knew of several colleagues who might be interested in contributing and it seemed that each time I mentioned this project it enthused people and they then offered to write something too. The book began to take shape and themes to emerge. I could then identify gaps and seek out people with expertise in these areas. Along the way, we have lost some valuable chapters for various reasons, but gained other important contributions, often through chance conversations. We have become a "storied community".

Each chapter focuses on a particular kind of belonging—with an individual, to a family, group, or community. While some are born into these environments and their identities are entirely shaped within that context, others have made a choice to follow a specific path. Others still have had an identity, and thus a route through life, imposed upon them from outside; poverty, lack of opportunities, overstretched family resources, and racism condemn many to lives on the edge. Each of these scenarios raises different challenges when the attachment turns bad.

The paths we choose may alienate us from family and friends, who don't understand or approve. If things go wrong we may assume that we will not be welcomed back, and we may be right. There may also be a great sense of shame for making choices that turned out to be unwise—and about which we may have been warned.

How to tear away from the old perilous life, redefine oneself and grow into a new life, become one's own person, when society pigeonholes you and you face constant, continuing prejudice? Perhaps the status quo would be tolerable were it not for the toxicity.

How to walk away from, or escape from the only life that is familiar? Maybe severing links with family, friends, partners, children? And possibly with no connection to others outside who may understand and help? The attachment instinct has ensured our survival, as individuals and as a species. But ultimately, survival trumps attachment; in many of the situations described in this collection, survival—and any possibility of thriving—demands *detachment*. The unfamiliar, especially if faced alone, can hold further jeopardy.

Authors here describe different kinds of danger. For Jacqueline Samuel, it is not a risk to life, limb, or sanity, but the damage done to the self by hiding or denying a vital part of oneself, the risk of losing a loving relationship, and, ultimately, the danger of living in bad faith. She acknowledges what she had to give up, a meaningful way of life that provided security, structure, and purpose. Jacqueline's chapter beautifully examines the inner conflicts and external challenges, the gains and painful losses for her. There is no inference that the path she chose, Orthodox Judaism, is in itself a danger, but we do hear stories of people leaving various faith groups, especially in small communities, where this can lead to dire consequences: individuals expelled from their families, parents who "abscond" denied access to their children, shame tainting the whole family, younger family members' marriage opportunities impacted, and so on.

For Ruthie Smith, discovering that a spiritual group she had chosen and been fully committed to, which had given her so much of meaning, had been corrupted was profoundly distressing, but the real spiritual trauma was the violation of her trust. When deeply held values are contaminated in this way, how much of oneself feels tainted, and what can survive the sense of defilement?

Others experienced actual mortal danger through persecution, violence, perverse sexual slavery, and addictions. For addicts, the drug of choice, whether that is a substance or the cocktail of chemicals produced in the body by compulsive behaviours, becomes the tantalising but potentially lethal "attachment object". Initially, as with secure attachment, this provides pleasurable feelings but over time its effectiveness wanes—it becomes unreliable. All attention then becomes focused on regaining the craved experience to the exclusion of all other connections, the same pattern we see operating in coercive relationships.

Leaving, whether a partner, faith group, cult, addiction, gang, or homeland, entails a myriad of losses. This book contains two chapters, by Hyun Suk Lee, and Zibiah Loakthar, about the challenges faced by people who were ultimately able to make that decision to escape their homeland and have often survived perilous journeys to seek asylum elsewhere. The "bad object" they have fled may be oppression by a brutal regime, poverty, religious or cultural practices that victimise. In some cases, not only is the journey fraught with dangers but the reception on arrival is regrettably hostile and dehumanising.

Each of us is shaped by our relational ecosystem. We learn how to behave in culturally accepted ways, how to communicate our needs, which aspects of our personalities can be expressed and which repressed. This process, though most influential in the first years of identity formation, continues throughout life as we adapt to new relationships and situations—humans are, after all, the most adaptable of all Earth's creatures. I believe, too, that the very landscape of our early years—the colours, seasons, sights, smells and tastes, flora and fauna of our environment—exerts an influence on who we become. Some people choose to leave, for education, employment, adventure, or love, knowing they can return. Some are displaced or forced to evacuate due to wars, natural disasters and, increasingly, climate crises.

Generally, families and neighbours who escape en masse are housed, at least temporarily, together. Others, however, who find themselves the target of persecution or poverty in their homelands face many of the same dilemmas as those escaping other dangerous situations and ask themselves the same questions, and more. Is it *really* necessary to leave behind one's home, family, possessions? Maybe culture and language? Where to go, and what risks will have to be faced? And what kind of reception might be waiting? Will it be possible to make a new life elsewhere, and what might that look like? These situations are fraught with ambivalence and, as with other escapees, decisions are made or postponed while in a highly stressed state when clarity of thought may be impaired, or when lulled into passivity by denial. How immediate is the danger? Is this *really* a life-or-death situation? Does escape leave loved ones in danger? It may be easier to make that leap into the unknown if it is undertaken with others, or to protect one's children, or if there are family members elsewhere to meet them.

From those early days working for ChildLine, I remember hearing stories of the "lovely, good, kind daddy" who sometimes disappeared to be replaced by a "horrible monster". This technique for preserving in the mind a wholesome object of love by splitting into good and bad is equally evident in those who have experienced a "good, loving partner/leader/guru" who unpredictably transmogrifies into an unrecognisable, terrifying presence. Thus, leaving entails walking away from the idealised attachment figure as well as the manipulative, cruel one, giving up hope of recovering or repairing that relationship. As Judy Davies describes in her chapter, it is the promise of change, the reminders of loving times, the pleas of vulnerability, and the sense of one's own importance to the abusive partner that evoke hope. Giving up all hope is a big, painful ask; sometimes it has claimed decades of one's life.

Fear, of course, pervades all these narratives; fear of humiliation, condemnation, litigation. Fear of loss. Fear of death and eternal damnation. Measures taken to manage fear include denial, numbing oneself with substances, dissociation. Splitting the other into good and bad is an effective defence. Another is radically splitting the self into fragments, each holding only some memories. Dissociation is an extreme, and extremely primitive defence against overwhelm: "Dissociation is learned early. Later abuse or other traumas did not account for dissociative symptoms in young adults" (van der Kolk, 2015, p. 121).

In Chapter 5, psychotherapist Nancy Borrett and client "Cora Hart" discuss together, with interjections by some of Cora's alters, how the therapeutic frame needed to be adapted to take into consideration their dissociative identity disorder. As van der Kolk reminds us, radical dissociation is perhaps the earliest physiological protection, before the psychological defences of denial and repression become available. In Cora's dreadful experience, dissociation spared her from full awareness of the brutality of her existence. Skilful but perverse and sadistic "attachment figures" manufactured massive splits in her psyche to protect themselves; the child who went to school had no access to memories of what she endured at home. In such thankfully rare situations, psychotherapists need to go beyond the traditional therapeutic frame to prove themselves reliable, secure allies in order for the client to risk seeking freedom from their family and abuse group, whose tentacles appear to be everywhere. Nancy's work with Cora has challenged her on many occasions to extend the therapeutic boundaries in order to provide the secure base her client has so desperately needed.

One theme that emerges in these diverse chapters is that it can take numerous attempts to finally break free from a hostile environment; there is frequently more than one "last straw". Due to the addictive quality of toxic relationships, when "addicts" walk away, committed to getting "clean", they are vulnerable to being drawn back in.

Another thread running through these chapters is that leaving is not The End. Relationships are carried inside us as threatening voices, watching eyes, injunctions, temptations. It takes many years to "relocate the abandoned object", to adapt Bowlby's phrase about the outcome of mourning. During this time, if there is no strong bond to provide an anchor and give some shape to identity: "We do not know where we are going, just that where we have come from is disappearing. Our bodies are burning with the shame of not belonging, and the feeling of longing …" (Jason, online newsletter of Refugee Action, 2 March 2023). It does not help that society frequently views refugees and asylum seekers, ex-gang members, ex-cult members, and those with a history of addiction as pariahs. Necessary resources to help with integration and becoming useful members of the community are scarce. No one can do it alone—we all need someone to attach to, and something meaningful to live for.

My own chapter concludes the book, gathering themes that have emerged and proposing a therapeutic model for those who, like me, work with a diverse client group.

What I had not anticipated at the inception of this book was that many of my colleagues would choose to write autobiographical, rather than clinical, accounts. It has been harrowing to read their stories detailing painful experiences, sometimes of mental cruelty, racism and assault, violation of beliefs and values that caused deep psychic wounds, or simply feeling that a fundamental part of oneself is perceived as unacceptable by those we respect and identify with. It is also unusual for psychotherapists to openly share their own narratives, coming out from the shadows of professional anonymity to tell their personal histories. For each of the authors in this collection who made that choice, psychotherapists or not, sharing such personal information has been courageous. It has also proved to be significant in the long, ongoing process of recovery. Difficult memories have been revisited, old ghosts roused. Traces of unresolved trauma and loss have been reactivated. As painful as it has been to read their experiences, it was far more challenging for these authors to reconnect with past events and process them by putting them into words, weaving them into a coherent narrative. I am touched that they have been prepared to do so, and that they now feel safe enough to share them in this book. This is triumph over trauma, the "adversity activated development" (Papadopoulos, 2021) that Zibiah Loakthar references in her chapter. This is also what I noticed that first meeting with Mary Kelly.

Despite the very different form of oppression each describes, and the unique voice of each author, those who have contributed their narratives of attachment, danger, and ultimate survival have become a "storied community". I thank each of them for their courage—we can learn so much about attachment and its central role in human nature by exploring their stories of walking away from their previous lives, their people, everything that is familiar, and making a new beginning. And, following Mary Kelly, I hope these stories help each of us recognise that a helping hand and warm welcome can be all it takes to make a difference to those driven to escape persecution, oppression, and danger in all its forms.

References

Fairbairn, W. R. D. (1952). *Psychoanalytic Studies of the Personality.* London: Tavistock (reprinted London: Routledge, 2002).

Papadopoulos, R. K. (1999). Storied community as secure base: Response to the paper by Nancy Caro Hollander's "Exile: Paradoxes of loss and creativity". *British Journal of Psychotherapy, 15*(3): 322–333.

Papadopoulos, R. K. (2021). *Involuntary Dislocation: Home, Trauma, Resilience and Adversity-Activated Development.* London: Routledge.

van der Kolk, B. (2015). *The Body Keeps the Score: Mind, Brain and Body in the Transformation of Trauma.* London: Penguin.

CHAPTER 1

Breaking the bonds: Escaping a long-term abusive relationship

Judy Davies

"What has he got to do before you'll leave him—kill you?"

It was January 1989. I was with a counsellor in her office at the Elizabeth Garrett Anderson Hospital, London, desperately trying to work out if I could somehow save my marriage. I was also in a state of shock following the death of my father.

I had learned of my father's death a week before, after arriving home in the evening. But not immediately, as my husband—whom I will refer to as H (H for him, H for husband)—first ushered me to the local pub where we had several drinks and chatted as normal. It was only when we got back that he said, "You had better listen to the answerphone." I then heard my sister's message, reporting my father had been found dead at his nursing home after suffering a stroke.

It was hard to take in. And upsetting to realise that H had deliberately delayed telling me—perhaps because he didn't want to miss out on the pub, or maybe to put off having to deal with my reaction. In any case, he retreated to the bedroom while I went into our tiny kitchen and, tears streaming, poured myself some wine, refilling my glass repeatedly until the bottle was empty.

Two days later, H told me that I had done enough crying. It was time to move on.

From then on, his behaviour became increasingly unpredictable and threatening. He shouted down the phone at me when I rang him from Rymans in Tottenham Court Road to tell him they were out of stock of his favourite 2B pencils. He picked up a bowl full of washing up and hurled it at me across the kitchen because something I said (I have no idea what) offended him. And, on the morning of my father's funeral, when I woke him up at ten past eight instead of ten to eight, he again lost his temper, accusing me of ruining his day.

After the funeral, with the words of the counsellor in my head, I more or less decided to leave. I packed a small bag which I hid in the airing cupboard, waiting for a good moment to make my getaway.

Then, a day or so later, my mother went missing. She lived in a small village in mid-Wales, having divorced my father several years earlier. A neighbour had gone round to her house to find the door unlocked and no one in, and was now searching for her in the surrounding fields.

I was waiting by the telephone for the neighbour to report back, when I accidentally trod on the wire connecting the phone to the wall socket. When H saw this, he had a complete meltdown. "You could have cut off the phone!" he yelled, and listed the dire consequences: missing a vital call, loss of work, loss of income, everything falling apart.

This hysterical onslaught terrified me. Grabbing my purse, door keys, and an umbrella—it was pouring with rain outside—I managed to open the front door, then ran along the passageway and down the concrete steps into the courtyard below …

To go back to the beginning

When I first set eyes on H at the start of the academic year (we were both students at the same college in London), I took an instant dislike to him. He was in a conspiratorial cluster with other members of his year group who were gazing at him with slightly shocked admiration. He was holding forth and, although I was too far away to hear what he was saying, I was struck by how angry he looked.

I next became aware of him when I saw a poster with his photo on the wall of the students' union, announcing that he was standing to be union president. He was wearing dark glasses. How pretentious, I thought.

Our first encounter was at the students' union bar where we were both ordering drinks. I challenged him about the photo, to which he gave some witty and disarming reply. We then very quickly got into deep conversation. He was not as I had imagined. He had a sense of humour, he listened. In this and subsequent conversations I discovered we had much in common: had read the same books, seen the same films, shared many of the same cultural references.

H had previously been a student at the Sorbonne and had taken part in the May 1968 events, hurling paving stones and embracing the graffitied slogans of the Situationists: "Live without dead time", "I take my desires for reality because I believe in the reality of my ideas", "Be realistic—demand the impossible!"

His radicalism attracted me and also felt familiar. I had grown up in a communist household where debates about matters political and cultural were common currency. At the same time, H offered a welcome alternative to my parents' blinkered idealism and their dismissal of any criticism of the Soviet Union as Western propaganda.

But the recognition went deeper. H was, I now see, the quintessential Angry Young Man, straight out of John Osborne's *Look Back in Anger* (1957), and, like its hero Jimmy Porter, a provocateur, contemptuous of the mediocre, and resentful of those whom he perceived as having the advantages of class. This was also my father.

I had battled with my father throughout my teens, a relationship that was only marginally repaired later in life after he suffered his first stroke. My attachment to my mother was much more positive, but complicated by her severe depressions. At such times she completely retreated from daily life and only multiple electroconvulsive therapy treatments seemed able to bring her back. Her depressions alternated with manic episodes which could be highly disturbing as well as excruciatingly embarrassing.

There I was at twenty, disaffected with my family, unsure of myself and feeling adrift. And so, I was drawn to H who seemed purposeful, full of ideas, and, to my surprise, interested in me.

Our conversations happened on and off over the course of a year, always in the students' union bar. Sometimes he was there with his girlfriend. Each time we conversed I became more attracted to him, and I started to fantasise about us being together.

At the beginning of the next academic year, after a session in the union bar, I joined a small group of students going for a meal at a nearby Indian restaurant, the Agra in Whitfield Street, overlooked by the Post Office Tower. H was also in the group. After the meal, as we stood on the pavement outside, we linked hands. That was it. A week later he moved into my flat.

It is astonishing to me, even now, how quickly H took over my life. I initially experienced this as beneficial. He helped me with my studies, suggested books to read, involved me in various projects. We did everything together: listened to music, went to the cinema and art galleries, met up with friends, ate out in restaurants, and patronised almost every pub in the West End. It was exhilarating and I had never felt happier or so nurtured.

But, from quite early on, a disturbing undercurrent began to threaten my sense of well-being. We had arranged to meet in Store Street in Bloomsbury, a turning off Tottenham Court Road. I walked up and down several times trying to locate it, becoming more and more anxious. When I eventually arrived, I was forty-five minutes late. H was furious. He shouted at me for keeping him waiting and refused to listen when I explained why.

The intensity and venom of his outburst was incomprehensible. In a state of emotional numbness, I compartmentalised the whole episode and wrote it off as an anomaly. And for a while, normal life resumed.

Some months later, another incident occurred. We were in the Underground waiting for a train when H, seemingly out of the blue, suggested we should get married. "But why?" I asked. At that moment there was a gust of wind from the approaching train. As it emerged from the tunnel, H took hold of me by the shoulders and pushed me towards the track. It was only at the last moment that he pulled me back. I was in deep shock. Something inside me collapsed, as if part of me had been annihilated.

I was now living in two parallel worlds: the first, the world as I wanted it to be, the second, too distressing to contemplate. I found myself agreeing to marry H. We went ahead with our plans and let our families and other people know. H joked about it: "We're only getting married to annoy our hippy friends."

Not long after this, and before we got married, H, his brother, his brother's girlfriend, and I were having drinks at my sister's wedding reception. H began to mock the other guests, deliberately raising his voice. I must have shown my discomfort because his brother's girlfriend said, "Oh, come on, H. Can't you see you're upsetting Judy?"

His expression suddenly changed and he dragged me outside. He was shaking with fury. "How dare you fucking show me up?"

I managed to free myself and ran down to the main road, trying to conceal myself in the doorway of a shop. The next thing I remember H had caught up with me and banged my head hard against the wall. I literally saw stars.

In the coming days a huge bruise and bump appeared on my forehead and I had swollen eyes with dark circles underneath from crying. When I looked in the mirror, I could barely recognise the person I saw reflected back.

Similar episodes followed, becoming more frequent after we got married. I tried to persuade myself that they were isolated and untypical events, and clung to the hope that things would get better. My body told a different story. There was never a time when I was free from bruises, some fresh, some fading.

H's physical attacks were nightmarish and sadistic. Fuelled by adrenalin, his face became distorted with rage, resembling the demonic transformation of Dr Jekyll into Mr Hyde. His expression was atavistic, his teeth bared: I was the prey about to be devoured. "Leave me alone," I would plead as he pinned me against the wall or struck out at me. But verbal protest and physical resistance were useless as they only upped the ante and inevitably increased the level of violence.

On one occasion, to avoid his blows, I managed to lock myself inside the bathroom. "Open the door, you fucking bitch," he screamed. I heard the door panel crack as he threw his weight against it and the lock gave. Once inside, he pushed me so hard that I fell into the bath, my head hitting the taps. But H was more concerned about the split in the door: "Look what you fucking made me do."

Despite the intensity of these attacks, I think H was able to measure how much force he exerted, whether it was pushing, striking or, on one occasion, driving the car at me. I was too essential to his own life for him to want to end mine.

To escape danger, I often took flight. I would stay away for hours, hoping that his rage would dissipate by the time I got home. A couple of times, I caught a bus, staying on until the terminus, then making the return trip. Other times, I would get on a Circle Line train, barely noticing the names of the stations as they went by: Tower Hill, Monument, Embankment, Victoria, South Kensington, Baker Street, Farringdon, all the way round to Tower Hill, then round again. Huddled in my seat, I tried to blot out the other passengers, hoping to avoid their scrutiny. I felt isolated and miserable. Often when I returned home, I would find the front door locked against me and would hover in the dimly lit hallway outside, staring at the Artex walls. Then at some point, often the early hours of the morning, I would hear the latch click and I would be allowed in.

Another ritual would then begin:

H: Apologise.
Me: I don't think—
H: Apologise.
Me: But I haven't—
H: Apologise.
Me: [*Reluctantly*] I'm sorry.
H: OK. Now tell me what you've done wrong.

All the while H held me in a vice-like grip, until eventually I relented and tried to find the right words to pacify him. I hated this as it felt like a betrayal of myself, but it was the only way I could escape and return to some kind of normality.

The following day there would often be an act of contrition, though never an explicit apology. On one such occasion, H brought me breakfast on a tray with the following note:

> *Transworld Enterprises*
> *Bill for Royal Breakfast No 5*
> I Grapefruit—no moaning for 1 week.
> Brown sugar—3 gay smiles.
> Cost of transporting cigarettes—10 kind looks.
> Marmite—friendly gestures.
> Toast—a sigh of pure love.

Individual pot of tea—one kiss, forehead variety.
Arrangement & decoration fee—a lingering embrace.
Total—No moaning for one month.
Compliments of the Chef

I was disarmed. I buried my misgivings. I forgave him.

Along with this alternating hostile and loving behaviour, H took control of almost every aspect my life. Everything I did came under scrutiny: the way I dressed, the way I spoke, the way I walked, my body shape, my views. I found myself increasingly unable to think for myself.

H kept tabs on my whereabouts and activities at all times. If we were apart, even for a few hours, he insisted on me calling him, and would throw a tantrum if I didn't ring at the appointed time. I spent many hours in telephone boxes—no mobile phones then—and can still recall their distinctive smell of disinfectant mixed with urine.

Being tired or unwell was not tolerated. On one occasion when I said how exhausted I felt after a day at work, H replied, "If you're not fucking well, go to the fucking doctor." He then frogmarched me to the GP's surgery. I saw the doctor on my own, while H remained in the waiting room, but found myself unable to answers his questions or explain why I was so upset. The doctor, clearly frustrated, gave up.

Another time, when I told H I was feeling sick during a visit to a pub in Charing Cross Road, he insisted I needed fresh air and forced me across the road to the deserted area at the base of Centrepoint. Here he made me run up and down several times between two concrete posts until he felt I had learned my lesson

H also put huge pressure on me to borrow money to fund our various joint writing and music projects and a lifestyle we could not afford. Advances from publishers and my full-time salary were never enough. Final demand notices began to regularly drop through the letterbox. I borrowed from anyone I could, including relatives and work colleagues, as well as getting a huge overdraft from the bank. Always short of cash, H also insisted I sell anything of value, including my eighteenth-century Italian violin.

I was not allowed to challenge any of this. If I mentioned that something had upset me, H would say, "That's typical of you, bearing a grudge, dragging up the past." And so, the usual script was reinforced: I was the wrongdoer while he was the person being wronged. In this way, the roles in our relationship were established. I was conditioned into being submissive, available to H at all times, dependent on his approval.

Unable to express how I felt, my distress tended to manifest in physical symptoms. My lip would start to quiver uncontrollably or I would have a facial tic. I also suffered regular crushing migraines. To deaden the emotional pain, I would at times resort to alcohol, for example sneaking a bottle of vodka into my workplace and taking small sips throughout the day.

Most people who knew us, including family, had no idea what was happening. We were seen as a particularly close and successful couple. And, unable to imagine my life without H, I felt I had to keep up the pretence.

But concealment, both from myself and others, was not always possible.

During the 1980s we lived in a council flat a stone's throw from the River Thames. The walls were sufficiently thin to hear our immediate neighbour and her young son through the bedroom wall, especially when we woke up in the morning. I particularly remember them singing along with the radio to Pink Floyd's "Another Brick in the Wall".

I was charmed by this until I realised that if we could hear them so clearly, they could also hear us. When I met my neighbour in the corridor—our front doors were adjacent—I put on a friendly face, as did she, and we exchanged greetings. At the same time, I experienced a deep shame wondering what she must think of me.

Another neighbour, a middle-aged man, approached me in the local pub when I was at the bar ordering drinks (it was always me who bought the drinks). He told me he had seen H in our local park grabbing my bag from my shoulder and emptying the contents onto the ground. I was mortified and struggled to respond.

More humiliating still was when my car was stopped by two policemen as I was driving across Westminster Bridge. H, who had never learned to drive, was in the passenger seat. They told me to get out of the car and drew my attention to the missing petrol cap. Then I noticed one of them pointing at my face and making a comment to his colleague.

I suddenly became conscious of my black eye which must have been visible despite the thick make-up I had applied. They both started laughing. When I got back in the car, unable to say anything to H, I felt more alone than ever.

As happened so often, I suppressed my feelings and got on with the demands of daily life.

Leaving—the first time

My denial of the real nature of my relationship with H was suddenly tested when I happened to hear an interview on the radio with Dr Susan Forward, an American psychologist. She was talking about her recent book *Men Who Hate Women and the Women Who Love Them*. At first, I didn't relate to what she was saying. After all, H didn't hate me, he loved me, and said so often. And I had never thought of him as a misogynist—he had women friends, admired many women writers, was ideologically on the side of feminism. But then came a moment of recognition as she described men who were excessively possessive and controlling, and whose behaviour, seemingly loving, could suddenly switch.

As soon as I could, I hunted out a copy of the book. It contained the following checklist:

- Does he assume the right to control how you live and behave?
- Have you given up important activities or people in your life in order to keep him happy?
- Does he devalue your opinions, your feelings, and your accomplishments?
- Does he yell, threaten or withdraw into angry silence when you displease him?
- Do you "walk on eggs" rehearsing what you will say so as not to set him off?
- Does he bewilder you by switching from charm to rage without warning?
- Do you feel confused, off-balance or inadequate with him?
- Is he extremely jealous and possessive?
- Does he blame you for everything that goes wrong in the relationship?

(Forward & Torres, 1987, p. 10)

I was able to tick off every item. That was a shock. I had known at some level that much of H's behaviour was unwarranted and damaging, but seeing it spelt out like this threw everything into turmoil.

The book contained the testimonies of many women in situations similar to my own. Also, advice on what to do. This included being assertive and calling out unacceptable behaviour, for example stating, "I am not prepared to put up with this." There was also a warning that if such challenges triggered further harmful behaviour to put personal safety first and, if necessary, leave.

After reading the book, I started tentatively to put some of the advice into practice. But H became highly belligerent each time I tried to raise my concerns, making it clear that any challenge to his power was non-negotiable.

At that stage I felt unclear about the way ahead. Then events took their own course.

It was a normal day. We were walking past St Martin-in-the-Fields church, on our way to Embankment Tube, when H took offence at something I said and launched into a verbal attack. I felt an overwhelming need to get away. To my relief, H didn't follow. With no conscious plan, I made my way up Charing Cross Road, then into Berwick Street, and finally Marshall Street. I found myself outside the Samaritans—I must have seen the sign many times as we were frequent visitors to the Cranks restaurant opposite. I located the entrance and rang the bell.

I was assigned a volunteer who showed me just the right amount of warmth and concern. For the first time I was able to open up and talk about my life with H: the violence, the denigration, the humiliations.

"Do you think he will change?" she asked.

"I don't think so."

"Well, I'm not supposed to give you advice, but, if I were you, I would leave him."

We talked further. She explored whether there was anyone I could ask for help. I mentioned my aunt who lived in North London and was then able to telephone her. With no hesitation, my aunt invited me round.

It was a relief to tell my aunt what had been going on. To her credit she didn't pass judgement, but she wasn't surprised—she already had the measure of H. She arranged for me to stay with her son and daughter-in-law who lived nearby, and meanwhile let H know I would not be back that evening. He was, my aunt told me, monosyllabic at the end of the phone.

The following day, I rang H to tell him that I had decided not to return home. He was in a desperate state and the conversation was torturous. He pleaded with me to come back, reminding me of the publishing contracts we had yet to fulfil. I compromised and agreed to meet him in a café in the West End, just to sort out practicalities.

When we met, H played his trump card. His sister, who had recently survived a suicide attempt, was coming to visit. He piled on the moral pressure, telling me I needed to be there when she arrived, insisting that I couldn't let her down.

As I write this, I am shouting to my younger self, "Don't do it!" But I persuaded myself that if I made it clear to H that my return was conditional on him changing his behaviour, things could get better. I suppose, at this point, I still imagined him capable of changing. And so, I went back to our flat.

That was my rationale at the time. Now, I see that I was drawn back by the belief that my very existence depended on my being with H. Not unlike Cathy in Emily Brontë's *Wuthering Heights* (1847), when she exclaims, "I am Heathcliff!"

Some weeks after my return, I wrote the following poem:

> A fuzzy ether
> charged with mission and misery
> where our souls united
> particle for particle
> where eyes averted
> mouth devouring
> you bludgeoned
> my cowering heart …

The following year was one of the most difficult in my life. There was an uneasy truce between us and for the most part H moderated his temper—certainly there were no overtly violent attacks. We resumed our old pattern of life, discussed work, took on new projects, signed new contracts. But it felt so wrong. I felt oppressed, coerced into doing things. My attachment to H was damaged and I felt an increasing antipathy towards him.

Who knows how long the situation would have continued had it not been for the death of my father, setting off the events described at the start of this chapter and leading to my second attempt to leave.

Leaving—the second time

To resume: terrified by H's violent outburst as I waited by the phone, I took flight. Outside, the rain was coming down in large diagonal sheets and I hastily put up my umbrella. I heard H's footsteps coming up behind me, but he ran past, not realising it was me. I managed to dodge round a corner and out of sight. Then, heart pounding, I made my way to the Tube, leaving my old life behind.

My aunt found me a temporary place to stay in the home of one of her friends, Joan, who lived with her husband Alf in Child's Hill, North-West London. They generously welcomed me into their household. At breakfast, I joined in the daily ritual of completing the *Guardian* crossword. And Joan and I really hit it off. We had animated conversations on many topics, often into the small hours. Joan was an accomplished pianist and I loved hearing her play, the sounds of the piano resonating through the house.

I stayed at Joan and Alf's into the early spring. Outside the house a beautiful magnolia tree came into bloom. Slowly I began to reconstruct my life. I found a flat share. I managed to get some freelance media work, writing and interviewing. I formed new friendships.

The presence of H still loomed over this period. We had a number of outstanding publishing contracts and so I agreed to meet with him in various cafés and public places to complete the work.

Each time we met H exerted pressure on me to go back to him. He said I was killing him, describing the heart palpitations he had experienced after I left. Then he threatened to kill himself. When I refused to be drawn in, he said, "I know where you live and there are such things as letter bombs."

He also tried to win me back with gifts and cards, often inscribed with affectionate messages. I particularly remember a postcard of Rembrandt's *The Jewish Bride*. The portrait shows a man embracing his wife. He is looking down at her devotedly, one hand on her shoulder, the other encircling the lower half of her breast. You belong to me, his pose suggests. Her eyes are slightly downcast, her expression docile and dutiful. To me, the image signified not just a bond, but bondage. It sickened me. I couldn't wait to get rid of it.

Another challenge came when we were booked to appear on ITV's *This Morning* with Richard and Judy to promote our most recent book. This was broadcast from the Royal Albert Dock in Liverpool.

We travelled up by train the evening before and arrived, as arranged, at the hotel. I had informed our publisher that H and I had separated and required a room each, but it turned out only one had been reserved. The receptionist was confused, especially as she understood that we were married. H meanwhile was saying, "No, the double room is fine," pressurising me to share with him. I persisted and managed to get my own room, but this battle of wills was exhausting. Added to this, I now couldn't bear to be anywhere near him.

Appearing on the show was a surreal experience. I remember seeing the weatherman relaying the forecast from a floating replica of the British Isles, before being taken to make-up and then on set. On air we were introduced as husband-and-wife team, H and Judy. It caused some amusement in the studio given that we were being interviewed by Richard and Judy, also husband and wife. The interview itself was all very upbeat. Meanwhile I was excruciatingly aware of the disjuncture between appearance and reality.

I was relieved when our joint projects came to an end. I no longer had to see H, though I still received a number of letters from him via my solicitor. In one he wrote: "I know sometimes things were hard for you, but that can change. Come back. We can have a baby together ..." Difficult to put into words how outrageously offensive I found this.

Recovering

As I set about establishing my new life, I experienced a number of post-traumatic stress symptoms. These included a prolonged period of restless nights and recurring nightmares. Often, they would feature H's face looming over me as I struggled to get away. Or he would appear as an intruder trying to force his way into the house, sometimes succeeding.

Despite this, my overriding feeling at this time was one of liberation.

There was, however, still some unfinished business.

I had taken nothing with me when I left the flat and, although my aunt had picked up a few clothes, there were other items I was anxious to retrieve. Most important were my family photos which I had requested from H on several occasions and which he had repeatedly refused to hand over.

An opportunity arose when I learned that he was going to be away for the day at his sister's wedding. I went over to the flat, accompanied by a friend for moral support—luckily, I still had my keys. Everything was covered in a thick layer of dust and, as I went from room to room, I was surprised to find many of my personal belongings in exactly the same position as on the morning I had left, my toothbrush and make-up bag in the bathroom, my clothes still hanging over the chair in the bedroom. "Bloody hell," my friend said. "It's like Miss Havisham in *Great Expectations*."

I eventually found my family photos and some essential documents. As we left the building, I bumped into two women who lived in the same block. "Thank God", one of them said, "you're alive. We thought he must have killed you."

Not long after I received a letter from H who had spotted my finger-prints in the dust. He was outraged. How dare I come to the flat in his absence and without his permission, the least I could have done was ask him, and so on … a long diatribe. I ignored it.

Breaking the bonds

I was determined to divorce H but decided it would be easier to wait for two years and divorce by mutual consent. Meanwhile I decided to change my name by deed poll. Given my problematic relationship with my father, I didn't want to revert to my maiden name and, in the end, chose my mother's maiden name.

When the two years were up, I instructed my solicitor to start divorce proceedings and the relevant papers were sent to H. Weeks passed and he did not respond. She then advised me to sue for divorce on the grounds of unreasonable behaviour. Sitting in her office in Kings Cross, I described some of the more harrowing incidents. She wrote them down verbatim on a yellow legal pad. It felt strange to be narrating such highly charged and shameful moments in these impersonal surroundings. A document was prepared and sent to H, but with the option of signing the original papers. Faced with this choice, he signed.

After the decree absolute came through, I continued to reconstruct my life. This included reclaiming the places in London where H had vented his fury so they no longer felt contaminated by his presence. I was beginning to feel safe in the world.

And then ...

I became a Samaritans volunteer, partly as a way of saying thank you for the help I had received. It felt like a good fit and, given my family and relationship history, I could relate to many of the callers. I learned a great deal from my Samaritans colleagues, though I did notice the impatience expressed by one or two about women who stayed with abusive partners: "Why doesn't she just leave?" they asked.

This attitude, I noticed, was fairly widespread and made me reticent about sharing my own story. I didn't want to be judged, especially as I noticed that women (and men, for that matter) were often blamed and pathologised for staying in abusive situations, as if there were some inherent flaw in their character. I also didn't want to be seen as a victim.

I became interested in training as a psychotherapist and enrolled in an introductory course. At the same time, I began therapy sessions, and started to talk about what I had been through. Unfortunately, the therapist, a trainee, was visibly overwhelmed by what I was describing—I can still picture the panicked look on her face. Her supervisor was involved and the sessions came to an abrupt end.

I went on to do a psychotherapy training. Through this I was introduced to the work of John Bowlby on attachment and an emerging body of research and clinical material on trauma, including the writings of van der Kolk, Judith Herman, and Sandy Bloom. It was here I came across the notion of trauma bonding and an explanation of why abusive situations can be so difficult to leave.

I became familiar with a number of psychological terms describing the feeling states I had experienced: hypervigilance, denial, dissociation, depersonalisation, derealisation, somatisation—all defences to counter threat and emotional distress. This was very validating as it indicated that my past responses to H had a rational explanation, however irrational and inexplicable they might seem.

From the literature on trauma, I learned that when individuals are subjected to danger, feelings and bodily impulses take over, shutting down the thinking part of the brain. This is to enable more primitive and instinctive survival mechanisms to come into play, including fight–flight and freeze–submit responses. The body's nervous system takes over. Adrenaline helps prepare the body for action, increasing the heart rate and respiration and causing muscles to tense. Alternatively, if submission is the only option, other chemicals slow down the heart rate and respiration, leading to exhaustion, weakness, shaking, and physical collapse.

Because the frontal lobes shut down in dangerous situations, traumatic memories are difficult to access and process. Instead, they remain unprocessed in the amygdala—the brain's emotional centre, and in the body. And because they are not time-coded they can be easily retriggered: by a sound, a smell, a gesture …

No wonder the recipients of abuse can find it difficult to make sense of what they are experiencing and can so easily be caught in a repeating cycle of violence and submission.

It is now understood, through the work of John Bowlby and subsequent attachment research, that attachment systems are primary and linked to survival itself. Being subjected to fear increases the need for attachment, especially when no alternative attachment figure is available, allowing the bonds of an abusive relationship to become even stronger.

Becoming aware of this made sense of my own experience. My need to appease H came from my fear of losing him, believing that only by making him happy could I be happy. I could now understand how H took advantage of this, fine-tuning his coercive and controlling behaviour until I was conditioned to behave as he wanted me to.

From theory to practice

The insights gained through my training and reading became central to my work with clients. Later on, I completed a training in EMDR (eye movement desensitisation and reprocessing). With its focus on the effects of trauma on mind, brain, and body, EMDR proved invaluable in my clinical practice, providing safe and effective protocols for accessing and processing traumatic memories.

Among my clients there were many (mostly women) who had experienced domestic abuse. I found this challenging and often complex work, especially when there were ongoing threats to safety, children involved, or complications because of police, social services, or family courts involvement.

This work inevitably had an emotional impact on me and sometimes reactivated my own traumatic memories. But I found it helpful to draw on my own experience, and especially rewarding when individuals were able to make the transition from despair to hope.

Some cases stand out, especially that of a woman who was referred to me after her ex-partner tracked her down to her new house and shot their seven-year-old daughter on the doorstep.

Such catastrophic endings are far from unique. According to Helena Kennedy, in Britain 1.4 million women a year are known to suffer domestic abuse, and there are likely to be many more. Half of all female murder victims are killed by a current or former husband or lover, and on average nearly two women die as a result of domestic violence each week. None of this is helped by what she describes as "an unsympathetic and obstructive criminal justice system" (Kennedy, 2019). The recent report of Louise Casey (March 2023), describing the Metropolitan Police as "institutionally misogynistic", also shows how far there is still to go.

I first became aware of H in 1970 when we were both students, the same year that Germaine Greer's *The Female Eunuch* (1970) was published. It is sobering to reflect that domestic abuse continues to have a devastating effect on millions of women across the world, often reinforced by institutional, political, and religious structures.

Concluding thoughts

This is the first time I have told my story in any detail. For various reasons, including timing and life's other complications, it wasn't something I was able to do in my own therapy. It has therefore been quite an experience to revisit my relationship with H here.

Bringing it to mind at this stage in my life has stirred up some residual trauma. I notice that H has once again appeared in my dreams and is certainly present in my thoughts. Picturing him, I can feel my throat constricting, a knot in my stomach, a sensation of nausea. Also, shame and guilt and some nagging questions: Why did I allow myself to be so totally dominated by H, to do his bidding, even when it felt completely wrong? And why did it take so long—more than seventeen years in all—to finally leave him? Hopefully this chapter goes some way to answering these questions.

I am now able to forgive my younger, more malleable self, the person who became intoxicated by love and for a while—undoubtedly too long—lost herself.

I accepted a long time ago that it is not within my power to make H take responsibility for the harm he did. But I have been able to take responsibility for myself and how I live my life.

I am a different person now. I am no longer a victim. I can speak with my own voice, make my own choices and mistakes, initiate my own projects and adventures, make wiser decisions about the relationships I have. I am my own person.

References

Baroness Casey of Blackstock DBE CB (March 2023). Review: Final Report. An independent review into the standards of behaviour and internal culture of the Metropolitan Police Service. https://met.police.uk/SysSiteAssets/media/downloads/met/about-us/baroness-casey-review/update-march-2023/baroness-casey-review-march-2023a.pdf (last accessed 1 May 2023).

Brontë, E. (1847). *Wuthering Heights.* Ware, UK: Wordsworth Classics, 1992.

Forward, S., & Torres, J. (1987). *Men Who Hate Women and the Women Who Love Them.* New York: Bantam.

Greer, G. (1970). *The Female Eunuch.* London: MacGibbon & Kee.

Kennedy, H. (2019). *Misjustice: How British Law Is Failing Women.* London: Vintage.

Osborne, J. (1957). *Look Back in Anger.* London: Faber & Faber.

CHAPTER 2

Obair idir lámha—a work in progress: The journey of recovery from an abusive therapy cult

Mary Kelly

Introduction

There are numerous kinds of cults: religious, spiritual, political, therapy, business, psychedelic, personal growth, wellness, and even sport-based, and can range in size from two persons to international members of millions. It is estimated that there are 1500–2000 operating in the United Kingdom, according to the Family Survival Trust (FST), a UK charity that supports people affected by cults. Many people find it hard to understand how intelligent individuals are drawn into such coercive groups, blaming bad upbringing and loss of religious faith that leads to people searching elsewhere for meaning and purpose. As a former cult member, I hope to help de-stigmatise those ordinary people who get drawn in, inform readers about how cultish groups operate and gain control over members, the obstacles to leaving physically, and the enormous psychological journey back to a reasonably healthy non-cultic way of feeling and experiencing the world. I'm hopeful this will help people with loved ones still in cults and be informative for those supporting survivors to rebuild their lives after leaving. The process of leaving a cult is colossal and the task of surviving and building a new life Herculean. I dedicate this chapter to my children, who are the most courageous people I've ever met.

What led me to get involved in a cult?

As part of my nursing training in a Cork hospital in 1972 I had to do six weeks' psychiatric secondment in Our Lady's Hospital, aka "the Mad House". A grey Gothic building overlooking the city, it was built around the time of the Great Hunger (the Irish Famine—*an gorta Éireannach*) in 1850 to house 2,500 patients, lunatics as they were called then. The experience of seeing humans living in such degrading conditions was shattering. Due to adverse social conditions, these vulnerable people, many with what we now call learning difficulties, anxieties, and depressive states such as postnatal depression, were sentenced to this hellish place. No curtains, no seats on toilets, no activities, broken windows, no privacy, no comfort, locked up in vermin-infested unsanitary confinement. Half-naked or dressed in ragged clothes, gibbering and making obsessive repeated movements, rocking, scratching, crying and screaming, yellow-skinned from doses of drugs now banned. Many were restrained physically. The stench of urine was pervasive, the atmosphere of captivity and hopelessness overpowering. We student nurses were locked in with these patients twelve hours a day. One fateful morning I was co-opted to assist doctors giving ECT (electroconvulsive therapy). No anaesthetic was used. It was terrifying to witness. I had no reference point as to why these poor people were condemned to such a grim place in the care of brutish attendants. Images of Dante's Inferno from *Paradise Lost*, which I had studied two years previously for my Leaving Certificate, matched what I was seeing. Though there were shared horror stories with my peers, there was no debriefing to help us understand anything about this mind-bending experience when we returned back to our general hospital. We were not socialised to ask questions, such as why must it be like that?

Within some weeks after this placement I had a breakdown and was admitted to a more modern psychiatric hospital. I was unable to understand or communicate about the sudden drastic change in my personality. Numb to all my previous interests, I was given medication for depression. It didn't occur to me to speak about working in the asylum which had deeply affected me. No one asked what had happened, the focus was on what was "wrong with me". It was "just another" tough learning experience that had to be borne during nursing training. A very supportive, loving relationship I had had with someone for five years also came to an end at that time. How I managed to return to training and sit my final exams is a mystery. Only now can I see how these events severely impacted my mental health and well-being.

A few years later I experienced depression again after the birth of my first child. At that time I was an unmarried mother. Though I had some support, I felt vulnerable and afraid, unable to break through the depression, scared to go for professional help. I knew by now the only help available was through the Catholic Church or the psychiatric institutions. I had read about and was drawn to emerging new therapies of that time, such as Arthur Janov's (1970) primal scream therapy and saw an advertisement for a "primal therapy commune". Before visiting, I read the recommended book by the commune leader documenting her very interesting therapy with a well-respected therapist. The leader, a thirty-seven-year-old Englishwoman, had set up a group in London encouraging people to take control of their therapy and not leave it to professionals. In soundproofed rooms, screaming therapy was used as the way to express childhood traumas. The group moved to a remote island off the Irish coast in the 1970s and advertised in alternative publications like *Spare Rib* and *Diggers and Dreamers*, attracting many to visit and learn about communal living, growing food, home education, home births, and smallholding skills. I was interested in learning these skills, but above all I was desperate to break out of crippling depression and hoped to learn how to communicate my feelings. Having once been outgoing socially and someone who loved sports, I was very quiet, with little self-confidence when I first visited. I didn't trust institutions or experts, and the anti-authoritarian counterculture impression of the commune was attractive. Like many other members, I was a bit of an idealist and wanted a better world, for my children especially. No one joins a cult; we join a group that says it is offering a way of life that will meet our needs on many levels. Little did I realise I would end up having every aspect of my life micromanaged by a charismatic bullying cult leader.

The public image was of a radical therapy commune that claimed to prize honesty and openness, and with a deep commitment to "get to know our true selves". In later years, when we relocated to South

America, the image changed to the latest "in thing"—saving the rainforest and protecting human rights. However, the reality was completely different. Under the guise of group therapy and getting in touch with our feelings, extreme violence was provoked and encouraged by the leader. Couples and families were split up and set against each other. There was no friendship or solidarity between members; we were pitted against each other and could never challenge the leader. Ironically, for someone who professed to be passionately interested in therapy, the leader never got to know herself as she was not challenged for being a manipulative bully who incited hatred, and encouraged verbal, physical, and sexual assault. She never earned money, but skilfully extorted it, and property, from members. All properties and land bought with money donated by members remains with her and her family to this day. Thus far she has not been prosecuted for any of these crimes.

How I became attached to this group

Though shocked and frightened by the extreme physical and verbal violence, I accepted what I was told—that this confrontational therapy was the only way out of my depression. I swallowed whole that these were the only people in the world who would show me my "true self", and that it was an act of real caring to confront me. Like all survivors of abuse and coercive control, I did anything the leader wanted. Everything about my life and my children's lives was subject to her control.

We were all branded as "fucked up" and, like all cult members, were led to believe we were special, the only people in the world actively facing our own demons, and that the leader was a pioneering psychotherapist who wanted to change the world. We engaged with and contributed to many environmental and humanitarian projects, but there was a dark side to this activism. Saving the rainforest, "educating" campesinos about sustainability, buying land for displaced refugees, being a voice for the families of the disappeared were among these good causes. Trying to right injustice is never-ending and all absorbing, and can make one feel useful and righteous. So much harder to fight the immediate injustices happening "at home".

Commune life was about endless hard physical labour, screaming therapy, group therapy, sex therapy. It was normal to witness blood curdling expressions of extreme hatred and threats of wanting to kill. Everything we did was manipulated and coerced, and informed consent or free choice was not allowed. Even sexual partners were chosen for us, and we were punished and humiliated when we didn't comply. Couples had to report details of their sexual relationships in the morning group therapy, alongside the daily work of breakfast being cooked, wood chopped, laundry washed, cows milked, clearing fields to plant crops, and many other endless farming chores. The leader would analyse the reported details and insist on confrontational exchanges which were very frightening. She had to be entertained, her loud laughter an indicator she was savouring the violence.

Brainwashing and thought reform

Research and testament from survivors of other cults show that there are common systems of control used by all cults and self-contained authoritarian societies. The dynamics of thought reform emerged from the work of the renowned research psychiatrist Robert J. Lifton with former Chinese and Western prisoners of war who were converted and brainwashed by the Chinese communist regime. His theory of thought reform has been found to apply to many kinds of coercive groups and abusive relationships. After leaving, I didn't know of any therapists with an understanding of cults, and it was some years before I would meet with survivors of other cults. Listening to their struggles about fitting into society and trying to catch up on lost years, I began to understand my own experience. Later still, I was very fortunate to meet Gillie Jenkinson, a psychotherapist (and former cult member) highly skilled in cult psycho-education. We worked through Lifton's Eight Components of Thought Reform, which helped enormously in making sense of my experience during those years in the commune—commune in name but in reality a cult.

It's very difficult to describe the highly demanding, controlled and chaotic way we lived, and to convey rationally the insane ideology that I believed back then is not easy. Though it will sound formal and academic, I will use Lifton's (1961) system to help convey a sense of my life during those years.

Milieu control

The most powerful of these controlling systems was used to keep a tight rein on the environment and achieve the self-suppression of members. With no electricity, telephone, television, or newspapers, all forms of communication in the remote locations where we lived was contained. Every aspect of our lives was planned and managed; our daily routine, working long exhausting hours with little sleep and certainly no rest, ensured compliance. We had a confused romanticised understanding of the dangerous areas where we lived. The weaponising of information was a core method of control. The leader was the only one who read newspapers and political magazines and she interpreted both the outside world and our immediate physical environment. She was free to act with impunity and there was never a democratic discussion about anything, especially our physical safety. Tragically there were two fatalities, debilitating infections, and many serious injuries. Every aspect of our lives was tightly controlled; our time, energy, money, diet, sleep, personal boundaries, relationships and sexuality, clothing, social life, bringing up our children, personal space and privacy, access to legal protection, medical care, and education.

In pre-internet times, all our incoming and outgoing letters were read aloud, interpreted, and pronounced on, relationships with birth family and friends were effectively severed. Our world was reduced to Us vs Them—everyone in the outside world was the enemy, deemed unenlightened and a bad influence on us.

Loading the language

Every behaviour and interaction was interpreted through the leader's self-styled therapy with the use of clichéd thought and feeling-stopping language such as *doing a number, being in/out of touch, in a pit, cut off, doing a poor-me, the outside world, good for your growth,* and *coming out with your feelings.* The use of these terrifying words was feared as they could alter one's life within seconds. The leader or very high-up member could decide at any given moment that an adult, child, or visitor was responsible for a *bad vibe.* Under the guise of group therapy, that person and anyone sympathetic to them were aggressively confronted, insulted, humiliated, and frequently assaulted violently.

Mystical manipulation

This was another method of control and designed to make the leader appear omnipotent. As well as "psychoanalysis", psychic readings, tarot, astrology, and other esoteric practices were used to add an air of mystique—our weaknesses and strengths divined, and what our futures held if we didn't do x, y, or z (for the group, of course). New visitors were drawn into having "interesting readings" and *love-bombed* into joining the group, jettisoning their previous lives, relationships, even properties, convinced they had been chosen and led to find a new and better way of life (of hard labour!) Synchronistic events were used to create mystery and prove the astrology or psychic readings were correct.

Sacred science

The belief system was that the leader was pioneering a unique form of therapy that would save humanity. No other therapy was as radical or *pushing the boundaries*, no one else gave free therapy and she didn't retreat after an hour of paid therapy like her contemporaries in London at that time, as she often liked to remind us. She was "the only therapist doing round-the-clock therapy"—sleeping with all male members to "analyse" their sexuality, and females by surrogacy (the men reported to her on their experience of the women). Her view on everything was accepted without question. Sexual humiliation and rape were normal, the twisted thinking was that we secretly wanted it. Only heterosexuality was tolerated, any hint of anything other deemed an abnormality needing therapy. Similarly, there was no leeway for anything other than the neurotypical way of relating. Anyone behaving differently was mocked and shamed.

Demand for purity

All cults have their own version of purity. In my group it was disloyal and a "sin" to be interested in anything outside the group. Separated from all previous interests, we were coerced into confronting our parents violently (a badge of honour) and all other friendships, ways of life, interests, hobbies, likes, and dislikes were discredited. Essentially we had to become like the leader, adopting her values, her ways of relating and seeing the world. Through thought stopping (killing off critical thinking) and feeling stopping, we suppressed our authentic selves to become what was expected of us—*getting in touch with* our real feelings as decided by the leader, and enforced by other members. Getting in touch with one's anger was the highest ideal. Through so-called primal therapy we were praised for feeling violently angry, especially towards one's birth family.

Dispensing with existence

A member could be GRO'd (got rid of) at any time. We were always in dread of changes in the hierarchy, and of what was coming next. The leader had faithful bodyguards ready and willing to use their fists without question. I remember one morning feeling shocked when her favourite bodyguard was GRO'd for shouting at her that she was incapable of feeling love. Her swift militaristic response was "might is right", ordering two teenage lads to "get the guns and shoot off shots", warning him off the farm. Anyone could be got rid of, except the leader, the only one who never had to run away.

Members rose in the group hierarchy and became favourites through ruthlessly mocking, humiliating, and aggressively confronting other members. Being *cut off* meant that you were refusing to communicate honestly, and had gone into *a pit*—a place of withdrawal, excommunicated from others, the worst place to be, butt of endless confrontation, humiliation, and degrading treatment, sentenced to harder work and isolation, an altogether untouchable status. Anyone speaking normally or showing sympathy to *a pitter* was challenged and put in the *hot seat*. You were only allowed out of the pit when you admitted to intensely violent feelings against your parents/children/spouse/lover/former friends. Alternatively, you could be let out by accepting an opportunity to confront someone the leader wanted taken down, something we all jumped on, as being in a pit was horrifying. Being cruel to other members was the price we paid, building up further layers of self-hatred. This wedded me more deeply to the group; how could I ever leave, having done such appalling things to others? I firmly believed what I was told—that everything about me was wrong, that I was not a *real* person, I was *an irredeemable pitter,* undeserving of any respect, and the worst parent ever.

Doctrine over person

The ideology of the group was that our everyday necessities and well-being were not important. The prime aim was to be a very productive worker and a source of *growth* for the leader and other members. Our individual needs, such as being able to parent our own children, were violated and utterly demolished.

As in many cults, specific and multiple methods were used to control and limit the bond between parents and children (Stein, 1997). We were coerced into accepting that our children were being raised in the healthiest manner in a collective childhood where survival skills were prized over education. We had high ideals, but little knowledge or understanding of actual child developmental needs. Our way of life placed their needs as the lowest priority. The cult positioned itself in the role of parent; we were not allowed ordinary parental contact with our children. Our parent–child interaction was manipulated and supervised by other members, usually in very traumatic group therapy settings. Members policed and reported on other parents' contact with their children. My own were repeatedly told that I hated and didn't care for them. This coercive dynamic meant that immense threat could be wielded against parents through our children at any time. I hung on for many years, hunkering down, twisting myself into every shape possible, desperately hoping to be allowed contact with mine.

A frequent phenomenon in many cults is the leader's parting curse. Being told repeatedly "You're not fit to be a mother" has been a serious burden to my recovery. The therapy was supposed to put us in touch with our feelings yet if we showed any of our real feelings, such as love, sadness, grief, shame, abhorrence at the violence being used, we were called humiliating names and told that our true selves were fascist and full of violence, while our softer feelings—especially love—were ridiculed.

Confession

The constant atmosphere of threat and violence ensured that there were no secrets, as everything was reported to the leader. Our innermost fears, failings, and weaknesses were openly shared and inevitably used coercively against us in a flagrant abuse of power. We were forced to confess to disloyal thoughts like missing our families, wanting to run away and leave the group, to vulnerabilities, guilts, and jealousies. This public purging was to rid us of our authentic selves and secret fears, another method used to control us and create an atmosphere of guilt and shame. We victimised one another, always wanting to be "in" with the leader.

The current of who was in or out of favour ran like wildfire through the group; everybody was expected to side with what the leader felt was happening, and act on the type of confrontation and level of violence that was expected. Unspeakable duress was used to force participation in degrading activities. Being silent was not an option and was interpreted as being extremely violent and *doing a number*. Protesting against this treatment was labelled as being a victim, or *doing a poor me*. There was an irrational law that one *only* had to come out with whatever truth was decided, and the violence would stop. This forced confession was one of many methods used for creating our cult identities. Often the violence was so extreme, members had to flee, leaving without money, passport, or belongings, and tragically leaving without our children. This deepened the separation and split in our families.

Breaking point

It's been a harrowing, lonely journey walking away and facing the depth of depravity that I have been part of. I had given all my work, hopes, and dreams to what I believed would be a good life, lived in community. Even though every relationship was dysfunctional and abusive, I was deeply bonded and attached through many experiences and repeated traumas. Like other members, I had left and returned many times. I prayed and fantasised often for interventions, that the state army would rescue us, or that there would be a massive environmental disaster! The realisation of how far detached we were from any outside help was overwhelming and on occasion I felt suicidal.

Within the cult, everything was turned on its head; very well-educated people treated as stupid and backward, nurturing loving people coerced into accepting they were cruel and brutal, the brute and bully given immense power over others. Everything depended on what the leader said and how she interpreted reality. Our barometer for danger was totally compromised. Therefore, we were all in denial about the seriousness of the civil war raging between the state-backed paramilitaries and armed guerrilla groups, and that we were living in a very dangerous region. We naively believed we would be immune and protected because we were "confronting our own violence". This proved disastrously untrue; we were robbed at gunpoint several times and, tragically, two young members (one of them the leader's grandson) were brutally executed by a faction of the guerrillas. This is a stark example of cognitive dissonance, common in cults, when untenable beliefs collide shockingly with reality. When things went disastrously wrong, inevitably and absurdly, this led to blaming oneself and other members for not being good enough, rather than question the leader and her hierarchy's illogical interpretations of reality.

Something detonated inside me and I began to wake up to questioning how we lived. I felt we were all responsible for these tragic deaths and that the way we lived had to be challenged. I was appalled at the brutal cruelty with which the leader treated her daughter, the bereaved and grieving mother. I tried to challenge the leader but with no solidarity from others, I withdrew my outburst after threats of violence. Secret feelings of wrongness grew.

Two years later, another experience further changed my perspective when I became trapped in a heavily armed siege. During the week it took negotiators to end the siege, alongside the possibility of a violent death, I experienced unexpected friendship and appreciation from those I was helping in a nursing capacity. This caused some disruption in my pseudo identity (that is, who I had been told I was) and very negative view of myself, which I believed to be 100 per cent true at the time. Bizarrely, I realised I was more terrified of the leader than any of the armed men! I knew then that I had to leave forever, which felt like stepping off the highest cliff-face. But even just having a rebellious thought about leaving was dangerous, other members being always highly attuned to any shift in allegiance.

Leaving: Physically out but mentally in—my cult personality came with me

The idea of leaving that closed, highly controlled environment and living outside caused immense fear. Leaving was not a linear exit. All of us had run away, returned, and run away again, unable to fully break free.

There was huge stigma about leaving; members who left were hated, vilified, and seen as betrayers. Runaways, or recidivists as the leader called us, were pursued by group members and pressured to return, all to please her. When I ran away, I was stalked and harassed by angry members, bombarded with guilt trips about how much I owed the group for "parenting" my children and persuaded (threatened) that I had to return. I was light years away from seeing that *they* actually owed *me* for years of unpaid physical and medical work, and for giving all my savings and family inheritance. Yet it was reconfigured to me owing them, and that I must return and pay back by way of slave labour.

Leaving forever is very complex; it meant giving up on years of service to a leader and way of life where I had hoped I would become a better person and parent. Aside from initial temporary relief, I felt I had betrayed the group for many years after finally leaving, and my life had lost its meaning. The dominant emotion was grief; my new life felt like a post-nuclear landscape where nothing could grow. I was so programmed to have every thought centred upon the leader and working for her, it felt impossible to have any interests or hobbies of my own; my ability to concentrate was zero. I couldn't read, and felt disconnected from news on radio and television. Thoughts of having failed the group plagued me. I had long ago accepted I wasn't a fit mother, and believed my children would be hating me as much as all the adult members for having left—the biggest sin.

In year two of leaving I came across a book about cults. I was both drawn and repulsed by it, refusing to browse it, convinced I'd be betraying the group even more by reading a few lines. It was a very strong physical sensation, as if I was still being watched. But I also missed aspects of that life, especially the communal effort to live sustainably and work with the land. Though I'd been living close to nature in view of majestic mountains, I had never been able to be present to the wonders of nature, *las montañas, los bosques y estrellas espectacular* (the mountains, forests, and spectacular night skies) all passed me by; fear had infected every experience.

Leaving meant losing all connection to my children. It meant facing up to struggles with money, finding paid work and a place to live, understanding society, making friends, finding meaning in life, all the time struggling with how to speak about my past. Not only had I nothing, in my soul I was so damaged and broken. Creating a curriculum vitae is very difficult for anyone who leaves a cult: how to fill in the long gaps of unexplained years, and how frustratingly unfair, after working so hard, to have no current hireable skills. I didn't know how to live an ordinary life and had to get over many phobias including accessing medical help, training, and education, and reporting crimes to the police. Ordinary language had to be reclaimed, and the idea that leisure time is healthy took a long time to sink in. I had an instinct to begin a peaceful path, very counter-intuitive as I was programmed to always go towards high adrenaline, conflict, rush, and breakneck chaotic involvement in all I did. It's been a long slow road before I could really trust myself that peace is vital to my recovery.

The long-term effects of being in an abusive group take decades to unravel. Coming out of a controlled and highly demanding environment, the outside world was full of uncertainty and a huge cultural shock. I was lost without the leader feeding "correct ideas" and without the group's constant criticism to keep me on track. Their voices were always in my head. My conflicts played out in traumatic and terrifying nightmares of being back there. I alienated people who didn't understand how the cult had affected me, and I didn't understand it either. I was confused and defensive, uncompromising, combative, judgemental, and extreme in my opinions. Too fearful of exposing the leader, instead I found myself in lengthy legal battles with other authorities. No surprise that I was unable to make genuine friendships as my pseudo/cult identity was still very active, and I was drawn mostly to people with coercive natures and workaholic addictions.

I was gifted an opportunity to study law in those years which kept me occupied with the pressure of passing exams. It gave me something to do and interestingly helped open up my brain to reasoning and nuance, as opposed to all-or-nothing thinking. Studying criminal law, I was amazed to learn that undue influence, incitement to hatred, extortion, verbal, physical, and sexual assault are all crimes punishable by imprisonment!

Dealing with introjected voices and fear of reprisal kept me in a frozen state for many years. The energy pattern of being *in a pit* and not allowed to speak until I *came out with the truth* was deeply etched in my being. I was totally inept and ill-equipped at normal communication when I finally reconnected with all my children. All our interactions had been in charged, confrontational settings, there was no trust and no words could bridge the impossible chasm between us. Building trust and connection has been a long and slow journey, with many stops and starts, gradually learning who we all are, as opposed to who we were told we were.

Leaving a therapy cult and seeking therapy help

Exiting a therapy cult is terrifying. When trust has been ruthlessly betrayed, how do you ever put your faith in a therapist again? I had to learn. I had been programmed never to say bad things about the therapist/leader. The real me didn't have access to myself for many years after I left. Even thousands of miles away I was still under the leader's control. I had been so dedicated, with such a sense of purpose. After leaving I didn't know what I thought or felt, or what I could trust in myself or others. I felt unbounded grief, anger, impotence, despair, confusion, depression. I needed help. Over a long time, and years working with many therapists, I learned that feeling all of these was at least reclaiming and reconnecting with myself.

Psycho-education about how cults work and the brainwashing process is a very important step in the recovery process. In writing this chapter I've come across an excellent workbook for those of us breaking free and recovering from cults (Jenkinson, 2023). I'm briefly referring to some of the material to give a broad outline of how cults operate and how one can start the recovery process.

Unmasking the cult leader as the traumatising narcissist she was and the people I idolised has been a very long, interesting process. My own authentic emotional world first began to slowly show itself when I received news that both my parents had died when I had been in the cult and estranged from them. I was struck by a lightning blow of loss (which was laughed at in the cult). Allowing myself, secretly at first, to feel that earth-shaking grief became the entry into very slowly starting to feel my own life again, the kind of feelings which were never acceptable in the group. Owning my grief was a very definite step away from the leader. Grieving for all I've lost is endless, especially my relationship with each of my children, my parents, and siblings. The separation and loss of parenting my children has been enormous; it comes like a deluge at times and leaves me gasping with unendurable pain. I know it will never leave me. I have grown around it (as Tonkin, 1996, describes in her theory of loss), as grandchildren and a beloved dog have arrived, and new experiences, events, and opportunities have shaped how my family is evolving now. So true is the saying "the best time to plant an oak tree is twenty years ago; the second-best time is now".

Surviving within the cult and undoing the pseudo cult identity

When working with people who have been in cultic groups,

> practitioners need to find the balance between not being overly neutral when listening to atrocities and being open to people's feelings of loss and grief when they leave the cult … the same skills needed to work with survivors of domestic violence where it may alienate the client to demonise their former partner. (Dubrow-Marshall, 2013, p. 22)

It has been immensely helpful to my recovery when very occasionally therapists were willing to voice their horrified reactions to some details of my experience. Being listened to and having our traumas finally witnessed is so healing.

Most therapists will have no understanding of the brainwashing process, of being recruited into a cult and the iron-tight grip it exerts over our lives. In working with a cult survivor, therapists will first be meeting with a pseudo identity. This is made up of introjects/beliefs and behaviours swallowed whole, implanted by the leader, enforced by the group through cruelty, name-calling, shaming, and manipulation, and accepted so as to protect ourselves and fit in. Using thought-provoking questions, a therapist can encourage the questioning of this identity and be a curious sounding board, which can lead to opening cracks that allow the authentic self to peep through on occasion. The introject will be recognised by the frequent use of verbs which incapacitate or put tremendous pressure on us (can't, must, should, shouldn't, and words of extreme self-criticism). Guilt and shame are used in the forming of this introject which takes over one's being. In the cult, accepting this alien personality was crucial to fit in and avoid violence. I was convinced I was the person the leader decided I was; thinking I was learning to communicate better, I was actually learning to obey her unquestioningly.

Once critical thinking has been switched off, this alien personality grows and takes over. Jenkinson (2023) describes this process in a visceral and graphic way as the authentic self being "buried under tarmac", an alien lump of "undigested stuff" which one is unable to "chew over". Working to uncover and chew it over takes time. For second-generation members born in cults (SGAs) this overlaying happens from birth. Cult recovery is a unique journey, and rational thinking does not happen overnight. Kindness and patience can help survivors make their own discoveries. Therapists can be curious about personal interests pre-cult, planting seeds about healthy routines, self-care, and a safe support system, encouraging the celebration of progress and achievements, championing the determination, resilience, and strength gained along the way.

Towards well-being

Learning how to calm one's nervous system that is constantly on alert is vital to managing triggers that take us back to traumas. Jenkinson describes triggers as a *pattern match* when the present feels similar to the past, often charged with adrenaline and a massive impulse to fight, freeze, or flee. It is said that victims of abuse are the keenest observers of human nature: it's a survival skill. The tone of someone's voice, a silence, the raising of an eyebrow can all set off internal alarms. All cult victims have a sleep deficit. Copious amounts of sleep help towards calming a tortured nervous system.

First-generation adults (FGAs) who join cults suffer huge levels of shame and self-contempt for having brought our children into an abusive environment. Developing self-compassion is exceptionally difficult. Guilt and shame are constant punishing spectres. Having compassion for the fact that I can't have compassion for myself is at least a starting point, and this has helped in the darkest moments. In my nursing training we had never heard of compassion; not having had much life experience, empathy and kindness were more easily available. I learned more about compassion when I trained as an end-of-life doula and sometimes found that through compassion by proxy I've been able to glimpse what an impossibly harsh critic I am of myself.

Internal family systems therapy (IFS) (Schwartz & Sweezy, 2019) has been helpful to me in my recovery. I write and speak not only to the inner wounded child, but several parts that dominate if I don't listen: the traumatised student nurse, the naive young mother who made unwise choices, the implacable critic, the optimistic adventurer, the victim and oppressor, the compulsive helper, the seasoned lonely woman, the powerful child, the sorrowing romantic, the hopeful fool, the gullible eejit, the raging survivor, and so on. I have a battalion of inner critics ready to pounce; it takes effort and a rare feeling of worth to say to them, "Back off! What exactly do you want to tell me here?" I'm exploring seeing my inner critics as protectors who helped me weather the worst traumas. We unconsciously act to ensure the best strategies for our survival. My numbed-out and people-pleaser selves kept me safe and stopped me losing my mind. Speaking with the persecuting part has been profound; I can see it has had a useful function, protecting me from further traumas, but also a punishing role, inherited first from early Catholic indoctrination telling me not to "get above myself" in trying to move towards a life of freedom and autonomy.

Compassionate inquiry (CI), developed by Gabor Maté, can help us reconnect with our authentic selves, and recognise the unconscious beliefs and behaviours that currently control our lives. It invites the possibility of letting go of addictive impulses and unhelpful beliefs. With relative ease, these behaviours can be traced to their earliest origins, when the only choice for survival had to be attachment to a protective Other at the cost of asserting our true self. The process involves tuning into and holding these beliefs with compassion, without judgement, not trying to change them, but recognising that the developmental needs contributing to these beliefs were not met. The emotional patterns we developed can be looked at with curiosity, asking: How do these beliefs benefit me, and can I train myself to self-regulate now?

Compassion is love. In this safe space, with the right questions being asked, self-compassion is possible, bringing curiosity about how I might move forward with lighter steps.

Another approach I have found useful is energy psychotherapy (Mollon, 2008), which works on blockages in the subtle energies of mind, body, and spirit and has relieved suffering in times of crises. Using unique therapies such as emotional freedom therapy ("tapping"), blue diamond therapy, and Chakra healing has also helped release some of the stranglehold energy patterns of oppressive traumas.

Sometimes my past is too much to bear. Learning to bear witness (letting it be), knowing that nothing can make it better, I have found is also an important way of accepting all that has happened that I cannot change. I attended Quaker Meetings for a time; learning how to sit in silence with myself was very difficult! I was privileged with an opportunity to volunteer as a Quaker hospice chaplain around the Covid pandemic time. Accompanying, and being a reassuring presence for, the dying as they enter into the mystery of death taught me that it is possible to experience deep peace and acceptance.

Gardening and connecting to the natural world have been crucial to my return to well-being. I found something to care about, immensely soothing and contemplative, and reflecting (in a safe way) many aspects of my life. Sue Stuart-Smith, a psychiatrist and psychotherapist who has studied the therapeutic effects of gardening, discovered that it has a profoundly healing effect, allowing our inner world to coexist, free from the pressures of everyday life, "a meeting place between our dream infused selves and the real physical world" (2021, p. 16). I can hear my own thoughts and my attention is free floating when I'm watering, planting seeds, tending, supporting, and pruning plants. My anxiety reduces, as does the tightness in my chest. It is very nurturing seeing new life grow from seeds, reaching out to become tall and strong.

In dark despairing moments I compare my alien/introjected self to Japanese knotweed, an invasive species that is impossible to totally eradicate. Thinking it's all been pulled up, it reappears through difficult triggers and overwhelming destabilising memories. As a parent who took my children into an abusive and dangerous cult, I often think recovery is impossible. I hear familiar echoes in stories about child soldiers of war-torn countries where families are forced to be unimaginably brutal to each other. I recognise the same brainwashing processes when I read how young idealistic people are recruited into terrorist groups. I feel horror, rage, grief, and disgust at the depravity I've been part of. I have wanted to find the leader and explode a hand grenade, annihilating both of us. I'm slowly learning to express my anger in healthier ways that are freeing me from that abusive bond.

In better times, I feel my life growing rich in opportunity, friendship, and love. Well-being is inching forwards in a gradual and spiral direction.

Second-generation cult survivors and recovery (SGS)

Children born into cults don't have a healthy experience of family. They've had constantly busy absent parents who have placed the leader and cult-related work above loving and caring for them, are often parented by other adults, and have suffered neglect and cultic abuse while being told they are receiving love (it is caring to be confrontational!) When they leave they are very frequently estranged from their birth parents who sometimes remain in the cult. In their journey of recovery, they are negatively affected by society's cultural myths about family—that family is forever, blood being thicker than water, family is all you have, a mother's love knows no end ... Post cult, witnessing loving healthy families is then very painful. Meaningfully reconfiguring the concept of family, managing triggering experiences, and developing coping strategies for family related milestones are vital to survival after exiting a cult. Finding ways to bear pain and loss is central to recovery; the grieving process is immense.

Children see no model of love, compassion, kindness, or forgiveness in cults. They adopt the good/bad polarised value system—we are right, the rest of the world is wrong. They've never seen middle ground, nuance, and negotiating, as happens in ordinary families. There is no model of how to disagree agreeably. They have often had no formal education, which is a huge obstacle to leaving. What they have learned is that independent thinking gets you into trouble. As a result of the leader's narcissistic need to be the most important relationship in their parents' lives, and the fact that parents' involvement with their children detracts from cult work, parents are most often separated from their children. Leavers/recidivists are cursed by the group and burdened with a sense of doom, negativity, and foreboding about the future. We were all told we would never survive outside the group and the task of building a new life and thriving is enormous.

My place in the world now

Despite my very adverse experience of community, I like learning, playing, and working with others. My doula community, local choir, gardeners' growing club, colleagues at my day (legal) job, and cult survivor's network all give me a sense of belonging and purpose. Importantly, I've reconnected with former nursing and school friends, and I'm beginning to feel part of my neighbourhood.

The process of writing has opened up very painful wounds. I've had to look closely at my life and what led me to join a cult. I am aware of patronising and dismissive attitudes towards people who get drawn into cults and fundamentalist groups. Fearing being judged stupid, I've held back from sharing my story. Surprisingly, it has been therapeutic, healing, and enlightening to excavate the layers of trauma from a long dark chapter in my life, giving me greater understanding and learning, especially glimpsing the bigger picture. Locked-away parts are stirring. I've been surprised to remember the experience of working in an asylum which I had blocked out. There's a possibility that I will reclaim my Irish heritage which I shunned. I've hated the actions of Church and state, the hierarchical systems of control which profoundly damaged our lives. Historically, I now understand that, after the War of Independence, the young Irish state was eager to show it could manage its affairs independently from the United Kingdom. The promise of universal human rights and equality of all citizens was most unfortunately hijacked by misogynistic leaders in the Church and government of that time. Wanting to present itself as a great cultural and Gaelic-speaking nation, the resulting Constitution was sectarian and biased against women particularly, not merely reinforcing but formalising that their place was firmly in the marital home. It took decades for the brutal cruelty of the mother and baby homes and psychiatric asylums to be unearthed, both dumping grounds for society's problems. It's a joy to see ensuing generations not standing for the hypocrisy so typical in the Irish way of law-making. Coincidentally, a recent referendum on the place of women in the home in the Constitution has failed. On International Women's Day 2024 the electorate voted a resounding *no* to the ineffectively worded double referenda on proposed changes to the outdated legal status of the family in the Constitution; also on the rights of women, carers, the elderly, and people with disabilities. It failed because the government—Dáil—didn't follow the comprehensive proposals of the Citizen's Assembly and the Oireachtas. *Ní saoirse go saoirse na mban*—there is no freedom until the freedom of women. As Brendan Kelly, one of Ireland's leading clinical psychiatrists, says: "We need a revolution in mental health care, and quite possibly a social revolution, placing human compassion at the centre of human activity, human connection and human flourishing" (Kelly, 2017).

Writing this chapter has been a gift. I've wanted to tell my story but feared vengeance from the cult, and so have withheld details that would identify them. I don't want threats to my family, or possible litigation.

I want therapists to know there are training courses on how to help those of us who have been in cults, as well as podcasts, seminars, and great books available to study. It took me many years to find these, but they have been invaluable in helping educate the professionals who have helped me. I have had years in personal development groups which helped me learn to relate socially. Counselling and therapy helped me navigate the many obstacles and stresses of life post cult. Trauma therapy is now showing me how to manage anxiety, recurring nightmares, and panic attacks. I'm learning tools to handle the triggered spaces, and emerge battered but wiser, less frozen and more hopeful. So many kind and patient people along the way have listened, encouraged, and helped me find hope in times of deep despair. I am eternally grateful to all of them. I feel privileged and blessed for all the opportunities I've had to recover a bit more, including the chance to contribute to this book on leaving coercive relationships.

A big obstacle for former cult members is that almost no one will understand our experience. A small cohort of brave people have been writing and speaking out about cults for many years, often facing real threats and litigation for doing so. In recent years, in response to a proliferation of cultic-type services being offered on the internet, and building on this earlier work, there has been a raft of informative documentaries, podcasts (including Steve Hassan's), and educational books (such as Lalich & Tobias, 2006), and a concerted effort to shine light on how undue influence and coercive control can physically and psychologically imprison and paralyse vulnerable, intelligent, and often very gifted individuals.

ICSA, the International Cultic Studies Association, holds an annual conference and has an informative website which is helping expose cults and educate the public about their growth. It's so important to have a body of well-researched work and credible voices to combat the power of cults and cult personalities, who are becoming more dominant on the political stage.

In the United Kingdom, the Family Survival Trust is campaigning and working towards dialogue with Parliament to have the law on coercive control amended so that crimes committed within cults can be prosecuted. We also need to teach our young how to reason, evaluate, and weigh the consequence of making decisions, and how to research, assess, and question information on how the world works. Educating young children in school and in the community about cults and how to question authority would be a very positive step to help prevent young people being recruited into coercive groups. There's much work to be done, by therapists, mental health workers, and community workers. Experts by experience, cult survivors have a wealth of valuable experience to bring to this work. However, funding for resources and support for the growing number of cult victims is desperately needed, especially as many struggle to find well-paid work to fund their own recovery.

References

Dubrow-Marshall, L. (2013). Working with cult survivors. *Therapy Today, 24*(4): 18–22.

Hassan, S. (n.d.). The Influence Continuum [podcast]. https://podcasts.apple.com/gb/podcast/the-influence-continuum-with-dr-steven-hassan/id1603773245 (last accessed 26 March 2024).

Janov, A. (1970). *The Primal Scream, Primal Therapy: The Cure for Neurosis.* New York: Dell.

Jenkinson, G. (2023). *Walking Free from the Trauma of Coercive, Cultic and Spiritual Abuse: A Workbook for Recovery and Growth.* Abingdon, UK: Routledge.

Kelly, B. (2017). *Hearing Voices: The History of Psychiatry in Ireland.* Kildare, Ireland: Irish Academic.

Lalich, J., & Tobias, M. (2006). *Take Back Your Life* (2nd edn). Berkeley, CA: Bay Tree.

Lifton, R. J. (1961). *Thought Reform and the Psychology of Totalism: A Study of Brainwashing in China.* New York: W. W. Norton.

Mollon, P. (2008). *Psychoanalytic Energy Psychotherapy.* London: Routledge.
Stein, A. (1997). Mothers in cults: The influence of cults on the relationship of mothers to their children. *Cultic Studies Journal, 14*(1): 40–57.
Schwartz, R., & Sweezy, M. (2019). *Internal Family Systems* (2nd edn). New York: Guilford.
Stuart-Smith, S. (2021). *The Well Gardened Mind: The Restorative Power of Nature* (2nd edn). London: William Collins.
Tonkin, L. (1996). Growing around grief—another way of looking at grief and recovery. *Bereavement Care, 15*(1): 10.0

Weblinks

Internal Family Systems by Richard Schwartz: https://integrativepsych.co/new-blog/what-is-parts-work-therapy-ifs
International Cultic Studies Association: https://www.icsahome.com/
The Family Survival Trust: https://thefamilysurvivaltrust.org/files/ugd/b17260_69b0d1c7ce134d44b7fe2aab640e567d.pdf

CHAPTER 3

Reclaiming sovereignty from the cultic power of the guru[1]

Ruthie Smith

What are cults?[2]

I came to write this chapter following my own experience thirty-five years ago when I realised a spiritual organisation I was in was becoming like a cult. Although there is no precise definition of a cult, I like the broad sweep of the Oxford English Dictionary where it is defined as: "a relatively small group of people having strong (religious) beliefs or practices regarded by others as strange or as imposing excessive

---

[1] This chapter is based on a paper presented at a Confer conference about "Spiritual trauma—the forgotten wound in the consulting room": 24 March 2018—London.

[2] CAVEATS

- I am grateful for discussions in a private online forum, which contributed to my understanding of why it is so very difficult for people to leave cults—anonymous personal quotations come with permission from members of this group.
- In speaking about a Tibetan Buddhist cult, I do not wish to malign Tibetan Buddhism, many of whose teachings I have found profound and beneficial.
- The spiritual community I speak of and its leader Lama "X" offer a raw example of the nature of cults, how they function, the organisation's leadership and the "inner circle". I have not named this organisation due to their litigious tendencies.
- *Vajrayana* and *Tantra* are the same path, *Sangha* means spiritual community, and the words *Lama*, *Guru*, and *Vajra master* are used interchangeably.
- The "Nature of Mind" is a transcendent awakened state of consciousness beyond the cognitive mind of ego.

control over members—a misplaced or excessive admiration for one particular thing".

If we think of the passion with which various organisations defend their ideals, many groups might qualify. It is only too easy to be part of an organisation—be it religious, spiritual, political, or whatever—where the group's ideals creep up on us. Not wanting to stand out or be too different, we adapt and acclimatise. For instance, when I first started out as a psychotherapist, some psychoanalytic institutions seemed very strict, and the analytic relationship somewhat peculiar. The "blank screen", with its inherent power imbalance, felt un-relational and infantilising, and I protested against external realities being dismissed as transference, abuse questioned as fantasy, or clients labelled resistant if they didn't agree with the analyst's view. The freedom of our thinking, our creative minds, and our curiosity are precious—as is our capacity to take fresh perspectives and question.

Inform, a UK charity that advises on new religious movements (a term used to mitigate against the shame and stigma associated with the word cult), comments that "Many cult members are very intelligent and skilled. The reality is that all sorts of people are involved in cults." A BBC television documentary, *A Very British Cult* (2023), showed how easily people who sincerely sought self-development were hoodwinked by a coaching cult. Another example in Africa (BBC, 2023) showed how hundreds of people seeking solace, strength, and support, including university graduates and high-ranking police, followed to their deaths a Kenyan starvation cult led by Pastor Paul Mackenzie. In both examples, the attachment to the cause was so intense that relatives were unable to prise followers away from what appeared to outsiders as evidently crazy behaviours and ideals.

Buddhism, with its many forms, used to enjoy a good reputation representing harmlessness in our wider culture but has become tarnished by the financial abuse of Myanmar's Thai Buddhists, the power struggles around succession in lineages, and reports of sexual, physical, and financial abuse in a variety of Buddhist communities (Tibetan, Zen, Thai, Western, and so on). Spiritual leaders are no longer seen as reliable holders of "truth", and victims of abuse and corruption are finally speaking out. For many, there is profound disillusionment.

After interviewing thousands of current and former cult members, relatives, and friends, Thaler Singer (2003) identified the key difference between cults and religions: in the latter, adherents' devotion is to principles or ideals whereas that becomes diverted into devotion and obedience to an individual in the former.

The hidden mystical truths of the East certainly attracted me to Tibetan Buddhism, but I would never have dreamed that I might be entering a cult. Steve Eichel identified several warning signs of cults,[3] including that the group typically uses deceptive means to recruit new members, and people often feel pressured to make quick decisions about becoming involved. Even though there may be outside followers, the group is closed, with an inner circle who, without question, follow the leader in secrecy. Typically, cults exploit their members—mostly financially, psychologically, emotionally and, all too often, sexually—and terror features strongly. People are inculcated into the idea that if you go against the group norms and leave the cult, horrible things will happen to you. The charismatic leader proclaims him—or herself as having special powers or even—perhaps unique to spiritual and religious cults—divinity.

Cults systematically induce states of psychological dependency, causing harm to members, their families, and the community. Shaw (2013) adds that, when a religious cult is led by a narcissistic leader who claims to have reached unity with the divine, these autocrats consider themselves exempt from social or moral limitations or restrictions. They are not held to normative societal standards of conduct, or subject to any system of checks and balances. Behaviour that would in any other context be considered amoral—if not psychopathic—is idealised by devotees as indicative of the leader's transcendent perfection and enlightenment. Thus, there is an additional dimension of manipulation and abuse in spiritual or religious cults.

Cultic groups are also elitist, depicting themselves as unique, with a strong organisational tendency to separate themselves off from other bodies and institutions, outside criticism, so they have diminished opportunities for internal correction or reflection. In summary, if you

[3] Notes from producer Paul LaRosa. "48 Hours": *The Family—A Cult Revealed* including aspects of an interview with Steve Eichel by Peter Van Sant.

wish to determine the cult-like status of a group, various helpful but challenging questions provide useful indicators:

a. Does the leader claim divine authority for his deeds and for his orders to followers? (cf. Eileen Barker from *Inform*)
b. Is there any deception in the recruitment of new members? (cf. Shirley Harrison)
c. Are members used for fundraising or missionary activities for little or no pay to line the leader's pockets? (cf. Shirley Harrison)
d. Does the group have an authority figure that everyone seems to acknowledge as having some special skill or awareness? (cf. Steve Eichel)
e. Does the leader set forth ethical guidelines that members must follow but from which he or she is exempt? (cf. James R. Lewis)
f. Does the leader make public assertions that he or she knows are false, that is, have a policy of routinely deceiving outsiders? (cf. James R. Lewis).
g. Is there any sexual manipulation of members? (cf. Janja Lalich)
h. Is there a major time commitment required for indoctrination sessions and group rituals? (cf. Steven Hassan)
i. Is there any deliberate holding back of, or distorting of, information to make it more acceptable—or outright lying? (cf. Steven Hassan)
j. Is there a buddy system to monitor, control, and report deviant thoughts, feelings, and actions to leadership of individual and group behaviour? (cf. Steven Hassan).

A Tibetan Buddhist cult

Here I share my own experience of following Tibetan Buddhism. In 1979 I went to a talk called *Meditation and Peace* by a revered Dzogchen Lama called His Holiness Dudjom Rinpoche. He transmitted a glimpse of the "awakened state" of consciousness, a spacious luminosity that felt profoundly grounding, like coming "home" to true reality—the feeling that *this is it.* There was no doubt in my mind that this was the spiritual path for me. I was very fortunate to receive teachings from several venerated masters, who have now long since passed. After the deaths of two of them, I witnessed with my own eyes that their bodies had largely dematerialised into rainbows as a sign of their enlightenment—known as *rainbow body** in Tibetan Buddhism—leaving little to cremate and demonstrating for me that this was a genuine path to enlightenment. [* See Glossary.]

After this awakening I wanted to study Tibetan Buddhism so joined a group, noting that its members were intelligent and committed, good-hearted souls from all walks of life including family-oriented people, creative artists, lawyers, doctors, architects, psychologists, and teachers. A significant proportion of the senior students were graduates from Cambridge University and, as a newcomer, I thought, "If all these people are following this teacher, he must be OK"—so I put my heart and soul into the study and practice of Buddhism for the next thirteen years.

The young lama was a gifted teacher. After many years—around the time that he became an international best-selling author—I was appointed a trustee of the organisation. These new temporal responsibilities required that I attend to external realities, and I began to realise that my critical faculties had gradually been eroded. I noticed that the teacher was becoming increasingly grandiose and controlling—delusional even—and previous doubts cemented and would not go away. I was very shocked when several women disclosed their experiences to me, as a trustee, of being sexually assaulted and raped by the teacher. Naturally I did my best to assist these women but when I raised this with the teacher and other trustees (retaining confidentiality of those who had disclosed), there was complete failure to recognise or acknowledge this as abuse. I was told I had no right to criticise the guru/lama, and threats of libel were made to another trustee who had agreed with my concerns.

The potential for abusing power is inherent within Tibetan Buddhism because the lama is accountable to no one and there are no formal complaints procedures other than the courts of the land. It was increasingly my view that people entering into this organisation as spiritual seekers were at serious risk, so after repeated attempts over several months to initiate dialogue and effect change, I left the teacher and organisation in 1992, resigning as a trustee and copying the Dalai Lama in to my resignation letter. I made a long report to the trustees and the Charities Commission stating my observations that the charity was behaving like a cult, where the culture of denial echoed the dynamics around disclosure of abuse within a family:

> One of the common features of sexual abuse is denial. No one wants to acknowledge that it is taking place [...] everyone denies and colludes with it, including the perpetrator because it is too uncomfortable, embarrassing, disappointing and frightening for people to face. The "family" holds together, firmly maintaining that everything is absolutely fine, so that the abused person's sense of reality is undermined. It creates a "conspiracy" of denial where everyone agrees to maintain a certain view of reality ... defined [within this organisation] with the "catch-all" phrase "pure perception", where the consciousness of the group does not allow the "child" to see that "the Emperor has no clothes on".[4]

What I initially perceived to be a legitimate spiritual path no longer felt safe. The teachings themselves were inspirational and of enormous personal help, but the teacher's behaviour was feudal, unacceptable, and criminal—I felt like one of the furies in Greek tragedies, utterly sickened by what I saw and, as my attempts to speak with the teacher had failed, I walked away. I was vilified by the community, shunned as a pariah and betrayer, and it took years of agonising grief afterwards to process and come to terms with leaving. In taking refuge in the Buddhist teachings, I had made a commitment "until enlightenment" so I could never have envisioned leaving this path and spiritual community. Though I was devastated by my departure, it was also a wake-up call to grow up and find my own sovereignty. However, it distresses me that I could not stop the guru's abuse. Some years later, a million-dollar lawsuit was filed in the USA by a young woman victim of this teacher, for which I gave testimony. Although this was suppressed, I was glad that I at least made a stand.

In 2017, a group of students wrote a public letter stating their wish "to break this veil of secrecy, deception, and deceit". Having suffered "subjugation" for more than twenty years, they felt they could no longer justify perceiving the teacher's violence in the terms he himself described it—as "crazy wisdom", "wrathful compassion", or "skilful means". They

[4] Quoted from my Statement to The Trustees, 10 July 1994.

detailed many instances of physical and psychological violence, sexual abuse, financial exploitation, and corruption. Subsequently, it transpired that the degree of violence and perversion was far worse than that stated in their letter. Those in the innermost circle felt enslaved in abuse, commanded to "serve" their Vajra master around the clock. This included debasing and perverse rituals such as women being forced to strip and have non-consensual sex with him at any time of day or night, (allegations amounting to rape) and regular beatings of the students, sometimes till they were unconscious or bleeding. One student said that although a hug was considered a blessing, *"being hit was allegedly an even bigger blessing. This teacher X really believes this. He really thinks he's some omnipotent being."* The student summed up being in the innermost circle as "like a dysfunctional, incestuous family with grave sado-masochistic tendencies, but without a safe word".[5]

A reputable London law firm subsequently investigated the letter-writer's allegations and concluded that: "Students of the teacher [...] have been subjected to serious physical, sexual and emotional abuse by him; and there were senior individuals within the organisation who were aware of at least some of these issues and failed to address them, leaving others at risk."

Deny and reverse victim and offender (DARVO)

Many Tibetan Lamas disappointingly closed rank. In a public teaching, one master declared the letter writers to be "possessed by demons [...] and [they] will go to 'Vajra hell' for breaking their '*samaya*'" (which means the purity of the spiritual connection with the teacher), at which point, the Sangha [group]—shockingly—applauded. The majority of students chose to stay in denial, and either would not or could not accept what had happened, swinging between horror and disbelief that the teacher they loved so much was capable of such atrocities. Devoted students who idealised their teacher chose to remain ignorant of the details of what had happened. Instead, the whistle-blowers were decried for speaking out against their Vajra master and the victims were blamed. This is the classic phenomenon of "DARVO": deny and reverse victim and offender.

[5] From correspondence with a former student.

The gut-wrenching disillusionment and mental gymnastics of denial employed by both victims and bystanders in the trauma of disclosure creates severe splits in the psyche. Students were heartbroken, confused that their idealised world was turned upside down and their teacher had feet of clay. What did this mean for their spiritual path? How could they try to square an un-squarable circle and make sense of the terrible abuses that were named? There was anger that the organisational leaders had known about the abuse for so long yet covered it up and allowed it to continue unchecked. Many felt betrayed that, while ostensibly professing "transparency", the management team—who failed to admit that this was abuse—spent thousands of pounds on professional consultancy to save public face rather than offering an unequivocal authentic apology to those who had been harmed. Far from truth and reconciliation, the organisational leaders sued one lawyer (who represented the victims) for calling the organisation a cult. The management lost their case, and the attribution of the word cult was upheld in court.

The shadow in spiritual groups: Idealisation, devotion, and manipulation

While the following are my observations of Buddhist and spiritual cults in particular, these features are relevant generally to the totalitarian nature of cultic regimes.

Devotion and idealisation

A Tibetan Buddhist Sangha is presided over by the master. Inherent within the secret Vajrayana teachings is the requirement to perceive the guru as the Buddha, and all beings as "deities".

Teacher X was gifted in transmitting the awakened state known as the introduction *to the nature mind.* To the uninitiated, this powerful spiritual experience is like going to a magic show—it is beyond the mind, beyond normal comprehension. When people first awaken and experience this higher state of consciousness, the usual reference points and concepts are gone. People can feel mind-blown—in a state of openness, awe, and transcendence. This inner light is exactly what people are searching for—it satisfies a deep spiritual hunger.

Such awakening can lead one to idealise a religion and project superpowers onto its charismatic spiritual teachers. Buddhism seemed to be the real deal. Experiencing this view of consciousness is a profoundly strengthening experience, and such glimpses of our expansive true spiritual nature provide rich ground for devotion to the teacher and the teachings. How could one not feel gratitude and want to serve, helping others to feel something similar? This leads to the commitment of taking the *Bodhisattva* vow of compassion.

A speciality of the secret tantric teachings is that one can realise enlightenment by cultivating *devotion* to the teacher, seeing all the actions of the lama as an enlightened Buddha. Tantra means sacred thread or link, so students are required to keep a pure connection—*samaya*—with the teacher. By practising *pure perception* in this way, it is said one receives the blessings of a Buddha rather than those of an ordinary person. The Vajrayana student is required to maintain this view at all times.

Mistaking charisma for wisdom and love

Kornfield speaks about a particular source of misunderstanding when we confuse charisma with true spiritual wisdom.

> Certain leaders possess the ability to evoke extraordinary states of mind. Amplified by our hopes, feelings of bliss and transcendence arise easily around charismatic ministers, priests, Zen masters, mystics, rabbis, and gurus. It is easy to mistake such spiritual powers as definite signs of wisdom or enlightenment or divine love. We forget that power and charisma are just power and charisma—that these energies can just as easily serve demagogues, politicians, and entertainers. It is possible for someone to be charismatic but not wise. (Kornfield, 2002, p. 255)

Spiritual seekers of truth may have a certain naive openness that makes them vulnerable to the guru phenomenon. The guru "knows best" and appears to offer longed-for certainty to followers whose emotional foundations are insecure. Charismatic leaders tend to attract idealistic acolytes. When students idealise teachers of whatever faith, they generally lose their discernment and capacity to take personal responsibility.

The shadow of idealisation

Devotion and idealisation pose equal challenges to the teachers. Like the pairing of Narcissus with Echo—who is a cypher, lacking self-worth—the child/parent model of guru devotion inevitably creates a fundamentally unequal, unbalanced, co-dependent relationship, in which the devotee/idealiser gives away their power and autonomy. Sadly, projections of adoration from the student may propel a teacher into grandiosity—especially if the spiritual leader has their own history of traumatic narcissism. Daniel Shaw (2013), who himself experienced harmful relationships in a spiritual organisation, writes that the abusive leader has often grown out of a transgenerational system of trauma. This is likely to be the case regarding Lama X, who was removed from his mother at an extremely young age in the Tibetan *tulku* system and brought up in a monastery. *Tulkus* are simultaneously deprived of maternal love, while also treated as special: it is easy to see how, while sitting on thrones in their infancy, dispensing initiations and blessings, their egos may become inflated. Shaw sees such early trauma as one cause and danger whereby gurus unconsciously act out their own unresolved trauma on the group. For Lama X, his original traumatic separation was compounded by China's invasion of his Tibetan homeland while he was still a child, forcing him to seek refuge in the West.

When idealisation is directed en masse at a leader whose charisma flows out of some ungodly wound, the pedestal will have at some point to topple. Lama X certainly nearly brought down the whole house of cards of his organisation.

Manipulation

Cultic leaders often reel in their followers by heaping praise, appreciation, and "love bombing" (a form of grooming) with *intermittent* positive reinforcement. This elicits total devotion. Spiritual seekers with backgrounds of childhood abuse are particularly vulnerable. Unconsciously drawn to such leaders who treat them as special cases, they mistake the seductive charisma of the teacher for love. Those who are susceptible to this intermittent positive reinforcement tend to have an insecure attachment style, are insecure in their relationships, and so feel compelled to work extra hard to people-please. Once the student has committed, the teacher gradually begins to mock, ignore, or mete out other types of cruelty, so the student then tries harder to win back that initial approval to which they became addicted.

The tactic of intermittent positive re-enforcement—to ignore, then pay attention to, then ignore again—lowers the bar for what constitutes affection, so the victim perceives themselves as diminishingly worthy of love. According to attachment theory, inconsistent and tantalising connection creates intense anxious attachment to the abuser. Feeling unsafe and confused, all attention is focused on the manipulative attachment figure, rather than on one's own experiencing self. This is trauma bonding.

While Vajrayana is not in itself a cult religion, Tahlia Newland (2019) argues that whether a particular community deserves the label of cult depends on how the lama teaches:

- *Devotion*: do they demand that you give up your discernment?
- *Pure perception*: do they demand that you see the lama's questionable actions as beneficial, and are the teachings of pure perception misused?
- *Vajra commands*: does the teacher demand complete obedience and consider that Vajrayana beliefs place the teacher above the law of the land?

A veil of secrecy is undoubtedly a warning sign. Healthy religious organisations allow open criticism and the free flow of information. They do not—as teacher X and his organisation did—demand obedience or devotion, nor reward favoured students with desirable teachings and attention, while punishing others through shame, humiliation, and fear tactics. A healthy organisation will not isolate nor condemn anyone who criticises, nor manipulate their members to give money and slavish service. The teacher would not think themselves above the law and would make it quite clear what is expected of the member at each stage of their spiritual path, so that the student can make informed choices.

Crazy wisdom

Tantra is particularly vulnerable to accusations of cultic abuse on account of secret practices which may occur privately between teacher and student. In Tibetan legends, many "mad" and *crazy wisdom* yogis used unconventional methods to bring their students to enlightenment very quickly—that is, in only one lifetime.

> I suspect some bad gurus … have been corrupted by that … insidious … notion that some rare souls achieve mystical self-transcendence so completely that they become morally infallible … [which] can turn spiritual teachers into tyrants and their students into mindless slaves, who excuse even their teachers' most abusive behaviour as "crazy wisdom". (Horgan, 2011)

Buddhism identifies the ego as the source of all human suffering, so *crushing* the ego is part of the teacher's agenda to awaken the student and bring them to the true nature of reality. Although the phenomenon of destroying an adherent's ego is found in most cults, the practice thus appears to be legitimised within Buddhist belief, and this can lead to abuses.

The *mind direct* transmissions by the Vajrayana master to *introduce the nature of mind* breaks through the student's egoic consciousness to *pure awareness*, beyond mind. Traditionally, students are required to undergo years of in-depth training and have developed a stable meditation practice before this introduction is made. However, Lama X often transmitted this initiation to completely new students with no preparation at all.

The guru may use various *skilful means* in the name of enlightenment—such as shame, ridicule, and humiliation—to crush the ego. I observed that this frequently ended up crushing the student, diminishing their sense of autonomy and self-confidence and causing post-traumatic stress disorder, especially when the teacher had serious and perverse character flaws, as did Lama X. Ironically, such cruel behaviour seemed to make the student more loyal and devoted. In psychological terms we could understand this as attachment to the bad object (Fairbairn, 1952), trauma bonding, coercive control, and—as Felicity de Zulueta described in *From Pain to Violence*—"attachment gone wrong" (de Zulueta, 1993).

In a cultic form of the devotional path, the devotee lives to please, and avoid displeasing, the guru/lama/god. The guru's displeasure comes to mean, for the member, that his core self is unworthy, defective, and dispensable, since devotees become conditioned to believe that loss of the leader's "grace" is equivalent to loss of the self. As students become more deeply involved, the anxiety about remaining a member in good standing increases. Extreme as it may seem, once deeply inside the group, this anxiety is akin to the intense fear, helplessness, loss of control, and threat of annihilation, that Judith Herman describes in her discussion of psychological domination induced in victims of terrorists and battering partners (Herman, 1992).

One of the whistle-blowers of Lama X said she put aside her misgivings about the teacher and just "went along with things". This included being enslaved in harsh unpaid working conditions and being cut off from families and ordinary life with little possibility of leaving. One nun was only able to escape and establish a new life in a different country because her father gave her enough money to pay for an air flight. As she looked back, she realised she had gradually been brainwashed into accepting behaviours, which, to an outsider, would appear completely unacceptable. The increasingly abusive behaviours of Lama X—erratic, demanding, and bizarre—were attributed as qualities of a crazy wisdom master. Abuse, however, is not crazy wisdom—as Mingyur Rinpoche wrote in his article on *The Lion's Roar* (2017), "The results of genuine 'crazy wisdom' are always positive and visible."

The narcissistic profiles of cult leaders and their devotees

People often seek spiritual help to heal the narcissistic wounds from their dysfunctional families. Those with histories of abuse often exhibit idealising childlike states of trust, longing for a sense of certainty, to be safe and cared for. Such seekers enter into highly dependent relationships with the teacher. While it is devastating if the supposedly trustworthy teacher turns out to be similar to their abuser and undeserving of that trust, we need to reach beyond the victimised position—from the soul's perspective, we are all responsible for our choices and there is something here to learn from and understand.

In 2003, clinical psychologist, Buddhist scholar, and meditation teacher, Jack Engler, published influential findings from his research (2003a). He discovered that narcissistic personalities represent a sizeable subgroup of those individuals with borderline levels of ego organisation who are drawn to meditation. For this type of personality, the ideal of enlightenment or nirvana offers a unique attraction: the possibility of establishing a mirroring or idealising type of narcissistic transference with spiritual teachers who are perceived as powerful, admirable beings of special worth in whose halo they can participate.

In Greek mythology, Narcissus and Echo were a co-dependent pair. Narcissists attract those who have people-pleasing/fixer empathic tendencies, who engage in false-self relationships where they are passive, submissive, and acquiescent. The Echo in this dynamic confuses caretaking and sacrifice with loyalty and love, so while he or she offers unwavering dedication to the master, the only reward is to be used and unappreciated. Co-dependent people yearn to be loved, but in choosing a narcissistic Other, their dreams remain unrealised.

Narcissistic leaders are frequently emotionally immature bullies and tyrants, often a feature of disorganised attachment. This double-bind relational template—the simultaneous desire for proximity and escape—creates a state of "fear without solution" (Main & Solomon, 1990). The conundrum of disorganised attachment is that of trying to find emotional stability when there is no safe "secure base". The ego uses whatever techniques/defences it has at its disposal to survive in an attempt to counterbalance anxiety. A common defensive strategy for managing the paradox of an attachment figure who is meant to protect but actually creates dread, is to idealise them—that is, keep them good—while simultaneously devaluing oneself and taking all the blame for having created problems.

Since maintaining proximity is fundamentally unsafe, the following strategies are commonly found with narcissistic personality/disorganised attachment. The relationship is largely concerned with *controlling* the object rather than having a relationship with it, and coercive control is but a step away from this. Winnicott (1971) speaks of *the ruthless use of the object* in the phase of baby/toddler development where the child is narcissistically self-invested and has not yet developed a sense of relationship with or *stage of concern* for the Other. Disorganised attachment skews development, the need to control is reinforced, and so inevitably there is a lack of mutuality or reciprocity.

A narcissistically invested guru who has not experienced relational mutuality or reciprocity is unable to respond appropriately to their students and has a tendency to re-enact and retaliate. Their disorganised attachment trauma is transferred onto and repeated with their relationship with the student who becomes a mere extension of the narcissistic guru's self.

The traumatised "disorganised" person may also identify with the aggressor (Anna Freud, 1936) as a defence. The teacher, in a state of infantile helplessness, may cope by hitting, sexually dominating, starving, mocking, publicly humiliating, and shaming their students, entirely unconscious of their acts of retribution against their own shameful sense of imprisonment which they cannot own for themselves.

Dependence is a significant factor in the mix. At some point, the cult leader realises how desperately co-dependent he or she is and despises his students as idiots or incompetents because he cannot tolerate his own need of them. He loathes his students, not only because they hold up a mirror to his own immaturity, but because he feels trapped and dependent on their slavish immaturity and devotion for his sustenance. The narcissist rages against these underlying infantile dynamics and, not content with his own psychological space, will predatorily invade the psychological territory of others, pushing victims as far as they will allow, invading their integrity and then pushing for yet more.

The narcissistic leader is unable to set limits or regulate his or her own emotions, resorting to addictions such as drinking, drug-taking, compulsive sex, gluttony, binge television watching, making large amounts of money, or adopting reckless behaviours (which in some instances has resulted in death)—the majority of which were strong features of Lama X's lifestyle.

When a guru is swayed by power and becomes grandiose, there is a complete lack of accountability. When the Tibetan Buddhist master Chogyam Trungpa died, Regent Osel Tendzi, who was HIV-positive, succeeded him. The regent continued to have unprotected sex with several partners and infected people without disclosing his diagnosis until the Vajradatu board persuaded him to inform his students. The regent eventually told a stunned community meeting: "Thinking I had some extraordinary means of protection, I went ahead with my business as if something would take care of it for me."

Tobias and Lalich draw a portrait of a typical cult leader which emphasises their narcissistic profile:

> an outstanding ability to charm and win over followers … Paranoia, … Megalomania … an inner world of rage, depression and fear … The profile of a sociopath. Glibness and superficial charm … Manipulative and conning … Grandiose sense of self … Pathological lying … Lack of remorse, shame and guilt … Shallow emotions … Incapacity for love … Need for stimulation. Callousness and lack of empathy … Poor behavioural controls and impulsive nature … Early behaviour problems and delinquency … Irresponsibility and unreliability … Promiscuous sexual behaviour and infidelity … Lack of realistic life plan … Criminal or entrepreneurial versatility … (1993, p. 60)

This shocking description exactly sums up the infantile features—which worsened—in Lama X, whom I came to regard as having narcissist personality disorder. His mind-control, manipulation, and exploitation caused untold harm on all levels. One well-known lama used to joke about the "slaves" of Lama X, caught in master–slave dependency. I observed that this resulted in mind-shattering trauma, severe post-traumatic stress disorder, and a total loss of faith for those who managed to leave.

Fear and obedience: "Following the commands of your Vajra master to the letter"

In cults, fear, guilt, threats, and stringent tests of loyalty are routinely used to produce unquestioning obedience and group conformity. The leader's decisions control and usurp the follower's right or capacity to make choices. Humiliation breeds loyalty: it demonstrates that a person's will-power is broken when they subjugate themselves to another's bidding.

Caught up in his narcissistic bubble, Lama X was unable to tolerate any dissent, and would go into tirades of uncontrollable rage if anyone dared challenge him. Tolerating these aggressive outbursts—either as the recipient or observer—was seen as a test of devotion. Many didn't ask questions for fear that they might be singled out for ritual public humiliation and bullying.

In managing Lama X's image, dissent was actively silenced. Organisational leaders employed expensive specialist consultants to convey positive news and manage information and social media. While Lama X lived an egregiously extravagant lifestyle, he exploited lower-ranking students by using their offerings and donations to pay his girlfriends large amounts of money.

The difficulties of speaking out

It seems baffling that people sexually exploited by charismatic religious leaders are reluctant to denounce their abusers. In the Canadian documentary *In the Name of Enlightenment* (2011), a woman called Mimi highlights Stockholm syndrome—the paradoxical reaction of individuals who bond with their abusers: "The person beating us is also the only one giving us affection and food and a roof over our heads." The most dismaying part is that, as the teacher's devaluing and loathing of the student escalates, so too does the devotee's need to see it as something else. While this is a tactic frequently used in all cults, there is a greater degree of perversion when abused individuals are persuaded to view such cruelty as an act of the guru's love. A commonplace declaration by students of teacher X was: "I am so lucky to be receiving the teacher's blessings in this way." Such denial of the reality of the situation was a psychological defence, as a means to tolerate the abuse.

Terror is probably the main reason victims of abuse stay silent. They don't want to speak publicly for fear of retribution and negative consequences—of damnation, of not being saved, of possession by evil spirits, of being attacked by negative forces, and so on. While the fear of leaving is a common feature of all cults, this terror of eternal damnation is specific to spiritual and religious cults.

If a student wished to express real doubts concerning Lama X's behaviour, they would initially be fobbed off by the middle management tier of the organisation. If they eventually managed to see a senior person in the hierarchy, the customary response was that the student's difficulties were merely their (false) perception, and that seeing anything wrong with the lama indicated their lack of devotion. Students were also bullied by being publicly ridiculed, shamed, and humiliated in front of hundreds of people in the name of "getting rid of ego", which was a strong incentive for toeing the line. Those who did manage to speak out faced blame, judgement, character smears—they were shunned and scapegoated by the group—all things which I experienced.

A serious aspect of spiritual trauma was the way Lama X used fundamentalist interpretations of teachings to terrorise his students—for instance threatening *Vajra hell* to those who criticised or spoke out (something he threatened me with when I left). For some, this curse continues to haunt them for the rest of their lives.

When a student has *taken refuge*—a spiritual initiation—into a supposedly safe and trustworthy path, and the teacher subsequently distorts the truth and the teachings, this is one of the worst kinds of spiritual abuse, creating mind-bending confusion and distress. Losing your safe ground and spiritual trust results in overwhelming trauma to the inner world.

Fear of leaving

As Lifton (1961) noted, abusive groups tend to suppress any kind of internal challenge to the leader's decisions, which disempowers students from independent thought. "You have to do what the group does … and are pressured if you fail to do so. Your view becomes moulded to fit the ideals. Any failure to conform will be reported to the management by other devotees." When I left, I was threatened and guilt tripped, and they tried to bribe me to stay.

Lama X kept an inner circle of attendants to rely on at all times, who had no time to engage in normal social and family relationships, and who were not permitted to leave at will. One of Lama X's closest attendants described a form of thought police where people were checked on to see if they were straying. She regularly witnessed students being summoned to the lama's private garden to report back on other students' behaviour. This was particularly pernicious, since it was not possible to gauge if a friendship was genuine, or if you were being love bombed at the dictates of the master. Duplicitous relationships abounded; those at the top of the hierarchy were guiltiest of double speak, professing friendship while reporting on you behind your back—the opposite of following the path of *dharma* (which means truth).

Another student recounted: "When you are dealing with a narcissist who relies on you, they make it very hard for you to get away. I tried to leave a few times over the years and got manipulated. Lama X had huge psychological control. I was trained to obey and not argue, to shut up on command and to make anything he wished for happen even if his demands were ridiculous. He commanded me back to him several times and while inside I thought I had decided NOT to return I noticed myself saying 'yes'—so I felt I had to follow through. I eventually figured out that the only way to escape was cutting off all direct contact."

Another commented: "Being a virtual prisoner, X's attendants frequently ran away because life with him is incredibly awful. The attendants who serve break down, but then X reels them back in, by love bombing. Once the person is back in, X restarts the cycle of infantilising, abuse and control as part of the person's 'training'."

Hall of mirrors

In aspiring to see the lama as a Buddha, the student lets go of normal perceptions. Flaws and human deficiencies in the teacher would be pushed away as the fault of the viewer and their impure perceptions, like a hall of mirrors. Denial is the first defence, so students would blame themselves for being wrong and seeing negative things, and so work harder to purify their vision and judgemental mind. However, if doubts and splits continue to appear in the students' perceptions of the teacher, it is profoundly destabilising, placing the students in a double bind. One student described how:

"I started to pay more attention to my 'ordinary' perceptions and common sense, which over the years I had dismissed as being 'impure perceptions'. I felt lost, fearful and confused, and it did not feel possible to check out these perceptions with fellow students, since this created the 'double bind' of breaking samaya. Can you trust your own mind? How do you discern things? What perceptions can you trust? Is this my projection or is it real? Or unreal? If the teacher appears to be bad, does that mean I am bad? This is crazy-making stuff and was a huge spiritual trauma. The ground beneath became dangerous and not to be trusted. It was very scary to decide to trust my own perceptions, over and above whatever the 'Master' or other students were saying."

If *pure perception* is taught dogmatically, students struggle to exercise discernment. When the teacher denies the student's perceptions, reality becomes distorted. What is truth? They are paralysed, unable to think for themselves or find clarity. The Dalai Lama said that *pure perception*, taught by an unethical teacher, was tantamount to *pure poison*. Such distortion can lead to mental breakdown. At a conference in Newport Beach, California he commented:

> Part of the blame lies with the student, because too much obedience, devotion and blind acceptance spoils a teacher ... Part also lies with the spiritual master because he lacks the integrity to be immune to that kind of vulnerability. I recommend never adopting the attitude toward one's spiritual teacher of seeing his or her every action a divine or noble. ... if one has a teacher who is not qualified, who is engaging in unsuitable or wrong behaviour, then it is appropriate for the student to criticize that behaviour. (His Holiness the Dalai Lama, 1989)

The term "gaslighting", originating from the 1944 movie *Gaslight*, is commonly used in clinical and research literature. Anyone is susceptible to gaslighting, which seeks to sow seeds of doubt by making people question their own memory, perception, and sanity. Narcissistic cult leaders are masters at such manipulation. Gaslighting occurs slowly, so initially the victim doesn't realise it is happening. When Lama X used gaslighting to crush the ego, this included the added dimension of spiritual abuse. Since the lama is perceived by the devotee as being of a more sound, all-knowing mind, this creates tremendous confusion, pain, and conflict. By bullying, the leader casts doubt on the devotee's appraisals of the world—and their perceptions of the leader. The student loses trust in his or her immediate senses and feelings, instead accepting the interpretations offered by the guru. The persistent use of denial, misdirection, contradiction, and lying, destabilises and delegitimises the person's own self-belief and perceptions. If the student is already fragmented on account of early childhood trauma, such ego-crushing totally undermines the person's sense of self and confidence, particularly when this is done with such cruelty and violence. This makes it even more difficult to walk away, to have agency to leave.

The effects of gaslighting bring persecutory feelings of guilt, shame (stupidity), and fear which damage ego functioning and self-esteem, leading on occasion to breakdown. Tragically, some students fragmented and literally lost their minds. One I knew ended up by taking her own life; others have been severely traumatised, including suffering from psychosis and nervous breakdowns resulting from spiritual manipulation and abuse.

Finding healing

Having myself held a wishful image of Buddhism as a sacred healing tradition, I was devastatingly disillusioned when I left. I temporarily experienced a total collapse of my belief system, though ultimately this trauma served to strengthen my aspiration to listen to and follow the truth inside my heart. Being a whistle-blower proved to be an extraordinary teaching (not one, I am sure, which was intended by the teacher), where I was forced to embark on the road of individuation.

When we relinquish our personal wisdom, discernment, and common sense, perceiving this to reside in the external source of the master, we lose our centre. This is complicated in Vajrayana where students are required to "obey the Vajra master's commands to the letter". Disillusionment, while agonising, provides fertile ground for post-traumatic growth. Viewing experience as opportunities for personal growth is taught in the Buddhist teaching as "May confusion dawn as wisdom." Apocryphally, an Eastern Buddhist observed that "It is well known that the personal self cannot be denied, buried or neglected without serious consequences ... Westerners get into a death struggle with their ego while in the east, people sit around enjoying cups of tea!"

The "ego" in our everyday understanding refers to the healthily functioning sense of self which operates in the realm of the ordinary mind, dealing with reality and our basic survival needs. Through psychotherapy and mindful spiritual practice, we come to terms with our childhood traumas, integrate the ego, and develop self-esteem. We do not want to crush this healthy aspect of ourselves. The *grasping ego*, on the other hand, is something different—stuck in overthinking, mental projections, and narcissistic preoccupations, it prevents us from accessing our heart's wisdom.

For many years after I left the group, my ego did cling, preoccupied with ruminations about what had gone on. Cult stories were emerging about Lama X and in particular a Canadian documentary recounted the shocking trauma of one woman's experience, which I found immensely upsetting. I made another attempt to write to members high up in the organisation urging them for accountability. This turned out to be absolutely futile—so ultimately, letting go was the only way to complete my mourning.

What helped me do this? When we are connected with our "true" nature—what Buddhism and the Dzogchen teachings calls our *pure awareness*—and follow the flow of our innate wisdom and intelligence, this "higher" soul's perspective honours that we are all responsible for the choices we make. There is no victimhood but only learning, which helps our consciousness evolve. Jungians might use the term "Self"—others our "higher self". I like to call it *soul-connecting*. In the new paradigm we aim to reach beyond the old hierarchies of the priest above, and instead go direct to Source (or God) to connect with own innate wisdom where it becomes possible to find hope, follow our own guidance, and rebuild our lives.

I am very grateful to energy psychotherapy and energy psychology methods which helped me through the trauma of my experience of the cult, as I gradually learned to trust myself from within and find my own sovereignty, rather than relying on the authority of an external idealised Other who supposedly knows better. However painful the journey is, it is possible to find transformation and healing. The damage becomes the very path itself to greater understanding, wisdom, and compassion.

Glossary

Rainbow body

Various esoteric traditions emphasise the capacity for the miraculous transformation of the human body. The energetic principle of matter to light is inter-cultural and universal (White, 2018) where, during the higher, final phase of enlightenment ("God-realisation") the body changes dramatically and alchemically from flesh into light. The transsubstantiated body is referred to variously as the resurrection body, light body, solar body, diamond body—and rainbow body is the term used in Tibetan Buddhism.

Vajra hell

In addition to the "fire and brimstone" aspects of hell, Vajra hell is said to be extra tormenting because of the terrible limitless regret you feel for abandoning your sacred vows, which blocks your spiritual path. When you die, you will see these mistakes with utmost clarity and feel unbearable remorse for having lost such a golden spiritual opportunity to realise enlightenment.

Sangha

The Sangha—our connection with the spiritual community and friends who accompany us on our path—is one of "The Three Jewels"—Buddha, the Dharma, and the Sangha—who help us on our journey to enlightenment.

Skilful means

The practices and rituals of Vajrayana Buddhism are also often described as a process of *skilful means*, whereby practitioners use the very misconceptions and confusions of mundane existence as the path from which to realise enlightenment.

Pure awareness

Pure awareness—or *Rigpa*—is the state of non-dual consciousness. This is the "zero point" of quantum consciousness, an experiential state of embodied light permeated by peace equanimity and compassion. This takes us beyond ego (third-dimensional consciousness) into the sacred realm of *pure perception*—the non-conceptual fifth dimension, where we perceive divinity in all things—known also as *Christ consciousness.*

The grasping ego

This refers to our habit of "grasping" at having a "self"; incessant movements of grasping at a delusory notion of "I" and "mine", self and other, and all the concepts, ideas, desires, and activity that sustain this false belief.

References

NB. Apart from citations from books, many quotations in this text are from former Buddhist students who gave their permission to be quoted anonymously. Others are from articles which have arisen as part of public discussion about cults.

A Very British Cult (April 2023). Directed by Benjamin Lister. BBC 3.

BBC (2023, 2 May). https://www.bbc.co.uk/news/world-africa-65423645

Engler, J. (2003a). Being somebody and being nobody: A re-examination of the understanding of self in psychoanalysis and Buddhism. In J. Safran (Ed.), *Psychoanalysis and Buddhism* (pp. 35–80). Boston, MA: Wisdom.

Fairbairn, W. R. D. (1952). *Psychoanalytic Studies of the Personality*. London: Routledge, 1994.

Freud, A. (1936). *The Ego and the Mechanisms of Defence*. London: Karnac, 1993.

Gaslight (1944). Directed by George Cukor. Metro-Goldwyn-Mayer.

Herman, J. L. (1992). *Trauma and Recovery: From Domestic Abuse to Political Terror*. New York: Basic Books.

Horgan, J. (2011, 3 December). Why I don't dig Buddhism. *Scientific American* [blog]. https://scientificamerican.com/blog/cross-check/why-i-dont-dig-buddhism/ (last accessed 28 December 2025).

In the Name of Enlightenment—Sex Scandal in Religion (2011). Directed by Debi Goodwin. CMF FMC, Canada. *Inform* https://inform.ac/ (last accessed 28 December 2025).

Kornfield, J. (2002). *A Path with Heart: A Guide Through the Perils and Promises of Spiritual Life*. London: Rider.

Lalich, J. (1997). Dominance and submission: The psychosexual exploitation of women in cults. *Cultic Studies Journal, 14*(1): 4–21.

Lifton, R. J. (1961). *Thought Reform and the Psychology of Totalism: A Study of Brainwashing in China*. New York: W. W. Norton.

Main, M., & Solomon, J. (1990). Procedures for identifying infants as disorganized/disoriented during the Ainsworth Strange Situation. In: M. T. Greenberg, D. Cicchetti, & E. M. Cummings (Eds.), *Attachment in the Preschool Years: Theory, Research, and Intervention* (pp. 121–160). Chicago, IL: University of Chicago Press.

Newland, T. (2019). *Fallout: Recovering from Abuse in Tibetan Buddhism*. London: AIA.

Rinpoche, Y. M. (2017, 26 October). When a Buddhist teacher crosses the line. *The Lion's Roar*. https://lionsroar.com/treat-everyone-as-the-buddha/ (last accessed 28 December 2025).

Shaw, D. (2013). *Traumatic Narcissism: Relational Systems of Subjugation*. New York: Routledge.

Thaler Singer, M. (2003). *Cults in Our Midst: The Continuing Fight Against Their Hidden Menace*. Hoboken, NJ: Jossey-Bass.

Tobias, M. L., & Lalich, J. (1993). *Captive Hearts, Captive Minds: Freedom and Recovery from Cults and Abusive Relationships*. Alameda, CA: Haunted House.

White, J. (2018). Death and resurrection: enlightenment and the body of light. *Journal of Conscious Evolution*, *1*(1): Article 7. https://digitalcommons.ciis.edu/cejournal/vol1/iss1/7 (last accessed 28 December 2025).

Winnicott, D. W. (1971). *Playing and Reality*. London: Routledge, 1993.

Zulueta, F. de (1993). *From Pain to Violence: The Traumatic Roots of Destructiveness*. London: Whurr.

CHAPTER 4

Finding freedom: A leap of faith from Orthodox Judaism to a secular life

Jacqueline Samuel

A random Saturday in 2014 …

Under the inky shroud of night, I slipped out of my house like a shadow, my movements calculated and silent. The air was dense with secrecy as I approached the car idling by the garages at the back. Janette, the driver, face obscured by the dim glow of the dashboard, nodded imperceptibly.

With a furtive glance over my shoulder, I slid into the back seat, a phantom evading the world's gaze. The engine purred to life, and we melted into the obsidian tapestry of the night.

Dinner in Camden, here we come.

The mission to dinner in Camden was executed with a level of cloak-and-dagger precision that would have thrilled a younger version of myself decades ago, when dreams of joining the army danced in my imagination. In my fantasy, the allure of life in the intelligence services (as a spy, no less) promised the thrill of everyday covert operations. Yet, it wasn't just excitement I sought from the army; the well-defined roles and clear hierarchical structures of the military offered a sense of safety I longed for. Life, however, had different plans for me: instead of pursuing a military career, I found myself on a path towards Orthodox Judaism, an alternative system that, in its own way, provided structure, safety, and meaning.

Religion trumped the allure of the army, offering a broader code of living that felt genuinely true to me. Over time, the sense of truth collapsed, and I eventually sought freedom from the confines of religious life, discovering in the process that I no longer needed the security blanket of an army or a religious system to feel safe or contained. When opting for Orthodox Judaism, and choosing to enter a religious seminary over the military, I never foresaw that the only covert mission in my future would involve escaping the constraints of religious living for a simple dinner outing decades later. Life, as it often does, surprises us with unexpected twists. Reflecting on it now, it's been more than ten years since that dinner and since I began the process of leaving Orthodox Judaism. The journey has unfolded in ways I couldn't have predicted, and each step has led me to a deeper understanding of myself, the path I've chosen, and of freedom.

The conflict: Gayness vs religion

It was never my intention to leave Orthodox Jewish practice. There had been so much I loved about the religious life I adopted when I was sixteen. Growing up in a traditional Middle Eastern Jewish family, I was steeped in the rich cultural rituals, close-knit familial ties, and a deep connection to religious practices. From vibrant celebrations of Jewish festivals to the aromatic flavours of traditional Middle Eastern cuisine, my upbringing was a blend of religious heritage and regional customs. Respect for elders, adherence to community values, and the passing-down of traditions through generations created a sense of continuity and identity within the family unit. However, in the midst of this cultural richness and a robust Jewish identity, there lingered a sense of incompleteness within the traditional Middle Eastern Jewish family. Despite the steadfast connection to heritage, the religious practices of home felt somewhat lacking, less exacting or precise than that of our strictly Orthodox neighbours, or what I learned at my faith school. Amid the celebrations and shared moments, there was a yearning for a more structured spiritual foundation, prompting a reflection on the delicate balance between cultural vibrancy and the quest for a deeper, more meaningful religious experience.

The meticulous specificity of Orthodox daily practices, from the exacting order of putting on shoes to the analytical questioning of kosher dietary laws, provided a sense of emotional and intellectual satisfaction. It was a world where every action carried significance, fostering a connection to tradition that went beyond the surface, creating a deeply fulfilling way of life. However, after many years as a closeted Orthodox Jewish lesbian, I felt like an onlooker: a marginal outsider who was excluded from a big portion of Jewish communal life. Marriage and family are at the core of an Orthodox lifestyle, serving as vehicles into the community. Unfortunately, there was no possibility of marriage for me (at least not to a man), and therefore, my role in the community was limited. The aloneness that ensued was multilayered: I was precluded from having a personally satisfying relationship, and consequently, there could be no family life of my own. Communal life was only partially accessible without a husband. That said, these challenges weren't enough for me to leave the faith. I would have stayed regardless, and indeed found creative ways to live my life on the fringe. The conflict emerged when I met Janette.

Along came Janette

Janette was so much fun. She was larger than life with a belly laugh to match. She exploded into my life, showering colour and sparkle and light wherever she went. Her energy was infectious and I simply had to be a part of her, a part of it. With her, things were starting to get seriously lesbian.

This wasn't the first time I had faced this conflict; years before, as a fresh-faced seminarian, I'd fallen in love with a woman, cheating on god for the first time. In Orthodox Judaism, views on lesbianism and homosexuality often adhere to traditional interpretations of Jewish law, which typically consider homosexual behaviour as prohibited. These perspectives stem from verses in the Torah that condemn certain sexual practices, including those between individuals of the same sex. Consequently, Orthodox Jewish communities generally regard lesbianism and homosexuality as contrary to religious teachings.

Today, the degree of acceptance or rejection of LGBTQ+ individuals can vary among Orthodox Jewish communities and leaders. Some may advocate for compassion and support for LGBTQ+ individuals while maintaining the belief that homosexual behaviour is sinful. Others may take a more rigid stance, viewing homosexuality as a grave transgression and advocating for efforts to suppress or change one's sexual orientation. Overall, Orthodox Judaism tends to emphasise adherence to traditional values and practices, which can lead to challenges for LGBTQ+ individuals who seek acceptance. The tension between religious doctrine and personal identity can create profound internal conflicts and challenges for individuals navigating their sexual orientation within Orthodox Jewish contexts.

Back then, before compassion began to seep into Orthodox communities, I chose god over and above the woman I loved. I felt sinful, tainted, and haunted by shame and guilt which clung to me for a long time after the relationship ended. I threw myself into rehabilitating my connection with god, praying, studying, and exiling myself abroad so that I was far, far away from temptation. Because I thought, and hoped, and *wanted* to believe that my attraction to women was only a deviation from the heterosexual me. Ultimately, I was living a double life, projecting a cheery and religiously compliant exterior while grappling with internal torment and preoccupation. I could (I told myself) comfortably and *easily* meet and marry a man to follow the traditional vector of an Orthodox woman. However, at the same time, I was resigned to a life alone.

In Orthodoxy, where god is a central, organising figure, marriage is how religious life is lived and expressed. From the earliest glimmers of life, the Orthodox path is planned out. As a closeted lesbian, the path that includes marriage to a man is not really accessible. I tried though—oh, how I really, really tried. I dated men on arranged dates, each one vetted for suitability with matching values. Every one to no avail. It didn't matter how perfect he was, he was not for me, not *my* perfection.

Then along came Janette. I absolutely could not lose her as I had lost my first love. And so emerged my old conflict: Do I stay faithful to god (who would never approve of my relationship with a woman) or be true to myself? There had to be a way to integrate who, and what, and how I loved into my Orthodox Jewish lifestyle. Surely a loving god would want that? God is not vengeful.

And so I went to find out how to reconcile my Orthodoxy with my sexuality.

Leaving—a leap of faith

Inadvertently, while grappling with Judaism's understanding of gayness, I found myself questioning Judaism's fundamental beliefs. I delved into tomes of religious texts, sought guidance from rabbis, and connected with groups of Orthodox gay individuals. Along this journey I encountered thinkers with perspectives that I hadn't been exposed to before; including archaeologists, scientists, and Bible critics. Crucial to my exploration was someone who had trodden the same theological path, challenging the very philosophies and arguments that had inspired me as a teenager.

As an adult, once challenged, my beliefs could no longer withstand scrutiny. And so, the foundations of my Orthodox Jewish practice started to crumble. Years of diligent adherence to Jewish law suddenly became redundant, and, like a house of cards, the entire structure collapsed one quiet Friday night.

It was time for the kiddush prayer. Kiddush is a Jewish ritual performed to sanctify and consecrate certain moments, particularly the Sabbath and Jewish holidays. A blessing over the wine is recited, followed by additional blessings that acknowledge the sanctity of the occasion. Kiddush also serves as a reminder of the commandment to observe and remember the Sabbath and other holy days. As the words of the kiddush prayer left my lips, they felt strangely hollow and devoid of meaning. I quietly questioned myself: "Do I believe in this god to whom I am praying?" The answer, a resounding "No," echoed through my mind. Outwardly, I had been continuing to practise in the Orthodox way, but internally, I was a non-believer, navigating this duality with a lesbian partner by my side. This internal struggle had persisted for some time, but on this particular day the lack of cohesiveness became an unbearable weight.

During the "Grace After Meals" (a lengthier prayer filled with praise for a god I no longer believed in) I reached a breaking point; I couldn't continue with the charade, offering praises to a deity I had ceased to acknowledge. With a deep breath, I felt the moment arrive—a time to take a leap of faith! Turning to Janette, I said: "Let's go for a drive." Her initial half-smile suggested that she thought I was joking, given that driving is one of the activities that is forbidden on the Sabbath. "I mean it. I'm done. Let's get out of here, please."

And just like that, it was over. My thirty-year relationship with god had come to an end. I picked up the car keys half-expecting a bolt of lightning to strike, but that didn't happen. I was doing it. I was truly taking this monumental step.

Janette was mesmerised. We talked for hours. She had been aware of my quest for some time, and though I had shared much of the process with her, I spared her the intricate details. Having herself left religious practice behind after a brief foray, it never held the same significance for her as it did for me. Despite not fully understanding my anxiety or torment, she was supportive and, more importantly, excited! Before I knew it, she had booked us a holiday to Italy, where we could relish the joy of previously forbidden, non-kosher food. Since our trip to Berlin a year earlier, Janette had been hesitant about visiting countries with limited kosher options. Many holidays were spent in search of rare kosher groceries or restaurants, which frustrated her. She believed that exploring a new place was as much about savouring local cuisine as it was about sightseeing—a perspective I had never fully grasped. Now that the kosher dietary laws were no longer relevant, the culinary world opened up, challenging not only my concept of a holiday but also reshaping my entire approach to navigating the world.

Shifting patterns—decisions, decisions

This freedom business was complicated. Believe it or not, prior to that moment at the Sabbath table, I had given little thought to what life might be like if I stopped religious practice. Until that moment, I never really imagined it possible or likely that my life would actually change. My quest had been to integrate my Orthodoxy with my sexuality, not to shatter or quell or dispel my beliefs. The rest of me needed to catch up. Was I really ready to eat a lasagne in Italy or drive on the Sabbath? Did I eat pork now? I didn't know how to answer these questions. Intellectually, the answer was "yes", but in the face of her excitement, Janette's zealous holiday booking, I felt myself shrink, hesitate, stall. I tried to explain it to her—this was a shift of a significant magnitude. There were so many things to consider, confront, overcome, including: What and how I would tell the world? To whom was I accountable? What do I say?

My entire world was about to change. I had taken a leap, but had no clue where I would land.

Before I could share anything of my journey with the world (or perhaps choose not to) I needed to navigate the transition for myself. I had been drawn to religion in my teenage years for reasons similar to wanting to join the army—unfettered freedom seemed overwhelming and dangerous. As a teenager, I was curious and energetic. Without an identifiable sense of meaning and purpose, I feared where that curiosity and energy may take me. Religion with its absolute truths, clear-cut values, and dos and don'ts, felt safe and meaningful. However, when the element of truth unravelled, there was no turning back. Despite my love for aspects of Orthodox life and values, without truth and without a god, it all felt meaningless. So, I couldn't stay, and found myself working out where to go.

The leap into the unknown had a profound impact on every facet of my life. Let's look at a small example—Saturday. What is this thing called Saturday? I had never had a Saturday; I only knew the Sabbath. Of course; I had heard of Saturday but it belonged elsewhere, in the lives of others. Sabbath was something I knew and prepared for all week—grocery shopping, laundry, cooking—all in the service and goal of a quiet, gentle, respectful Sabbath day filled with prayer, family, and food. No cars, no money handling, no shopping. If there was no Sabbath and only a Saturday, did I now have a whole extra day, just for me? For Janette and me? What does one do with this newfound time, with a "Saturday"? And, more significantly, what then scaffolds the week without the structure of the Sabbath?

Just as I grappled with the construct of what constitutes a Saturday, questions of identity loomed large. I was never a fussy eater; I loved food and cleared my plate. As a guest in the Orthodox world, when asked about dietary restrictions, I proudly declared none; but this was within the confines of kosher dietary laws. Outside the Jewish world, I don't eat pork or shellfish or any of the animals that are forbidden by the Torah. In fact, I struggle to consume any foods that aren't kosher in its broadest sense. When asked now, I list the things I do eat. I have become that "fussy eater". The shift in my beliefs meant renegotiating not just my understanding of time but also reshaping my identity in the broader context of the world.

Resources

With my identity in flux and so many choices to make I was so grateful I had Janette as my support system to help me figure it out. Even though I had been quite outward looking in my Orthodoxy, the shift from "looking out" to "living in" was a wholly different challenge. Janette became my bridge to the outside world; she knew the struggles I was facing. She understood both the Orthodox world and the secular realms, identifying the gaps that needed bridging for me. Introducing me to friends beyond the community, she skilfully translated and filled in the cultural holes, even those I couldn't perceive. For many years, I had been detached from mainstream cultural phenomena—no television, cinema, or radio. The Spice Girls? A phenomenon that had passed me by entirely. If it happened during the 1990s, chances were I knew little about it. Janette mediated, seamlessly filling in the cultural spaces and paving a new pathway. She walked alongside me, holding me as I ventured into this uncharted territory.

Despite Janette's support, I found myself consumed by anger. Anger directed at my former teachers, whom I felt had misled me. Anger towards the Orthodox community, which I perceived as the eyes and ears of god, for the shame, isolation, and guilt they had unwittingly fostered. The frustration deepened as I grappled with the realisation that the community (from which I had already distanced myself) still held a lingering influence. Their gaze, felt long after my departure, cast shadows of guilt and shame upon me; this time, for choosing to leave.

While in the midst of all my anger, I didn't want to look back. I wanted none of it, not even the good bits. I wanted no part in the aspects of Judaism I previously enjoyed, refusing to join in with anything that had the whiff of religion attached, even a non-Orthodox Friday night meal. At the same time, my anger began to turn towards myself—for not being able to take the steps into secular life that I wanted to. I simply couldn't eat pork, despite my best efforts, and retched in my attempt to consume shellfish. It was as if my body, conditioned to a life in which it is so taboo, was simply unable to ingest it.

By accepting, embracing, and channelling my anger, I found a reservoir of strength with which to withstand the emotional turmoil of my departure. It allowed me to navigate the painful aspects of leaving behind a community, beliefs, and practices that had defined a significant part of my life. In this unexpected empowerment, anger became a transformative force, guiding me through the process of redefining my identity outside the confines of Orthodoxy.

Rebuilding and reconstructing

In time, as the anger subsided, I found myself increasingly able to reconnect with the parts of Judaism that I wanted to retain—elements that were ingrained within me. With patience and care, I painstakingly began to reconstruct a relationship with Judaism on my own terms. Moving to a new home, away from the watchful eyes of the Orthodox community, we settled into an area with a thriving secular Jewish presence. Free from the gaze of the Orthodox world, I had space to re-evaluate decisions about practices that were once taken for granted. One such decision was whether to affix a *mezuzah* (an encased parchment scroll with scripture) on our front door. A mezuzah serves as a cultural expression, signalling that the home is a Jewish household. Despite my departure from Orthodox practices, I realised that culturally, I still identified as a Jew. Omitting this Jewish symbol from my doorpost felt like a rejection of my Jewishness. After careful consideration, the mezuzah found its place on our door, affirming a nuanced connection to my heritage.

Gradually, I learned to not only tolerate but also enjoy a Sabbath meal with secular Jewish friends, realising that, at its essence, it was simply a shared dinner. I found a certain pleasure in this brief return to "ritual-lite". Last year, I accepted an invitation to a Passover *seder*, a ceremonial meal commemorating the Israelites' exodus from Egypt through readings and rituals. Initially hesitant, my friends assured me of the brevity of their seder to coax me into attendance. Surprisingly, I felt a bit short-changed by the abridged version and was more than willing to participate in the ritual. This experience underscored the realisation that not everything from my past had to be left behind; there was room for selective reintegration into my evolving relationship with Judaism.

Ongoing challenges

After more than a decade of embracing secular life, I am at ease living a culturally Jewish life where religion no longer occupies much of my brain space. From time to time, however, challenges still do pop up. One such challenge was my nephew's bar mitzvah celebration.

Several years prior, Janette who had been my rock, became ill and heartbreakingly died. Without her guidance, love, and support, this religious family event felt particularly overwhelming. Venturing into a synagogue, especially an Orthodox one, carried the weight of expectations—codes of dress, adherence to gender roles, and participation in rituals and prayers. Moreover, re-entering the community meant encountering faces from my past, with the looming sense of their gaze and potential disapproval. It all felt like too much to bear. I didn't want to conform to the expected norms—wearing a skirt or sitting upstairs in the ladies' section—nor did I want to feel judged. I had to find a way to be present on my terms while respecting the community's values.

Wearing a skirt felt unnatural, like donning a uniform or a costume that didn't align with my beliefs. However, I actively chose not to wear trousers to avoid detracting attention from my nephew's significant day onto myself and my attire. Being alone at the event bearing the invisible grief of my wife's death added another layer of difficulty. I felt marginalised once again in the eyes of that community. Recognising that I couldn't face it alone, I leaned on my resources, seeking a support system. I invited a gay friend to join me for the service. With an ally by my side and a firm belief in my freedom to make choices, I found the strength to relax and enjoy the festivities.

Another ongoing challenge involves driving through an Orthodox area on the Sabbath. Initially, it was an anxiety-inducing experience, leading me to take detours to avoid the discomfort. Even today, my heart races, palms sweat, and my body becomes tense as I navigate the streets, scanning for familiar faces. Despite the lingering unease, I now choose to drive through the neighbourhood, confronting it head-on rather than avoiding it.

These challenges, whether large or small, continue to shape my journey, pushing me to find ways to navigate the intersection of my past and present, cultural identity, and personal beliefs.

In conclusion: Thoughts for therapists

In my psychotherapy practice I specialise in working with people who have made significant life transitions, with a special interest in people who leave faith groups. When working with these individuals, therapists might consider that, as illustrated by my personal journey out of Orthodox Judaism, leaving a faith group is a complex and nuanced process that varies for each person. Indeed, leaving a faith group can be likened to moving countries; characterised by culture shock, loss of familiarity and identity, and a prolonged period of acculturation. Support systems and resources, such as language proficiency and access to secular education, can significantly impact the ease of this transition. While my focus in the chapter has been on leaving Orthodox Jewish practice, there are common denominators in the transition process that cut across various religions and experiences.

While my experience involved primarily internal challenges and the pursuit of personal autonomy, others may face external battles, including being shunned or persecuted by family and community. It's important for therapists to recognise the diversity of these experiences and approach each case with sensitivity.

When encountering someone who has left or is grappling with leaving a religious group, it may be useful to consider the following:

- **Motivations for leaving:** People leave religious groups for various reasons, including personal autonomy, seeking relationships, or escaping unsafe environments. Understanding the motivation behind leaving is crucial, as the decision is often a nuanced process that extends over years. Individuals leaving religious communities may experience a range of emotional and psychological challenges, including anxiety, depression, existential angst, and trauma. It's essential to provide a safe and non-judgemental space for clients to explore and process these experiences.
- **Transitional space:** Upon leaving, individuals may need a transitional space to land in, whether in the form of a new community, friendship circle, support group, or safe space. This transitional space aids in the acculturation process and helps individuals navigate new norms, attitudes, and perspectives. Individuals who have left religious practice may experience cognitive dissonance as they navigate

conflicting beliefs and values. They may struggle to reconcile their past religious teachings with their evolving worldview. Helping clients explore and resolve cognitive dissonance can be central to their process of self-discovery and personal growth.

- **Supporting identity exploration**: Leaving a religious community often involves a process of identity exploration and redefinition. Clients may be grappling with questions of who they are outside their religious identity and how they want to live their lives moving forward. Providing support and validation as they explore new aspects of themselves can be empowering and affirming.
- **Learning practical skills:** Regardless of the religious group left, individuals often need to learn practical skills such as making friends, dating, dressing, or finding employment. Social support becomes crucial for managing feelings of shame and inadequacy during this challenging adaptation period.
- **Ongoing challenges:** Challenges may arise even after significant progress in the transition process. This could include attending family events in the religious group, facing significant religious holidays, or encountering specific geographical areas associated with the past. Therapists should be prepared to address these individual challenges as they arise.
- **Respecting autonomy and agency:** Moving from a community-based culture to an individualistic culture is a significant shift. Individuals may grapple with the need to conform and comply, ingrained by their former community. It takes time to shed the sense of accountability and develop faith in one's freedom of choice. As a therapist, it's crucial to respect clients' autonomy and agency throughout their journey. Clients should feel empowered to make their own choices and decisions about their beliefs, values, and lifestyles without pressure or judgement. Creating a therapeutic alliance based on trust, respect, and unconditional positive regard can foster a supportive environment for clients to explore their authentic selves.

Overall, therapists working with individuals leaving faith groups should approach each case with empathy, recognising the unique challenges and providing support tailored to the individual's needs and experiences. It is an ongoing process that requires patience, understanding, and a collaborative approach between the therapist and the individual navigating this complex transition.

Postscript

A Saturday morning in 2023 …

Basking in the morning sun, I stepped out of my house, rocking a burst of colours to match my mood. The air buzzed with anticipation as I practically skipped to the waiting car—a kaleidoscope against the day's canvas. Each step felt like a dance to an invisible beat, a happy preview to the festivities waiting in London's heart.

Grinning ear to ear, I hopped into the car, joining friends decked out in equally vibrant gear. Laughter spilled from the open windows as the car rolled out, setting off on a journey painted in the lively strokes of camaraderie. The road to Pride in London stretched out like a celebration ribbon, carrying us into a day where love and acceptance splashed the city in the boldest of colours.

I paused, taking a moment to soak it all in.

Freedom.

CHAPTER 5

Can I join your planet? Escaping intergenerational abuse

Nancy Borrett and Cora Hart

Introduction and background

This is a story about the unbearable; how our survival need for attachment can keep us stuck in hidden trauma, or support an escape to safety. It is also about intergenerational violence, courage, and humanity.

My client Cora and I are writing about our therapeutic journey: Cora's search to find her place in the world, and my parallel path as witness, adapting my therapeutic approach to meet the complexity of both her internal and external realities.

As I start writing, I find myself struggling with how to share this material—how much do we let others know? First, Cora needs to remain anonymous for her own safety. And I worry that using language which truly matches her experience may overwhelm readers, leading to disbelief or dissociation. However, toning down the language feels like a betrayal.

Cora has dissociative identity disorder, also known as DID. DID is a survival mechanism that develops in earliest childhood, typically as a result of extreme and chronic abuse and results in compartmentalisation of the personality. People with DID develop with discrete altered identities, sometimes also described as alters, parts, different selves or personalities, and varying degrees of amnesia between these identities. Some people with DID refer to their internal world as a "system". Cora is describing her different identities as "alters". Many people with DID use plural pronouns as this more accurately represents their experience of self. Cora has decided to use singular pronouns for this chapter to make it less confusing for the reader.

DID remains a poorly understood condition, underdiagnosed and not covered in any depth on the vast majority of mental health trainings. Despite being extensively written about, spoken about, and previously known as multiple personality disorder, some senior practitioners still consider it a controversial diagnosis. Who wants to believe adults abuse small children repeatedly in such sadistic ways as to create such extreme dissociation? However, society's lack of acknowledgement, denial, and disbelief further harms survivors—how do you accept or seek justice for something when facing denial that it exists?

DID is a cross-cultural phenomenon, spanning all classes and ethnicities. It also appears to exist on a continuum. Fragmentation of personality into discrete identities will happen organically, given enough trauma during earliest life and the absence of a safe attachment figure. However, some clients also report abuse within organised criminal groups who use specific hypnotic and torture techniques to deliberately create dissociative splits within young children. This is often referred to as installed DID, or mind-controlled DID, and is typically associated with less co-consciousness (awareness) between different identities. Installed DID enables abusers to mould and train parts of the person to be obedient, compliant, and have specific roles that are useful to the abuse network. It also ensures there are identities who remain loyal to the network and may have little or no awareness of life outside, akin to brainwashed slaves. The alters who are more familiar with day-to-day life may be completely unaware of these more abuser-loyal alters, due to dissociative amnesia and the phenomenon of structural dissociation of the personality (van der Hart, Nijenhuis, & Steele, 2006).

Cora was born and raised within a multigenerational abusive criminal network and experienced extreme abuse—physical, sexual, emotional, psychological, and spiritual—from infancy and continuing into middle age. The abuse network has strong links to international organised crime, while much of her torture took place within the context of ritualised pseudo-religious belief systems. She describes an overview of her childhood experience below.

Cora's background

Cora: Unknowingly, for many years right into adulthood I was living two parallel lives within the one body and having DID meant one side was not aware of the other side's life: almost like identical twins separated at birth, unaware of the polar opposite life their identical sibling is living somewhere else in the universe. On one hand my life consisted of the everyday home/school life of a child in the UK: on the other I was experiencing extreme abuse, terrifying ritual activities, manipulation and sexual exploitation by an organised abuse network. It was part of an international criminal network linked to the church and I had the bad luck to be born into it. My parents and other family were active members.

I now know the sexual abuse and exploitation of me and other children funded their other criminal activities. I was subjected to ongoing violent and degrading sexual abuse by multiple perpetrators which was photographed and filmed, in addition to me being sexually trafficked to outsiders. I don't know exactly at what age the abuse began but because I have baby alters, and from what I witnessed, I suspect it started at birth. By the age of eight, I was being trained as a specialist BDSM (bondage, discipline, sadism, and masochism) sex worker and I continued to be trafficked in this role until a few years ago. As well as being actively abusive, my father was the doctor and my mother oversaw my trafficking hence set the boundaries, which meant they had confusing dual roles in my life as both abusers and caregivers.

The abuse network was also connected to a satanic ritual abuse group. The rituals were particularly violent, comprising horrific and terrifying psychological, sexual, and physical abuse of me and other children. This supposedly spiritual aspect of the abuse created a heightened terror and fear of retribution from a supreme being if I didn't comply. Did the ritual abuse stem from the abuse network's genuine spiritual belief system or was it another way to terrorise, abuse, and control vulnerable children? I'm not sure and I may never know the answer.

The abusers created confusion by treating my alters differently from each other. Some alters experienced painful and terrifying abuse, while others didn't. Alters who complied with the abusers' heinous orders were rewarded with special privileges, pleasurable sexual feelings, and promises of a long and happy life. After abuse the perpetrators would praise some child alters, emphasise how special they were, and how much they belonged and were needed. Naturally this made these alters feel valued and important, and kept them loyal, despite the pain and horror.

Sometimes my parents would even rescue me from other abusers who were hurting me so badly I thought I was going to die. This made me feel they must care about me. Because alters were experiencing situations other alters had no awareness of, some alters loved my parents; some were terrified of them, and some hated them and wanted to kill them.

There was no warmth or love or human touch in my life, except when I was being raped or abused or when the abusers were tending to wounds and injuries caused by abuse. Children need human touch to survive and therefore some alters grew to crave the sexual violence as it was the only time our body was touched and held.

Drugs and alcohol were used to sedate me, frighten me, and reduce pain after rituals and extreme abuse. This led to issues further down the line. These substances were called "sweets" or "your medicine" and "get better juice"; this was a mix of alcohol, drugs, and body fluids. How clever of them, because if I mentioned outside the abuse network that I'd had "get better juice" or "sweets" or "medicine", people would think my family were taking care of me … not the opposite.

DID kept the organised abuse network side of my life hidden from me until I was well into adulthood. It may be hard for people to understand how I experienced this much trauma with little awareness for so long: it is because I have installed DID, which means the abusers tortured me in particular ways to deliberately create splits and alters with allocated jobs/roles who would simply obey and be super-compliant and loyal to them. Individual alters held things in a highly compartmentalised way with amnesia between them. This meant my alters who managed day-to-day life had no awareness of the abuse network and vice versa.

Then there was my "ordinary life", not that it was without unhappiness and cruelty. I was born into a middle-class family and lived in a big house with my brothers and parents who had professional jobs. I went to school, although I was absent a lot. My parents were mercurial—either detached and neglectful, or angry and frightening. My mother didn't make eye contact except when she was hurting me.

There were many harsh rules, like I had to use a cold cloakroom downstairs where there was only a toilet and a tiny wash basin, instead of the main bathroom. I never had a bath or shower. I wasn't allowed to talk to anyone outside the family without my parents' permission or to mix with other children once school was over. Music, television, and magazines were not allowed. When I broke a rule, my mother would scream at me and hold me down while my father beat me with a belt or a piece of rope. When my mother lost it, she would hit and kick me. My brothers and I were quick to blame each other to avoid punishment, and our wariness and mistrust of each other developed into hatred as we grew up.

And then there was school. I was sent to school washed and in clean clothes, thus seen as a well-cared for child. Multiple red flags were missed. For a start, there were my school reports full of comments about my strange behaviour plus a shocking number of absences. I remember one where I'd been absent for twenty-one days out of a possible fifty-nine. But nobody said or did anything about it. A combination of factors led to my missing school: the abuse network's schedule of activities; my parents being absent; my abuse injuries were sometimes too severe for me to be seen; or because of the day-after effects of the drugs and alcohol they forced into me. In those days, schools were not vigilant about attendance and there was little communication between school and parents.

Children naturally pick up when there's something odd about another child. My strange ways, my wariness, and my jumpiness meant they kept their distance and I had no friends. I would watch them and long to be invisible so I could join in their conversations without them knowing I was there. Because to have friends was far too scary and alien. I was regularly in trouble at school and was accused of lying and of saying/doing things I had no memory of. Retrospectively I know this was due to the dissociative amnesia and identity alteration as I switched between alters. I thought I had a very bad memory because this switching left gaps in my memory. The alter who was being told off had no memory of what the other alter had been doing. My denial of what had happened or blank looks of puzzlement angered school staff, and I was disliked by them as well as by the children. As I grew older I learnt to just nod and apologise even when I had no idea what people were talking about. My life was one of sadness, loneliness, confusion, and anxiety with a deep longing for something I didn't have but didn't know what it was.

At the age of six my school referred me to a psychiatrist because of my unusually disturbed play with dolls and my insistence I had a large black wolf by my side. This was a protector alter my mind had created to help me feel safer. I heard voices inside my head and got into trouble for being "an attention-seeker" when a teacher overheard me talking to them.

Other obvious and shocking missed red flags (that I hope professionals would pick up on today) were my childly suicide attempts—drinking toilet bleach, running in front of a car, jumping out of an upstairs window with my brother, hanging myself with my school tie from the playground bars … all before the age of nine. By the age of twelve I was on antidepressants but the self-harming and suicide attempts continued. Still no one did anything. In my early teens I would collapse in the street, be taken to hospital by ambulance and kept overnight. Whether this was because of the drugs and alcohol or dissociative seizures or whether I was desperately trying to seek help, I don't know. The following day I would be discharged into the hands of my seemingly respectable parents without a word being said.

Without knowing why, I believed everyone could see how evil and disgusting I was and was repulsed by me and hence kept their distance. Little did I know I was being programmed to believe this, in order to keep me apart from other people and attached to the abuse network, to ensure I remained loyal to them. I never questioned why I was different as I blamed myself and felt ashamed.

I believe this was exactly what the abuse network wanted, as it increased both my dependence on them and their control of me. Life was so bewildering and exhausting that I withdrew and tried to fly under the radar where no one would notice me.

The following is told by Julie, a young child alter who managed the difficulties of day-to-day life, with no awareness in childhood of the more extreme abuse and trauma.

> Mummy and daddy goes away a lot and leaves us on our own. They say Philip's in charge but he's only three years older than me. He's

a little boy too. I brush their soft hair and help put on their shoes. I'm good at laces. I change Richard's nappies like he was my baby and put them in the bucket with the lid in the garage. Philip did the blue pin 'cos I can't work it. I wanted a baby doll but not allowed one. I cuddle Richard and feed him when no one there. When we was hungry me and Philip went to the corner shop and stole food. We eat a little bit of the food and Philip makes us save some. When he's asleep I nick a bit and eat it fast in the toilet. Sometimes we go down the road at night and look for food in the bins. We sleep in the same bed when mummy and daddy aren't there 'cos we scared we going to die. Sometimes strange grown-ups stay in our house we don't know who they are and they're scary and mean to us.

I like school but the teachers tell me off and are cross with me 'cos I fall asleep and don't learn properly. I jump out of my skin when a teacher says my name and the children laugh at me. I love Mrs Cook and I ask her to be my mummy. She says no but she lets me hold her hand when I walk across the playground. I feel warm and happy and I want her to hold my hand forever.

At home mummy and daddy don't ever touch me 'cept when they hit me. I don't think they like me but I try to be a good girl.

Nancy: Cora's childhood experience makes painful reading. However, from my work with many survivors of extreme abuse, and that of my colleagues, I am aware it is sadly not unusual.

DID is not an especially rare phenomenon. International research suggests it exists in around 1.5 per cent of the general population. I believe the hiddenness of DID in conjunction with our societal denial and the lack of help and understanding unfortunately serve to facilitate the continuation of this kind of abuse.

In extreme abuse situations the kinds of attachments that develop are sometimes referred to as trauma bonding (Carnes, 1997) where extreme and frightening experiences take the place of love and care and remain confusingly associated with them. Contact with an abusive caregiver may be both feared and longed for, as abuse is often all the child has known and its inevitability is not questioned. Through repeated torture and near-death experiences, children with DID are trained to transfer their needs for love and attachment on to handlers/controllers who also act as rescuers within this sadistic relational dynamic.

We know attachment is a survival necessity and our biological need for this means we will do whatever we need to do to maintain proximity to our caregivers. If this means dissociating from our own reality—both internal and external—then that is how we develop.

There is also the human longing for love. The absence of emotional connection expressed through indifference can seem more terrifying than abuse. Cora describes how the only eye contact her mother ever made was during abuse, and the way sexual violation became normalised—even longed for by some alters—as a substitute for tender touch or care.

Sachs (2008) expands on Kahr's original writing about infanticidal attachment (2007), distinguishing between symbolic and concrete infanticidal attachment; and I have found this distinction helpful in understanding the interpersonal dynamics of extreme abuse. Concrete infanticidal attachment is described as being the result of repeated deliberate torture and death threats within the attachment relationship. Sachs describes how within such a dynamic, "the deepest and most powerful engagement with these parents is in the midst of abuse" (Sachs, 2010, p. 79).

In intergenerational abuse families like Cora's, it seems likely that parents who abuse their children in extreme ways may also be highly dissociative, adding to the complexity. Shame relating to these painful connections, in conjunction with the deliberate manipulation, distortions, and criminality of the abuse networks bond survivors to their perpetrators, making it almost impossible for them to imagine life in the outside world. When people continue to be actively abused into adulthood, as Cora was, the continuing loop of trauma and dissociation prevents connected thinking. For people in this situation, knowing their own reality may be too painful or impossible without psychic breakdown, and dissociation remains a necessary survival mechanism.

Working towards freedom: The therapeutic process

Nancy: Cora, can you say something about how you gradually became aware of your DID and the more hidden aspects of your life?

Cora: Looking back there were many indicators I had DID but I only found out in my early forties during private therapy for something unrelated. My therapist back then told me I was dissociating and she was meeting other altered identities. I was gobsmacked but over time as I learned more about it, it made sense of many bizarre aspects of my life. People would say I seemed schizophrenic or like Jekyll and Hyde as I was unknowingly switching between alters. I would regularly lose my temper and get into fights and at other times I would cower and hide under tables, though I could not always remember this afterwards.

There was unaccountable missing time and I lived with a perplexing dread of being found out, though I didn't know what for until much later in life. Now I understand other alters were holding the threats of the consequences of speaking out or people finding out about the abuse network through me. I lost many jobs because I was viewed as unreliable, a bad timekeeper, deceitful, and untrustworthy.

As an adult I repeatedly moved home because I was constantly messing up—friendships, relationships, and jobs. People first became suspicious, then turned against me probably because they couldn't understand what was going on—nor could I most of the time. It was easier to move to another town or country and start again. In hindsight I realise this was a kind of geographical dissociation, dissociation being my default mode, that prevented any connectedness in my life.

Eventually following my repeated suicide attempts my GP took action and after a long and complicated battle I received a formal diagnosis and was referred for specialist DID-informed psychotherapy.

On being diagnosed with DID there came a mixture of responses from different alters including shock, denial, panic, but also some relief that there was a reason for being the way I was. I would much prefer not to have DID or the trauma that caused it and for years I fought against accepting it. I wanted proof and even when the proof came in numerous examples of what I was like, things I did or had done, I still didn't want to believe it. Accepting the diagnosis meant accepting my truth and I didn't want to be that person or that child. Retrospectively I can see it was unbearable to think of my parents as being that abusive and cruel, or that I had been so badly harmed by those who were meant to protect me.

Nancy: It seemed the attachment to your family was one of the most difficult aspects to explore in therapy. There was so much pain and conflict inside about your mother in particular. Many alters were amnesic of her as a perpetrator and were convinced she had not known about the abuse network. This always seemed unlikely or impossible to me, bearing in mind the kind of abuse you were describing, but it felt like an off-limits area for thinking, which in itself raised my curiosity. However, this is complicated territory as trauma practitioners are cautioned strongly about the dangers of suggesting possible memories to clients.

We've since learnt how some alters were specifically groomed by your mother to do certain "jobs" for the network. One of them, Star, has shared the following.

> **Star:** She's my mummy and I don't like people saying nasty lying things bout her. She's nice to me and gives me nice presents like she buys me a pretty dress and pretty knickers when I do what she says. She says I'm special and like her. She gives me important jobs and she says I'm good and I try to do them like her then she thinks I'm more special then she don't hurt me and hurts the other ones not me. I hate my jobs and I tell her I like them 'cos I mustn't make her cross. She's proud of me for being the baddest and the best baddest of them all. She gives me nice sex as a prize. I know others say she's bad and she's done lots of mean stuff. I don't want her to be bad and mean I want her to be my mummy 'cos she's my only mummy.

Nancy: Star has struggled with the more recent knowledge she has learnt from other alters inside about your mother. She has needed a lot of support and has thankfully now developed strong, loving connections with others internally.

During the earlier years of sessions, as we worked directly with many of your alters who brought trauma memories, some trust developed and your life appeared to improve and stabilise. I was aware there were areas we could not approach but did not realise the extent of what remained hidden.

Then came a profound internal change. Something highly taboo inside you was spontaneously disclosed to me by a specific alter for whom therapy had been quite transformational. This was a turning point, and alters who had been deeply hidden inside suddenly became more able to make themselves known, opening up about serious dangers which were ongoing.

It was a time of both crisis and opportunity when I began to realise you were still being actively exploited by the abuse network. Although I had considered this previously, it was something that had nonetheless remained hidden. Tell me what you remember about that time?

Cora: More and more alters were emerging, bringing with them their pieces of the shared history in an outpouring of emotions and horrifying memories. Therapy was intense, deep, and exhausting. Do you remember how alters would argue and vie for time with you in sessions and we had to negotiate sharing therapy time? I felt terribly vulnerable and exposed as raw painful emotions ravaged me week after week. Thankfully, I'd built up enough trust in you over the previous years to lean on you more than I'd ever needed to before.

One day I opened up about a hidden aspect of my current life—sex working. For me sex working was an angry, contemptuous "screw you" to the abuse network, whereby I used the skills and knowledge from their training to make decent money and fund the lifestyle I wanted. Over the next few weeks you gently and steadily challenged me as we explored the issue. The more other alters talked about punters they recognised, you and I came slowly to realise something was seriously amiss. But I still arrogantly and angrily believed it was my choice and I was in control. Then the day arrived when the mounting evidence led you to say, "You are being exploited." The horror of my reality flooded through me as things fell into place and I knew you were right. Facing the truth that the sex work was being run by the abuse network and realising once again I was just another pawn in their sick game broke me. I sobbed and sobbed as you held me and let me cry it out. Agonisingly painful, but an important turning point.

Nancy: Some of you understood the links between the abuse network and the sex work but for most this was new knowledge, though essential to know if you wanted to find safety. You're also referencing my "holding" of you in this section and I want us to write more about that. You are referring to a level of physical contact as well as emotional holding, which is a sensitive, potentially controversial matter in most psychotherapies.

Cora: I feel strongly about the use of touch in therapy in the right situation at the right time. The debates in the therapy world about whether it's OK or not quite honestly frustrate me and make me want to yell to therapists to be braver, respond to their client rather than a set of rules. The following is my perspective as a vulnerable client with a long history of negative touch through extreme physical and sexual trauma.

In the early days when I was building a relationship with you, touch could easily have been misunderstood by some alters and could've been a problem. No touch at this stage was the right thing for my alters and me as it wasn't necessary. However, once I started the deep trauma processing work, words were sometimes not enough. When my alters and I were sobbing brokenly and distraught, there was no way any of us could take in your words. Moving to sit beside me, placing your hand gently on my arm or my back let me know I was no longer alone, you were there, understanding how utterly awful it was and how body-breaking the grief was. It held me emotionally, helped me to stay sane and prevented me from shutting down. Frankly, to have left me alone on the other side of the room, breaking my heart, particularly when young child alters were out, would have been inhumane and harmful and would've damaged our therapeutic relationship.

Some survivors grow up receiving positive touch from caregivers as well as abusive touch. I didn't. Touch for me was either non-existent or abusive and it was a developmental deficit. It impacted my mental and physical health as well as meaning I grew up craving touch but with no understanding of its boundaries and what was OK touch and what wasn't. My abuse-created attitude to touch was so skewed it kept me trapped in abuse as an adult. To break free, heal, and keep myself safe in future relationships, I needed to experience safe and boundaried touch from someone I trusted. Touch in therapy was about me and what I needed, never about you. You always checked if it was OK with whichever alter was out and it was my/their choice.

Nancy: I think this is valuable for other therapists to hear, though I'm also aware of how easily touch can be misused, especially in the context of powerful projective processes. I remember times when some highly traumatised alters were so distraught they seemed to stop breathing and turned purple in the face. At these times, talking, encouraging body awareness, or suggesting so-called grounding techniques felt next to useless.

As you know, the issue of touch can be a highly charged one within psychotherapy practice, especially with a survivor of sexual trauma. I think it's important to notice the pull within the countertransference but to hold on to a "third" position too, including discussion in supervision and with colleagues. But we need to be brave when working with extreme material and I believe there can be a role for touch with some people at some stages of the work. In our sessions, it also led to important discussions with child alters about body boundaries and self-agency.

Ultimately, I understand how safe touch was important sometimes for some of you, to help you connect to your humanity, bring you into the present day, settle into your shared body and manage to bear your own reality.

Cora: Bearing my own reality became tougher still when I realised the abuse network was still controlling my life, not only the sex work, and with this came greater clarity and understanding about my whole life. Unexplained injuries to the body that I'd put down as dissociated self-harming were in fact the result of ongoing severe abuse. Several months later I discovered through an alter that the abuse network had set clear limits about what I could and couldn't talk about in therapy. That explained why I/we had previously been unable to tell you we were still being accessed and exploited. Over the next year as I ignored their rules and directives and talked with you about the forbidden taboo matters, they upped the ante on their control of me. Their attempt at increasing control eventually led to my coming to accept it was time to get away if I wanted a future.

I was discovering another side to my system where there were many terribly traumatised child alters who had been hiding a harsher reality from me. I noticed your therapy approach changed at this time as you were working largely with these very young child alters. You would gently welcome each one of them whatever they were like, respond individually and respectfully. You started to develop a stronger relationship with key alters which later turned out to be crucial to our decision to escape. You were clear every one of us was an equal part of our system and you had no favourites. Some alters jostled and protested and wanted to be the most special one, but you stayed boundaried and consistent in your acceptance and valuing of each and every one of us. Even those of us who were vile to you or to each other!

Nancy: Do you remember how hard we worked to encourage you to listen openly to each other's stories, to gradually put the pieces together to enable you to fully know what was happening? Some of you were furious with me initially and believed I was an interfering liar, the kind of person the abusers had warned you about …

Cora: Yes, this was long and painstaking work as my system was created by the abuse network to deliberately make sure all the alters held different parts of my story and didn't know about each other. It seemed almost impossible to listen to each other's stories and there was massive resistance to it. It meant overcoming huge fear of the repercussions of going against abuse network commands, and alters having to do something highly taboo they'd not done before. Some alters were adamant this was not going to happen and made it clear to you without holding back! One of my alters, Duke, has written the following about you.

> **Duke:** When I met you I hated you and thought you was a stupid dangerous woman and going to betray us. I knew we must never trust a therapist. You pissed me off big time 'cos you was interfering and I got mad with you. I was horrid and called you names but you was never horrid back. One day I said you was talking out of your arse. You was curious and asked me to explain it to you. No one ever asks what I think. Then you said thank you and said you looked forward to talking to me another time. Huh? This made me think you was even more stupid. But you kept being kind even when I was snarling at you. Then one day when we was by the river I felt weird inside 'cos I knew you was on my side and I'd been conned by the bad people and you wasn't bad and I cried a lot and hurt a lot inside. Your voice was soft and kind and you asked if you can hold my hand. I liked you holding my hand. No one ever done that before. You never ever said anything bad bout me. I waited and waited for it to happen but you never did. You even seemed to like me.

Nancy: I remember those conversations with Duke, his initial disdain and how his feelings changed over time. So many of your more hidden alters had a rough-tough facade but seemed to be the ones who held the most horrific trauma memories. They'd never known safety or respect and the veneer of hostility was shrouding pain, confusion, and terror.

Just around this time the Covid-19 pandemic hit the world and we had the first UK lockdown. It was awful timing, as it interrupted face-to-face therapy at a crucial moment when these most highly traumatised alters needed to learn to feel comfortable with me if you were to stand any chance of getting away.

We tried online sessions but they did not work well, partly as you had been filmed as part of your abuse and also because many of the newly known alters became confused about the idea of a talking image and really needed an embodied experience of therapy. Additionally, many of the external resources you'd used to manage distress were no longer available and you were isolated in your home. It felt really important to find ways to stay emotionally connected during the pandemic and creativity was needed. Almost by chance, we discovered that exchanging WhatsApp voice notes seemed to calm your whole internal system. You could listen to them as a resource, reminding you I was still there and that we were working collaboratively towards safety.

About six weeks into the first lockdown, we agreed in-person therapy was indeed necessary and that was also sanctioned by your GP—a relief for us both. We changed the therapeutic frame to meet the challenge of the situation and had intensive weekly sessions lasting three hours, working directly with the more hidden alters to process their trauma and help them become more orientated to the present day.

Cora: Thankfully this happened as, unknown to us at the time, the pandemic was going to change the way I was being exploited with the abuse coming closer to home, and the severity and danger of the sex trafficking increasing. Furthermore, neither of us knew then how much the violence and threats from the abuse network were going to increase in the coming months as I started to disobey them and begin to break away. When this happened, I needed an increasing amount of intense support and this would have been impossible with online therapy.

Being back in the therapy room together while the world was self-isolating felt like a one-in-a-million gift where the risks were greatly reduced of someone finding out I was breaking the abuse network rules of silence, obedience, and loyalty. It was a chance to tell you everything and I took it. Therapy intensified as alters hidden deep inside came out to talk to you and revealed the extent of our past and current horror. I wonder what it was like for you to realise how much danger I was returning to when I left the therapy room?

Nancy: It felt devastating at times, like sending you back into a war zone. The visceral connection I had with you had a profound impact on my worldview around that time. I developed intimate knowledge of what felt like a parallel universe, something most people are blissfully unaware of and might not even believe could be true. At times I felt stupid and ashamed I'd not realised sooner that your life was still being controlled by the abuse network.

I worked hard to remain able to think clearly in the midst of chaos. Some of you were functioning developmentally as highly traumatised and brainwashed young children and did not appear to have any concept of safety. One challenge was my perceived need to sometimes be more directive than any therapy training would typically suggest and, associated with this, my fear of becoming just another controlling person in your life. However, for you to survive and have any chance of freedom and safety I believed I repeatedly needed to challenge some of your perspectives pretty robustly, though I always tried to do this respectfully. This felt like an important positive risk to take, to be working outside my own comfort zone with your most severely traumatised child alters, frozen in time within the adult body.

Cora: I remember initially feeling slightly discombobulated and apprehensive when you became more challenging and directive, yet within weeks I realised it was unequivocally what I needed at this stage. Paradoxically, the dissociation that had protected and saved me was now threatening my survival by preventing me from confronting my truth. But it wasn't easy for either of us. Some of my alters fought your challenges and didn't want to hear the facts and links you were making between alters' stories which were making the truth undeniable. It felt unbearable. How could I live knowing significant people in my life were continuing to deliberately abuse and exploit me when some of my alters desperately wanted to believe they loved them/me, even a little bit. Gradually alters began to understand they had distinctive perspectives from each other about the family and abuse network and internal communication improved.

Alongside this, there were times when you advised me directly not to do something when I was about to put myself in a situation of potential great danger. I know you were uneasy about this degree of intervention and directness; however, my barometer of what was OK for others to do to my body and mind was so skewed I needed this. You were modelling that when someone cares about you it means they don't want you to get hurt and they want to protect you. An alien concept to me. Far from feeling controlled by you, it enabled me to consider that I had a choice and that I deserved not to be hurt.

Nancy: The timing of this work was also complex and involved weighing up potential risks and benefits. There were emotional risks from alters sharing material with each other prematurely, but seemingly greater risks from you remaining oblivious to your ongoing connection with the abuse network. There was no way to avoid the distress associated with this new knowledge. However, experience had also taught me you were likely to dissociate and "switch" if you were not ready to know something another alter was disclosing.

It seemed to me that the brutality of the programming and indoctrination governing your thinking needed a reciprocal toughness, though coupled with kindness and benevolence. I needed to meet you where you could be met, both metaphorically and literally, which leads me to something else important. Do you remember the days I visited you during the third lockdown when you were too unwell to travel to me, so we could walk outdoors and still meet face to face? You showed me places where you had been abused, drugged, picked up to be taken to ritualised ceremonies and so much more. What was it like to have me physically on your patch for the first time?

Cora: Your visits to my home turf had a considerable impact. Having DID means things often feel unreal, plus my brain stores things separately without connections which makes it difficult to recognise links. When we walked and I tentatively showed you places I'd talked about, the atrocity of my current life became startlingly real and fused with the extensive and profound work we'd been doing in the therapy room.

Nancy: Looking back on our work around that time, I remember some key elements including you repeatedly arriving at sessions with new injuries. Initially you'd minimise these—partly as the whole story was never known by any single one of you—but it soon became clear to me your life was at serious risk. Helping you collectively accept that and take it seriously when the backdrop to your entire life had been near-death experiences was a huge challenge. We needed an internal consensus—much more than a 48/52 per cent Brexit-style one—to work towards the concept of freedom as an overarching goal. I think you needed to know I believed this was possible.

Some of you felt you and I were on such different planets that you would never be accepted or acceptable. As a way of trying to conceptualise a life outside the abuse network, some of you asked me about my own life for the first time. I sensed a greater level of self-disclosure was needed from me to enable our attachment to deepen enough for those alters to achieve a closer connection or perhaps an element of identification with me. After some thought, I opened up a little more to you about myself and my life—just a few key aspects.

Cora: Thank goodness you took this risk ... It was another pivotal moment. Four months previously I'd despondently explained how I lived on a parallel planet to yours and despite many times trying to join your mainstream planet, I'd failed and been propelled back to my own depraved abuse network planet. I could see no way of joining yours, though I desperately longed for it. Worryingly, the deeper I shared in therapy sessions, the more alienated from you I felt. The gulf between how I perceived myself and you was widening at a time when the opposite was needed. I remember descending into despair and being on the point of resigning myself to the remains of my life being in the hands of the abuse network.

Your self-disclosure had an instant positive impact in several ways. You became more real and the substantial new 3D you was someone my child alters trusted far more than the 2D therapist they thought lived in the therapy room cupboard between sessions. Child alters are developmentally children and respond to people and situations from a child's perspective. It also made your planet seem less alien and hence more reachable. What's more, it showed a level of trust in me which improved my confidence in the belief that I could do the seemingly impossible and escape. Our attachment to you strengthened and hope returned.

Nancy: This is where societal denial is so harmful. If the systematic organised abuse of children was better integrated into our understanding of the world, you may have felt less alienated and part of a shared planet.

I remember working with those of you who remained frozen in trauma time, still believing we were in the 1980s. These alters were not impressed or convinced by anything I said and did not accept we were in the 2020s, whichever way we approached it. However, we finally had some success asking Google Assistant the current date, time, and place. Those of you with no connection to the physical body seemed to relate much more easily to technology than to me for this kind of factual information! Perhaps there were no attachment anxieties getting in the way with technology and no perceived personal agenda? Within the urgency of the situation, humour was also sometimes our friend and despite—or maybe because of—the horror you were facing, there were times when we really laughed together. These were moments of shared humanity and, retrospectively, emotional re-regulation for us both!

Cora: Yes, the times we laughed were hugely important. You can only belly laugh when you're relaxed and with someone you feel comfortable with. It felt good to laugh together as it affirmed a connectedness and a shared deep understanding and acceptance of my reality.

Nancy: But you supported and helped each other with adapting to reality much more than I helped. I just encouraged you to ask each other inside, to share feelings and fact check with each other. The slow, steady work we'd done together over several years came into its own here, as those of you who'd known me longer could vouch for me being acceptable to others inside who were struggling with even fundamental trust.

So many of you'd had crucial roles in holding secrets and perpetuating the cycle of dissociation–trauma–dissociation. Some had only known night time, darkness, terror, and torture. Do you remember when I suggested those of you who had never known daytime or felt the sunlight might choose to become aware from the inside next time you went for a walk, to try to feel the warmth of the sun or notice the colours of the flowers and grass? This was to help them connect to their/your place on the planet, your human rights, and offer a glimpse of an alternative world. It felt so important you could experience a sense of what life could be, might be, away from the abuse network.

Cora: I remember one alter screaming at the brightness of the sunshine, another thinking the body was being burnt alive, yet others were excited and awestruck by the colours, scents, and sounds of this strange, beautiful world and wanted more. As a compromise, I started going for a walk every evening during the golden hour when the contrast between the world these traumatised younger alters knew and this new world was reduced. The setting sun was cooler, the dusk chorus was peaceful and grew quieter as the birds began to roost and the sweet perfume of the jasmine was heightened. These special times helped bridge the two worlds and reduce the anxiety about moving into the unknown.

Nancy: I think strengthening your connection to the natural world was crucial at this time, as we were grappling with such deeply traumatic material. A key element of our work was understanding the degree and nature of the manipulation you'd been exposed to by the abuse network, mostly seemingly designed to increase terror and make sure if you spoke out you would sound mad or be discredited. One of your alters used the word "conning" to describe the abuse network's tactics and we continue to use her word to this day. It has been eye-opening to me to understand the lengths abuse networks appear to go to, to create terror and manipulate children's imaginative capacity, alongside use of drugs and alcohol.

Cora: There were numerous therapy sessions with you where different alters would come out and over time understand how much they'd been conned by the abuse network. For some alters the conning had affected choices they'd made, things they'd done and were continuing to do. For them this was particularly upsetting and it was only within the safety of the therapy sessions and their long-term relationship with you that they were able to face the unimaginable truth. It was the start of deep healing as they realised how wrong they'd been because they'd believed the cons.

Nancy: Possibly the biggest challenge for us was to sit with the grief as individual pieces of narrative merged to bring you into a more complete, shared, and felt sense of reality. This was harrowing work for you all. I remember some of you sobbing so much at times that I feared you would pass out. I needed to just be with you and hold on to some hope within the messy and complicated reality. It's hard to describe quite what an intensely harrowing time this was.

Cora: Gradually the abuse network noticed I was becoming less compliant and turned up the heat. The threats got worse and their message was clear. I was hypervigilant, frightened all the time, constantly assessing for threats and living on my nerves. One day after a particularly vicious threat I lost it and impulsively rang the police. They handled it well and were supportive, but I was too scared to name names so they were limited in what they could do.

Nancy: I am aware some readers may be wondering about the role of the police and safeguarding processes here. Safeguarding issues can be complex when working with people with DID due to the different perspectives inside and the existence of alters who will come out during interviews and mental capacity assessments to deny the external reality and sound convincingly stable. Your particular situation was no exception. It felt really important that safeguarding discussions with external agencies were sensitively timed and took place in collaboration with you, rather than superimposing a plan on you before you were ready or able to manage it. The safeguarding aspects of the situation needed a nuanced approach, not a knee-jerk one. The abuse network is, after all, an organised crime group, and some of you knew police were involved.

Cora: Years of building trust between us would have been undone had you raised a safeguarding alert without my agreement and I don't know how we would have come back from it. Time was running out as the abuse was worsening. I knew I needed to escape and I reluctantly knew I couldn't do it on my own. I would have to take a leap of faith and trust you and my handful of friends more than I'd ever done. To do that I needed you all to repeatedly demonstrate you were dependable and had my back 100 per cent.

The safeguarding alert raised by another agency did nothing to help me; in fact, sending two local inexperienced police officers to my house to ask me if I was safe (!) potentially put me more at risk. By then the abuse network was monitoring me closely so I would have denied everything for my own safety. It would've ticked the box for professionals and protected them. They didn't need protection: I did.

The violence, abuse, and threats continued to escalate until one day came the last straw.

I remember it like it was yesterday. It was a bitterly cold winter's evening and without thinking I did something impulsive that took me into a carefully planned trap set up by the abuse network. I regret my recklessness to this day and probably always will. What followed was a brutal physical and sexual attack in which I sustained serious injuries needing hospital treatment. In addition, they psychologically tortured me with drugs, images, and verbal triggers, including threats to important people in my life, until my mind was scrambled.

I strongly believe they wanted me gone because I'd become disobedient and they knew they were losing me, which meant I was proving to be a liability. It's my belief they wanted me to self-destruct by pushing me to suicide, rather than killing me directly. A far better outcome for them.

Nancy: I remember that time so clearly. What seemed key was that a specific alter who seemed to have a lot of control internally unusually remained present throughout the attack and experienced the conning and horror first hand. This enabled her/you to shift alliance and loyalty away from the abuse network. Movingly, this alter spoke with me directly in session afterwards and we were able to unpick things together. The abusers had used specific hypnotic cues to bring certain alters to the front and had also used threats relating to people they believed you cared about, including me. Your hard-won increased internal connection led to a percolation inside of the horror and the manipulation. So, if the abuse network wanted to push you to suicide, they failed as your newly won capacity to dissociate less seemed to strengthen your motivation to leave and find safety, rather than the opposite.

Cora: It did, and the decision was made. However, even then, some alters resisted and the conflict inside raged. Wanting to leave but not wanting to. The strength of attachment from some alters to the abuse network brought pain and grief and needed oodles of therapeutic work. Escaping would mean breaking contact with them and anyone who might be connected. It was a sprawling network and I had to let go of anyone I wasn't 100 per cent sure about, which included the whole of my family. I could count on one hand the number of people who would still be in my life. It felt like everything familiar was peeling away from me and I would be left raw and empty.

Memories of the extreme threats to me if I ever tried to escape meant I was terrified of it failing or them finding me. And underneath it all was a fear of this unknown planet I was hoping to join, where my life would change radically. How hard it was to leave something familiar, despite its depravity and danger. The intense shame and self-blame I carried meant I thought I would contaminate any future life or relationships.

In therapy we started to deal with the huge vat of conflicting emotions the decision was bringing. Terror. Dread. Panic. Anger. Self-doubt. Disbelief. Grief. And the impact of all this on my physical health, which was deteriorating fast. Escaping to safety seemed unachievable and I started to lose heart. At times I thought death would be preferable and I came close to suicide. As my hope faded and despair increased, I needed a lot of reassurance and extra support from you. Your commitment to me and my survival, and belief I could do it gave me courage. Simple things made a significant difference. Like when I said I couldn't see any future, just darkness. Your quiet reassurance you'd carry the light for me whilst I couldn't do it for myself was all I needed in that moment. I was many traumatised children in an adult body needing the gentleness, encouragement, and reassurance a child needs when facing the terror of the unknown.

Nancy: Both your physical and mental health were fragile at this point. Together, we talked through in forensic detail the complicated process of leaving your home and town. This felt very strategic and not something that typically falls within a therapist's role. However, having a deep understanding of your internal world, the different identities, feelings, fears, and realities that you had not shared with others meant I was probably best placed to do this. Other agencies were, of course, involved but didn't have the detailed understanding of your internal system that was needed. I was able to act as a link person with these agencies, encouraging you to communicate with them in the safest possible way.

We devised a three-stage plan—first, you spent a few weeks in hiding with a trusted friend; you then moved into a residential living facility with 24/7 medical support for some months before moving into a new home. You needed to move to a new area where no one knew you and to change your name and identity.

It felt extremely important that our contact continued while you were in the medical facility and I travelled to work with you weekly wherever you were during this period. I was fortunate that my work timetable offered this flexibility. As there was not always a therapy room to work within, at times we needed to walk and talk or meet in a (large anonymous) café, where we could still speak privately to some extent. This was not ideal, but it did seem that therapeutic containment was offered primarily through the security of the relationship and the regularity of contact, rather than the venue at this stage. We were adapting to meet the reality of the situation and emotional connection and consistent contact were paramount. I also worked with the staff at the residential facility to help them understand DID so they could support you. A lot of our work around that time was about helping you manage a new environment and living without abuse—something very new to you which also led to decreased dissociation. I'm aware that in some ways this has been really hard for you ...?

Cora: It was frustrating to discover I was so used to being abused that I didn't know how to live in a non-abusive setting. Although I was being looked after and treated well, I was suspicious of the kindness and found myself waiting for the abuse and control to start. The waiting was so triggering that sometimes I almost tried to provoke abuse from other people because then I would be back on familiar territory. I'd taken the first steps onto this alien planet and I didn't understand the "rules" of how to live on it and its strange ways. It was exhausting and frightening and I hadn't expected it to be this hard. The contact and continuity with you during this time was crucial to prevent me from giving up and going back to my old life which often seemed easier at that time.

Nancy: But importantly you did not return and have remained safe. Can you say more about the process of adapting to an abuse-free life?

Life today

Cora: Adapting to life on the other side has been complex, exhausting, and harder than I thought. So much was alien in this abuse-free life that I had to set about a fast-track programme to learn how everything worked and how to become a functioning part of my new community. In the early stages, freedom felt too immense, fast-moving, and alarmingly emotionally charged. A maelstrom of powerful emotions contributed to feeling confused and overwhelmed. Yet tiny moments of intense joy and excitement were emerging, something I'd not felt before, and they kept me motivated. I wanted more!

Several particular aspects of my new life stand out for me.

First—choice. The abuse network made decisions for me that I had to obey; I was not allowed to choose unless instructed to do so. During rituals they sometimes told me I had a choice, but they were torturous heartbreaking double binds that I was forced to make quickly before the last grain of sand in the egg timer fell. Hence I wasn't skilled in making choices and the word itself filled me with fear. Because I was used to other people making decisions, even when free I waited for the same to happen, including with you. When they didn't, I would turn to them and ask what I should do! Every time they said it was my choice, I panicked, froze in fear, and felt like I was being abandoned and thrown to the wolves.

Dealing with choice became a key part of our therapy. I needed to experience and practise making choices with someone I trusted—it was never enough to read it online or hear the theory in therapy. Gradually you helped me make small choices with support and no time pressure until I became more confident and could do it on my own. It was uncomfortable, slow going and I felt embarrassed at times because I was admitting I couldn't do something most ten-year-olds could do. But, wow, how liberating it was when I got the hang of it and realised choice could be exciting and life-enhancing even when it was hard. When I started to take my time, not feel pressured, and make good choices or even say to people I wasn't sure and I needed longer to think about something, I started to feel proud of myself. Again, a feeling that was new. Life-changing.

Second, my attitude to wanting to live or die changed. In the past, my life had been threatened so regularly that I expected every day to be my last. Not only that, but I used to want to die. The waiting would be over and even if death were a nothingness, that felt better than living with extreme pain, terror, and threat. Several months into my new life, I realised I now truly wanted to live and that had a huge impact. If you want a future then what you do today matters, whether that be your attitude, choices, or lifestyle. This was a mixed bag of both great delight in making exciting plans, but equally high anxiety as it was such a challenge and I didn't know where to begin.

And then, my changing emotions. As my fear lessened, my hypervigilance slowly decreased and I became calmer and able to think more clearly, although the hypersensitivity to other people's body language, tone of voice, and word choices still remained high. It was then the grief began to hit. Overwhelming vast wave after wave of grief. It was time to mourn what happened and what didn't happen but was longed for, what I never had but needed, and what was taken from me. For the realisation of what life could/should have been like and the pain of knowing and inexorably accepting my own history. I am still grieving. It has manifested as intense emotional and physical suffering—anguish, sorrow, depression, anger, resentment, bitterness, guilt, despair, and body pain. Most of it is disenfranchised grief and has reawakened feelings of being alone and isolated.

Being less dissociative now has reduced the amnesia between alters, improved inside communication, and increased connection to the body. All good stuff, as my alters and I are working better as a team to manage life and take care of our health. The downside is it has resulted in greater awareness of physical pain and of the irreparable physical damage a lifetime of abuse has done to our body. So, while being free from control and abuse, I'm finding I'm partially disabled and need help with some physical aspects of life, which feels like a limitation to my freedom.

I think the therapeutic relationship with you has acted as a bridge to help me develop deeper relationships with my close friends, while also enabling me to reach out to, and begin to trust new people, including professionals from whom help is now essential. I have found the latter particularly hard and struggle with opening up to them and wish I didn't need any help. However, some have listened well, responded in an empowering way, and helped bring about positive changes in my life. Gradually I am starting to gain a bit of trust. Do you remember when I told you I was worried a neighbour was grooming me? I am still learning to adjust to kindness and accept no payback is expected when someone is kind to me or helps me.

Nancy: Yes, I do remember your worries about the friendly neighbour but I'm pleased you were able to talk about it openly so we could think about it together. Beyond helping you get away and find safety, I have always wanted to support you to be able to trust other people—including professionals—and form relationships based on openness. This started with working on strength and trust within our relationship and the multiple experiences of rupture and repair. I feel so happy that you now have a much more extensive personal and professional support network than I could have previously imagined possible.

Cora: Now I am free I am able to draw from the bank within me, rich with resources from years of therapy. Resources I was able to store, but not apply until I was secure enough in our therapy, attached and trusting enough of you to be able to make the leap to leave. It is all there and most days now I am drawing on it, with new realisations and little changes that are building a new understanding and knowledge of life and how it can be on my new home planet. My new life is so much better and richer. However, unsurprisingly it is not all smooth sailing. Setbacks hit me really hard and I can be thrown back into a bad place much too quickly for my liking. I am sure with time this will happen less as I become more confident of my rightful place on this new planet.

Nancy: Our sessions continue weekly and I hope I am supporting you to live a more integrated life on this shared planet of ours. In our work overall I have needed to challenge some mainstream therapy practice, taking the work out of the therapy room at times and being directive about your personal safety in order to model something you'd never had. I've also sometimes had to move between roles, working creatively to match the differing needs of your alters. I continue to think openly and critically about ways of working that are genuinely in your best interests. This has felt so much more important than ticking professional boxes to preserve my personal comfort.

Throughout this process, consultation with my very experienced supervisor has been key, as well as drawing on my own internal supervisor at times when I've needed to make complicated and spontaneous decisions. Changes to the therapeutic frame have been discussed and agreed with you as far as possible, along with the rationale for them. We continue to revisit our work on maintaining fundamental safety and understanding the concept of freedom, especially for alters who were trained to be loyal to abusers.

As you have undergone profound life change, I have been on my own parallel journey as therapist and witness. Working with extreme abuse, especially active abuse, has brought out both the best and the worst in me and I have needed to acknowledge and draw on my own human vulnerability. At times I have felt frightened and despairing about a world that has a dark, brutal underbelly and offers little help or recourse to justice for victims and survivors. I've sometimes felt useless or alone, despite having good professional and personal support. I have needed to work on my own self-care.

Looking back, I am aware I made numerous mistakes along the way, including times when I misunderstood or misattuned to you. And there were sometimes things I just didn't get! I've tried to own my mistakes—even when uncomfortable—and spoken with you openly about them, doing my share of the necessary repair work.

Cora: The first time you made a mistake, apologised, discussed it with me, then moved on I was shocked and scared. Didn't you know it was dangerous to own up to making a mistake? In my experience of life within the abuse network this would lead to severe punishment. You'd just owned up to making a mistake rather than cleverly covering it up! Over the years of more mistakes and you owning them, I gradually learnt it wasn't the end of the world and slowly began to risk it myself, practising on you to start with.

These days I am happy to own up to my mistakes with confidence and be honest with other people. Then I move on and my world doesn't worsen. I have discovered that showing people I am fallible generally means they like me better, rather than hurt me, and the reciprocal honesty and openness deepens our relationship. I have learnt that ruptures can be repaired and relationships can be better for it. No longer do I feel the need to leave town and keep starting over because of my mistakes.

And finally …

Cora: I was thrilled when you asked whether I would be interested in writing this chapter with you and delighted to have the opportunity. Telling my story to others is important for my healing and doing it in conjunction with you, who I knew and trusted, made this possible in a safe and supportive way. The timing was ideal and it has benefited our therapeutic relationship.

It has been challenging in ways I hadn't considered, as you and I are very different! It gave me a unique insight into what it's like to be a singleton and at times I was quite envious. When you have DID it's like being an employee in a large company. Major decisions have to go to team meetings where you accept your views might be overruled by another of your alters. This made writing long and complex for me, having so many alters. With you as a singleton it seemed much more straightforward! You were a sole trader and my goodness, was I envious of how uncomplicated and time-saving that seemed to be when it came to writing.

Joint writing with you meant we (my alters and I) had to work together, listen to each other's stories, believe each other, and then produce one piece of writing. We collectively have never written jointly as a system before and it helped us become more co-conscious and compassionate with each other.

Having DID means everything is compartmentalised and kept in little separate nuggets. Naturally then, I planned to write my part of the chapter on my own while you wrote your part and then we'd put it together at the end. This was my approach to our writing, but not yours … I'm glad you persisted with helping me understand the concept of writing in an interconnected way, which was incomprehensible to me to start with. Eventually I got it and loved the new experience of working in a connected way with another person. I am now excited about trying it in other areas of my life.

Co-writing meant I learnt another useful skill I wanted in my new life. I had to tell you honestly in a respectful way when I disagreed with the content or style of your writing. Phew, that was difficult. However, it was great to practise on you because I knew you wouldn't be mean to me or reject me! I've now done it successfully with other people.

Nancy: This process has not been without complexity! We've spent many hours talking through the meaning of writing together, how much to share, making sure you had internal consent and agreement at each stage. This included adapting a consent form for all of you to agree and sign collectively and considering the potential changes to our therapeutic relationship. Reflecting on things together and finding a shared narrative seem to have enabled you to process the many layers of trauma in greater depth. Without embarking upon a second chapter, I cannot begin to describe how much I have learnt through both our therapy work and our shared writing!

My priority has been to keep your well-being at the centre of this project. I am so very appreciative of all your hard work, the internal negotiation and discussion that's been necessary, and your courage in sharing so much candidly with others.

It feels so important to me that we have worked collaboratively on this writing, combining our interconnected perspectives. I hope it's helped ease you into your rightful place on our shared planet!

Cora: Postscript

Getting away from the abuse group and beginning a new life has been the best thing I've ever done as well as maybe one of the hardest things. I would not be free and living my best life today without the courage and determination of all my alters and their willingness to take a risk and trust an outside person, our therapist and her support team. I include myself as an alter! It needed an extended period of support with a therapist who my alters and I had built a strong attachment to, and who had similar levels of courage and determination, as well as a willingness to take risks. I feel I am one of the lucky ones. My life today on our shared planet is one of relative freedom, choice, control, belongingness to a community, and moments of joy; gradually the intensity of the memories and wounds which will always be part of me are softening. But I am having to come to terms with the limitations on my mind and body of having been subjected to decades of severe trauma.

My hope is for a future where all therapists working with survivors of extreme abuse are able to draw strength and courage from those who have gone before. This includes taking considered risks and working outside the box in response to the needs of their clients. I wish with all my heart for this to happen to enable more survivors like me to get truly free.

References

Carnes, P. (1997). *The Betrayal Bond: Breaking Free from Exploitative Relationships*. Deerfield Beach, FL: Health Communications.

Kahr, B. (2007). The infanticidal attachment. *Attachment: New Directions in Relational Psychoanalysis and Psychotherapy*, *1*(2): 117–132.

Sachs, A. (2008). Infanticidal attachment—the link between Dissociative Identity Disorder and crime. In: A. Sachs & G. Galton (Eds.), *Forensic Aspects of Dissociative Identity Disorder*. London: Routledge.

Sachs, A. (2010). As thick as thieves or the ritual abuse family. In: V. Sinason (Ed.), *Attachment, Trauma and Multiplicity: Working with Dissociative Identity Disorder* (2nd edn). Abingdon, UK: Routledge.

van der Hart, O., Nijenhuis, E., & Steele, K. (2006). *The Haunted Self: Structural Dissociation and the Treatment of Chronic Traumatisation*. New York: W. W. Norton.

CHAPTER 6

Leaving the life of an addict: Transformations

Charles Brown

Which is a wonder how his grace should glean it,
Since his addiction was to courses vain,
His companies unletter'd, rude and shallow,
His hours fill'd up with riots, banquets, sports,
And never noted in him any study,
Any retirement, any sequestration
From open haunts of popularity.
—Shakespeare, W., 1599

Introduction

This chapter is a personal narrative that captures some aspects of my life growing up in the UK as a Black man and my experiences of active addiction. I attempt to articulate the influence these experiences have had on my life and my thinking, including my physical and mental health. I give an account of some of the events that may have contributed to my addiction. The main point of the narrative is not about what happened but how I learned to feel safe enough again. I outline what circumstances made it possible for me to leave my addictive lifestyle behind. My story offers a reflective account of the journey to recovery from addiction without the accretions of myth or romance. I acknowledge that every addict's journey is a personal one and subjectively different, however, I maintain the process of recovery remains broadly similar.

Addiction

Etymologically, "addiction" comes from the Latin *addictus*, meaning to contract or pledge. While the concept has existed for centuries, the word "addiction" itself didn't exist until Shakespeare coined it in his play *Othello* (1604), the first use of the word in the English language. Addiction has been understood in many ways over the years. Rebecca Lemon (2018) calls the word "addiction" a "semantic palimpsest". Her research into English texts beginning about 1550 shows "devotion" or "dedication" were synonyms for addiction in early modern writings, which has been obscured by more modern links to disease, compulsion, and the science of illness. Lemon advocates understanding addictions as "forms of attachment that simultaneously shape and unravel identity, clarify and overcome the individual, without devolving into moralism or medicalisation" (p. 167). She argues that a mother's addiction to her totally dependent infant is spiritually nourishing.

It is with knowledge of opium dependency that addiction took on the negative connotations that it has today. Contemporary definitions of addiction are framed as someone not having control over doing, taking, or using something to the point where it could be harmful. The individual becomes obsessed with the activity or substance, and not having it causes withdrawal symptoms, whether physical, emotional, or psychical. It is, therefore, possible to be addicted to just about anything. The impact of active addiction stretches beyond the individual and affects significant others as well as society. Most people with addictions do not realise they have a problem until they try to stop and discover that they cannot.

Background

In the aftermath of World War II, Britain called out for workers from its commonwealth citizens to help rebuild a broken and depleted country. The result was that 46,800 people from the Commonwealth had settled in cities across the United Kingdom by 1956. By 1961, an estimated 172,000 West Indians were living in the UK. My father arrived in the mid-1950s and settled in Nottingham, a city in the East Midlands. In 1957 Harold Macmillan declared that the British people had "never had it so good". However, the economy had sunk into a steep decline by the beginning of the next decade. The economic boom that had brought post-war Caribbean migrants to the UK had well and truly dried up, and a time of heightened race and class tensions had replaced the feel-good atmosphere. The British began to feel that the migrants were taking opportunities that should have been theirs, and the end of the decade saw violent race riots take place across many UK cities.

For most of the people coming from Jamaica and the other Caribbean islands, migration was a positive experience. It was seen as an opportunity for a better life for themselves and their children. They could work and afford to save some money to get a mortgage and perhaps send some money to help their relatives who were still in the Caribbean. Many immigrants were able to build houses in Jamaica, where they planned to retire. I never met either of my grandfathers, but I did meet my paternal grandmother and spent a few weeks with her. I understood my grandfather had left the island as a young man to work in Cuba, Panama, and Costa Rica, joining immigrants from other parts of the Caribbean, Latin America, and the United States, and was able to purchase land and property in Jamaica. He lived in England and worked here long enough to receive a pension.

My father, the eldest in his family, was expected to stay home, work on the land, and manage the family properties. His siblings went to school, gained an education, and pursued careers as electricians, nurses, and lawyers. However, he decided to come to England in 1955, where he found work as a miner in the Nottinghamshire coalfields. He arranged for my mother to come to Britain a year or so later, and they married in a Catholic church. I remember how happy my parents seemed in the black-and-white photograph of their wedding day that proudly hung on the dining room wall, surrounded by their friends and relatives from Jamaica and England.

My mother worked as a cleaner and domestic at the City Hospital. She was also a "banker" and would *throw pardna money*, a system in which friends save a set amount together on a regular basis, usually once a month, to be able to pay for goods and services they would otherwise have no way of affording. The set amount is called a *hand*, and the person who organises the group and collects the money is the banker. The banker hands over all the monthly contributions, called the *draw*, to the person whose turn it is to get paid.

The early years

While my parents were at work, an Irish neighbour looked after my older sister and me. I have warm memories of a woman who treated me with loving kindness.

I was raised in a typical Jamaican authoritarian household where children were seen, not heard, and adhered to the strict rules established by my parents. My parents valued obedience, hard work, and good manners, as these characteristics are deemed necessary for social mobility. They also recognised and held legitimate fears about the safety of their children in British society and believed physical discipline was necessary to keep their children off the streets, out of prison, and out of police officers' sight.

At first, we lived in a small house in an enclosed terrace that ran between two roads and had high walls at each end. I would delight in sliding down the stairs in a pillowcase as a child and was fascinated by fire. I remember my mother would take us to the arboretum at the end of the road, where there were always loads of Black kids playing, many of them friends whom I missed terribly when we moved house. I felt a sense of disloyalty and betrayal by this dislocation brought about by my father, who chose to leave the Black neighbourhood to move to a white area.

My sister and I attended the Catholic infant school that was near our home. There were no other immigrant children there. The nuns would dole out physical punishment liberally, and I would be smacked or made to stand on one leg in a corner, holding my opposite ear for what seemed like hours at a time.

When I was about four years old, I came home from school to see two girls I didn't know sitting in the middle of the sofa in the living room. It was a great surprise when my mother said, "Say hello to your sister dem who come from Jamaica to live with us." I never knew I had any more sisters other than the one who was a year or so older than me and liked to boss me around. The taller of the two girls was nineteen years old, with huge eyes, and slim with coffee-coloured skin; the smaller one was younger, fourteen years old, had shiny black skin, and didn't say much more than a quiet hello. My sisters! My immediate reaction was total shock. Why had no one ever mentioned them, I thought? I subsequently developed a strong attachment to my eldest sister and would often visit her in Jamaica.

My parents moved to a larger house in another area of the city, where my younger brother was born soon after. The new house was much larger and had two toilets. I soon had three younger sisters and another brother. There was a large park at the end of a nearby grove where I would play football with my friends. We supported one or other of the local teams, Nottingham Forest or Notts County, and aspired to play football professionally.

I remember sitting reading at the dining table one evening while the rest of the family were watching television when a brick came through the window, shattering the spell of the TV show they were watching, narrowly missing my father, who was sitting in his favourite armchair, and landed with a dull thud in front of the fireplace.

I read a lot of comic books as a child and enjoyed the encyclopaedias my father kept in the front room, nestled on a shelf between the cabinet and the radiogram.

My father would go to the pub on Friday nights and often return in the evening with snacks or some fried chicken for us. On Saturdays, he bet on the horses and often sent me to the bookies on the corner to place bets or collect his winnings. He would hold blues parties at the house, where alcohol and food would be sold. The police were often called out to deal with the disturbance caused by the large gathering of people and the loud reggae music.

I started at my new Catholic primary school much further away from where we lived, across the bridge that spanned the river. Everyone there was white except one Black brother and sister older than me. The John and Mary children's books by Grace James formed the realistic adventure tradition in children's literature, and together with Enid Blyton's books of adventure and magic were what we read in school. These stories involved children doing things and having adventures on journeys through labyrinths of adolescence, which were alien to me.

Once, a male teacher took me into the toilet, told me to drop my trousers and abused me. I ran home and told my father what had happened. He came to the school the next day. Everyone talked about the big, angry Black man who had come to the school and confronted the teacher and the headmistress. None of my younger siblings ever had to attend that school after that but travelled to another further away.

Trauma and loss

When another Black boy, whose parents had recently arrived in the UK, joined my class, we immediately formed an attachment. We would often swim in the river together until, one day, he drowned. I watched as the police divers recovered his lifeless body. Disturbingly, the incident was not mentioned at the school assembly the next day. I did not have contact with his family, and my family never discussed it. The whole thing felt like a bizarre mix of fact and fantasy. This was my first encounter with death and dying. No other Black boys came to the school. Shortly after, I and another boy who lived nearby went camping with the Boys Brigade and, on return, discovered his father's decomposing body in the kitchen. He had taken his own life.

Instead of going to church on Sundays, I would spend the money my father gave me to put in the collection plate at the bowling alley. I reasoned that, as the school and the church were conjoined, there was no reason for me to collaborate in my own demise. The money would be best used for my own enjoyment. I half expected something uncanny would happen, but I was not struck by lightning coming down from the sky.

My first day at secondary school was memorable because I was beaten up when some boys refused to let me onto the school grounds because I was Black. My father asked me what had happened when he saw my bloodied and bruised face. When I told him, he said to me that I was not Black. This was a perplexing and vexing statement at the time. Was it about Blackness, or was it about not being normal? My father made no further reference to it. The words didn't make the difference in my life that would make me acceptable to other people. I was still forced to wear the mask of self-hate. This fantasised image meant I was disembodied from a firm relationship with reality.

Typically, as a racially minoritised subject in a dominant cultural setting, I was dehumanised while being perceived as physically powerful and agile. I was encouraged to play a lot of sports at school. I was on the football, basketball, and athletic teams. However, I had no real interest in sports or athletics, and education insisted on preparing me for nothing more than living as a disembodied ghost in society.

I had plenty more fights at school. It was in my first year at secondary school that my addiction began. At first, it was about seeking recognition, being part of, and fitting in with my peers. I would smoke cigarettes and drink alcohol with my friends. I made other friends and progressed onto marijuana, sniffing glue, and taking hallucinogens. In the beginning, taking drugs gave me a sense of a shared connection with people who were like me and who understood me. But they were not like me, their lived lives were different to my life. I would always want to drink more, take more drugs, and party longer than everyone else did. Inevitably, the drugs began to exert their effect on every area of my life. I began bunking off school and sneaking out of my bedroom at night to hang out, drink, and smoke with the older boys on the corner who went to clubs at the weekends.

My English teacher, Mr Woodcote, was encouraging. I enjoyed his classes and learned something about writing. I was also fascinated by the biology classes and harboured the idea of a career in medicine. During my third year at school, discussions about careers and further education pathways were held. My form teacher told me that I was aiming high. My father thought I should go straight to work when I finished school or join the army like many boys in the neighbourhood had done, where I would learn a trade.

My uncle was an established and successful international lawyer who I regarded highly because he told us stories of how judges often held him in contempt for wearing traditional African dress in court. He urged my father to allow me to pursue my ambition but to no avail. I left school dispirited and went to work in a factory.

Reflecting on my school days, I struggled with identity shame and a pervasive sense that I didn't belong. Education did not provide a coherent, meaningful sense of identity to help me understand the world in which I found myself. My experience of education felt disempowering and alienating, and I sought validation of my racialised body in increasingly unhealthy and self-defeating ways.

I grew up in the 1970s disco era, a time of glamorised fashion, sexual freedom, race riots, protest, and rebellion. I soon grew tired of manual work, stopped working, and, after arguing with my father, left home. I became involved with the Rastafarian movement, an African-centred spiritual philosophy, and grew my hair, which brought me a sense of belonging and an expression of liberation.

I trained as an engineer but later developed an allergy that prevented me from continuing with this work. In any case, working in cold, draughty factories felt soul destroying. Unemployed and homeless, I began writing and performing my poetry, but I wasn't earning enough money to eat and buy drugs. I then started shoplifting.

Blaxploitation

In the early 1970s, Black superheroes suddenly began appearing in the comics that I was reading and in films. The Black actors appeared to be in control of their own narratives. The characters were pimps, prostitutes, street hustlers, and drug dealers. There was often violence and the racist dogma was challenged, furthering the process of decolonisation. They were some bad motherfuckers, in a good sense.

The term "Blaxploitation" is a portmanteau of the words "Black" and "exploitation", coined by Junius Griffin. Similarly, the term "slavesploitation" came into use around the same time, through the films that emerged in the United States during the 1960s and early 1970s. They are visible from that time in the context of self-determination when Black people began to reclaim power over their own image and representation. Slavesploitation films, as the name suggests, centred on the ruthless exploitation of slaves. The films criticised dominant cultural frameworks and galvanised key political movements of the seventies. In UK Black communities, the films reflected the reality of inner-city life and usually portrayed the triumph of Black protagonists over white emblems of domination, thus appealing to Black urban audiences.

I was first arrested when I was sixteen and kept on getting into trouble with the police throughout the following decade. During this time, I met a group of Black visionaries who were seeking to develop recreational, social, and educational activities that met the needs of the African Caribbean community. Through their help, I found somewhere to live. These social activists expressed a level of self-determination and did not subscribe to the belief that because of the colour of their skin, they were not good enough, that they should accept their position in Western society, remain where they were, and not progress. Their insistence on freedom and equality of opportunity within the African Caribbean community was based on the valuation of Blackness and Black culture that incorporated economic, spiritual, and revolutionary aspects. Working with them gave me a sense of selfhood, direction, and meaning.

They would eventually create an African Caribbean organisation whose activities included a supplementary school, a surgery to advise members of the Black community about welfare rights and related issues, trips for Black youth, political meetings, recreational activities, and a senior citizen's luncheon club.

I began working as a peer group educator with the probation service on developing a community strategy for young people focused on the reduction and prevention of crime and I later helped establish a non-profit, voluntary organisation supporting the rights of sex workers and those at risk of being exploited.

A rising fear of a crack epidemic in the UK of the kind experienced in the United States was at its peak. At the time, there were no drug programmes to cope with crack victims. Drug dependency units mainly treated white male heroin addicts. A group of us set up a radical—and successful—approach to drugs, specific to crack cocaine, that was funded by the social services and the local health authority, working directly with dealers and pimps to encourage addicts into rehabilitation. The project utilised outreach workers who had a good knowledge of the community and possessed the ability to work with dealers to safeguard the well-being of addicted individuals and refer them to rehabilitation treatment facilities.

A series of events, including the death of my parents, disrupted this sensitive deconditioning and unlearning process, and my addiction accelerated. I tried crack cocaine when someone told me that it was better than sex. We called it the white lady. I started using heroin to help with the comedown. I got involved with gangs stealing pharmaceuticals and dealing drugs. My lifestyle was putting me at very serious risk, and my use of drugs led to encounters with dangerous people. The company

I kept was based on convenience and easy access to substances. I was attacked and was found lying in the street after being stabbed, and was taken to the hospital. After one attack, I was told that I might never walk again. I was living in survival mode, using a cocktail of drugs, and was a physical wreck.

Meanwhile, I managed the community rehab team until my own problems with addiction came to light, and I was forced to resign. The person who took on this role was concerned about my issues and subsequently managed to get me a place in a detoxification clinic.

Recovery

My admission into a detox centre came as a shock. I had no conscious desire to stop using drugs or to change my lifestyle significantly. It happened during the Christmas holidays. I was at home by myself, using, when I overdosed. I was discovered unconscious by the team manager and taken to the detox unit, where I woke up.

I had never thought about not using drugs and did not know anyone who had stopped using drugs for any significant amount of time. I knew that I was an addict a long time before going into detox. I used the knowledge as justification to continue using. People I associated with had used detox as a way of maximising the effects of the drugs so that the next high would be like the euphoria of the first time. I saw the people there and compared my addiction with theirs; surely, I was not as bad as they were, I reasoned to myself. They were white people. How could they relate to my life? Their experience was very different from my own. I struggled to remain in the detox, but the people there, strangers, literally sat on me whenever I expressed any wish to leave.

I remembered what it felt like when I was at school. Without drugs in my body to numb me, I started feeling isolated and alone once more. I was remorseful, thinking about how my addiction had caused a lot of damage to my family, whom I was estranged from. Even the people from my community wanted me off the streets. The counsellors worked on bringing me to a place where I could no longer deny the truth of my addiction.

The residents in the clinic were not allowed to go outside for the first two weeks. When going outside later, we had to be escorted by a more senior peer. Twice a week, we had to attend twelve-step recovery meetings. At the first meeting that I went to, a Black man shared about his addiction which triggered a huge craving in me such that I had to leave the meeting. At the third meeting I attended I was given some heroin by someone standing outside the meeting. On one occasion, I went to the pub and spent an afternoon there playing snooker with a peer. However, I did not use drugs or alcohol.

When returning to the clinic, residents were submitted to drug tests. The facility provided staff who cleaned and changed the beds and prepared all the food. I was given a mug for drinking tea and coffee and told that my only responsibility was to keep this mug clean.

Being clean was disorientating. I felt that I was in a state of heightened awareness. The snow that lay outside the window seemed extraordinarily dazzling. I could clearly hear my heart beating in my chest. I felt different, and the fogginess in my brain had cleared away. I wasn't sure who or where I was without the internal compass of my addiction.

William Griffith Wilson, one of the founders of Alcoholics Anonymous, put it this way: "Suddenly, my room blazed with an indescribable white light. I was seized with an ecstasy beyond description. Every joy I had known was pale by comparison. The light, the ecstasy—I was conscious of nothing else for a time" (1984, p. 121).

After a month in the detox unit, the counsellors suggested that I needed further treatment. I knew that I needed—and wanted—to get clean, or I would be in a mental institution or prison, or dead. It was then that I decided to stop using drugs. I chose a treatment centre that was out of town. I was told it was not likely I would be able to stay clean if I stayed in the same environment.

I spent four months at a secondary stage treatment centre. I chose a facility near the seaside, which I thought I might enjoy. When I got there, I was greeted with a racist joke from a well-to-do white man. We had to do chores and would be given pocket money. This was offensive and belittling. It reminded me of school, and I felt restrained by the treatment centre's attitude. There was a palpable tension between me and the counsellors. It was not surprising to discover that I was the only Black person there.

The counsellors recommended a further six months of treatment. I went to a male-only rehab. There were Black guys in this rehab.

Some of the counsellors in this rehab were Black, and there were other Black staff, too. I felt at ease. I was less guarded around Black people but felt vulnerable to negative racialised influences. I had a conflict with one of my Black peers and the Black male counsellor. The dynamics between loyalty and betrayal evoked old internal conflicts in me.

Individual and group therapy sessions took place, psycho-education was provided and various other activities. Active addiction had occupied all my time, and when I went to treatment, I was left with empty hours that I did not know how to fill. At weekends, a group of us would go to nightclubs.

With hindsight, I could see that addiction had interrupted my life and had anaesthetised my feelings. Temporality does not operate in addiction, and years pass unnoticed. Psychological development is arrested, and the capacity for learning is hampered.

The treatment utilised language in a way that brought new insight and newer understandings; for example, discovering that alcohol is a drug was revelatory. It presented some key spiritual principles for living a more balanced and fulfilling life. Understanding and applying these principles has had a tremendous impact on my life. I had been a polysubstance user and was using any drug I could get my hands on at the end. I was cross-addicted, and my addiction had manifested itself in a variety of ways. Having grappled throughout my life with issues of identity I thought I had found one as an addict, not realising that was not my identity but a false self-representation. My identification as an addict is a reminder that my drug of choice is any mood-changing, mind-altering substance or experience. Using was my response to living life as a social non-being.

I learned that I cannot change people, but I can change some things that I cannot accept. I learned that parents let you down, that families are not always a place of trust, and that some friends will not always be there for you. I also learned that I have lived with betrayal and been hurt by love and that it's hard for me to trust.

From a very young age, I had learned to turn the other cheek, but in doing so, it felt like I was killing off a part of myself. Through narrative storytelling and identification, the value of each one teaching the other is unparalleled. This narrative exchange becomes nourishment. The value of each other is not fungible but gives a protective space without ownership that is safe, creative, and meaningful. The significance of spiritual principles frustrates insecurity, self-rejection, and isolation, creating a positive sense of self. There were many times when I was close to being thrown out of treatment and, at times, picking up drugs again.

Treatment never offered a cure, which was what I had expected. It took time for me to understand that what was being offered was the key to freedom from active addiction and my dysfunctional attachment relationships. Having an authentic connection with others began in early recovery. They helped restore my sanity and supported me in my recovery.

When I was discharged from treatment, they helped me move into a small flat. When I discovered there was no electricity or gas supply there, I felt unable to deal with the situation on my own so I went back to the rehab and they helped me contact the energy suppliers.

Leaving addiction

Like me, many people think that addiction is when someone uses drugs all day, every day. While that was part of my experience, I found addiction is an experience of relapses until there is a substantial period of abstinence, character and lifestyle changes made.

After five years in my recovery journey, my siblings finally came to accept that I was no longer using drugs. They thought I had reinvented myself through my former identity as an addict. Relationships with my immediate family have remained difficult, but those with my wider family have improved. The miracle has been simply gaining a fuller awareness of reality and undoing the illusion that I am separate in any way from my fellow human beings.

Living clean has taught me that the world is bigger than I imagined and not as far out of reach as I had feared. When I first got clean, I worried my life would become boring! Instead I went to university, trained as a psychodynamic counsellor and had some more therapy; then further training, first as an addiction counsellor which led me to working with addicts who were seeking a new way to live without drugs, and later as a psychoanalytic psychotherapist. Throughout my experience at various academic institutions, I have been the only Black person in the cohort.

Although I met with some difficulties, I managed the damaging, pervasive effects of my earlier experiences. I have since worked across the voluntary sector, in residential settings, community settings, in the National Health Service and in independent practice.

I now have an understanding that we are essentially spiritual and that people are bodily impacted not only by their relationships with others but also by their social environment, which in turn shapes personality. Remaining abstinent is contingent on certain factors, two of which are important—awareness and change. When you have an addiction, not only does your physical health suffer, but you are emotionally arrested, and your capacity for learning is severely impaired. At the time of writing, having been drugs-free for almost thirty years, I can say that the benefits have far exceeded all expectations. My relationships and quality of life have improved. My life has meaning and purpose, and I have come to know a new freedom.

I lived for years and years with feelings of betrayal and injustice, feeling like a fundamental part of myself was constantly being attacked. Perhaps the drugs were needed to keep a part of myself silenced and essentially killed off. Growing up, being told to "do as I say, not as I do", was confusing, and having little faith in authority left me feeling isolated, alone with myself. I can now acknowledge the past but it does not define who I am. I recognise that I have a right to demand human behaviour from others and to express that part of me that has been denied a voice. I deserve everything that life offers.

References

Alcoholics Anonymous (1984). *Pass It On: The Story of Bill Wilson and How the A.A. Message Reached the World*. New York: Alcoholics Anonymous World Services.

Lemon, R. (2018). *Addiction and Devotion in Early Modern England*. Haney Foundation Series. Philadelphia, PA: University of Pennsylvania Press.

Macmillan, H. (1957, 20 July). Speech given at Bedford Town football ground.

Shakespeare, W. (1599). *Henry V*: Act 1, Scene 1.

Shakespeare, W. (1604). *Othello*: Act 1, Scene 1.

CHAPTER 7

Bad company? Street gangs and child exploitation in Bristol and beyond

Joe Secrett and Linda Cundy

Our estimates suggest that approximately 14,000 children were identified as at risk or involved in child criminal exploitation in 2022 to 2023, and we know this is likely to be a significant underestimate on the scale of the problem.
—Home Office, County Lines Programme data, 16 December 2024

The victim and the offender are frequently located in one single damaged young person.
—Boswell, 2013

These young people are actually a doubly traumatised cohort, traumatised by their developmental experiences and further traumatised by their gang experiences, the gang having been their attempt to find a "cure" for their ailment.
—Minne, 2023

It is ... a hard truth that while we readily recognise that street gangs cause significant harm to communities and to young people themselves, they also are very often the only constant within the life of that young person. For a young person that has had a challenging background, the structure and protection offered by a gang—no matter the cost—can be hard to turn down.
—Centre for Social Justice Report, 2018

Introduction

There are numerous types of "gang" in the world, each with its own version of perverse attachment, dangers, and challenges involved in breaking free. Many operate in regions with a long history of poverty, lawlessness, and violence; membership provides perceived protection and a chance of an income. We see images from around the world of men, young and not so young, with bodies, heads, and faces crudely tattooed, badges of belonging but also intended as a threat to others, a clear "back off, don't mess with me" message. CECOT, a "mega prison" in El Salvador incarcerates up to 40,000 such tattooed men, jailed, often without trial, for violent gang-related offences including kidnappings, torture, and murder. The regime these prisoners are subjected to has been denounced by human rights groups as amounting to state torture on an industrial scale. In Russia, mafia-type gang members also wear their criminal lives on their skin. Each new killing, new prison sentence is etched onto their bodies. "The hand was a virtual curriculum vitae, with tattoos marking criminal convictions and specialities, whether a second-storey cat burglar or a convicted armed robber" (Galeotti, 2018, p. 70).

Being inked in this way is for life, making it impossible to reinvent yourself as a mainstream citizen. Many lives are cut short by rivals, by law enforcement, or sometimes on order from the top. It would not be surprising if those at the bottom of the pile turned to the very narcotics they traffic in order to cope with their harsh and hopeless reality, with inevitable further risk.

There are highly organised mobsters with a clear hierarchy involved in running drugs, guns, black-market services, and protection rackets. They are also responsible for people trafficking, money laundering, and contract killings: anything lucrative and illegal. These mobs include well-established crime families where those in positions of power deal ruthlessly with any challenge to their reputations or business activities. There is serious money involved and worldwide networks of influence. Serviced by crooked accountants and lawyers, facilitated by corrupt police and politicians, their orders carried out by gangster "enforcers", these mafiosi crime lords often move in powerful circles, gaining legal immunity through a combination of bribery and intimidation.

All by proxy, of course; those at the top of such cartels as the Sicilian Cosa Nostra, Calabrian 'Ndrangheta, or Russian Vory keep their own hands clean. For the lower ranks, life is not so charmed. Violence and murder are rife. How can they, or the children of big crime families, break away?

One controversial measure in Calabria attempts to intervene in the intergenerational cycle of violence and corruption. "Influence and trust, especially in 'ndrangheta clans, are established and preserved through family bonds … the sons will carry on the family businesses and lead the clan's activities and the daughters will forge and strengthen alliances through marriage" (Sergi, 2018, p. 6). By defining the culture and values being transmitted to children of crime clans as child abuse, revoking parental or paternal authority, children can be removed, relocated, and fostered in different regions to protect them. If any members of crime families, including women, decide to make an escape and are willing to share information about the gang's dealings, they are given witness protection and new identities, but must always remain vigilant to retribution.

Closer to home, knife- and gun-related violence are always in the news in the UK. Street, or postcode, gangs may not have the same deep historical roots or political influence; they are often loosely affiliated groups made up of people who are disenfranchised. They do the dirty work of selling drugs imported and distributed by others higher up in the hierarchy. These narcotics are, perhaps, the very same substances as those handled by gangs in Latin America or Asia. With that comes a host of dangers.

I do not work with gang members but have had clients who do, and others whose lives were blighted by living in areas or on estates where muggings at knife point, open drug dealing, street fights, police sirens in the night, and other evidence of gang activity make day-to-day existence unsafe.[1] I have known children who were drawn into gangs and, in one tragic case, a teenaged boy was killed after being recruited. Worries for children, family, and friends add to the stress for my clients. One woman asked me to see her teenaged son. He was quietly spoken and articulate.

[1] Sarah Coleman's book, *Life and Hope Out of Darkness* (2025), describes her work with women in a South African township blighted by gang activity and likened to a war zone.

He denied being affiliated but had somehow got caught up in inter-gang conflict and been stabbed in the abdomen. He was fortunate to survive. Had he been prepared to cooperate with police investigations he was entitled to criminal injuries compensation, money that would have been most helpful to his single mother. But, although he knew his assailant, he was reluctant to disclose, partly from fear of retaliation against himself or his family but also mistrust of the local police. As a young man of dual heritage, he had been stopped and searched without cause on many occasions. All I could do to help was write a letter to his Member of Parliament asking for her support to get the family moved to a different borough.

To help me understand the attachment dynamic in street gangs, what draws young people into that life, the dangers they face, and the challenges involved in breaking free, I spoke with Joe Secrett. Joe is a freelance youth specialist in Bristol in the West of England. His particular areas of expertise are serious youth violence and child criminal exploitation, working from a relationship-based, trauma-informed perspective. Joe explains: "I grew up in inner city Bristol and started volunteering at the local youth club when I was seventeen. I was being groomed into selling class A drugs and my youth worker got me out of that really early. I got lucky. I saw the impact on myself, and that was the motivation for working within my community, because I knew how needed it was. For me, it was about having those role models that I could look up to outside the family. Then about ten years ago, we were seeing so much serious youth violence and that was where I really wanted to focus, where my expertise is most able to have an impact."

What follows is a conversation between us that focuses on Joe's experience working predominantly with young men in his home town.[2] My questions and comments are shown in a different typeface from Joe's responses.

What is a gang? Who gets involved and why?

To start, it's helpful to look at what a gang is *deemed* to be. While there are organised gangs that recruit people, there are also groups of friends

[2] A report by the Centre for Social Justice into gang-related violence, published in 2018, addresses issues primarily related to London, highlighting regional differences and needs.

within inner city communities of high poverty, high deprivation, that end up getting into low-level crime and then are seen as a gang. Then sometimes they take on that persona. Also, you may have a group of young, mostly Black, boys from St. Pauls in Bristol selling drugs, and they are viewed by everybody around them as a gang, even if they are a just a group of friends who got caught up in some stuff. You can have a group of university students who are selling cocaine to other students in an organised manner, and they're never seen as a gang. So, I think it's also really important to look at society and how gangs are portrayed.

We don't use the word "gang" much in the work. We say we're serious youth violence specialists or child criminal exploitation specialists, and those things all tie in with gangs, as well as other avenues that young people can get involved in that may be nothing to do with being gang affiliated. But then there are also young people who do identify as a gang: they have a name, and they have conflict with other gangs.

If we're talking about child criminal exploitation, I've worked with young people who are just being exploited to sell drugs. You've got somebody who's the big guy who doesn't sell anything himself, but he's got people who get people to run for him. They are very good at identifying vulnerable young people; they know who to target, they know how to target them. Some young people are groomed by being befriended or given perceived protection. Other young people I know have been forced into it. I know a twelve-year-old who was forced to go on a county line, threatened that if he didn't go, his mum would be stabbed. He'd never been involved in anything before. They just saw that he was from a vulnerable single parent family. There was no man in the house. He ended up in a trap house in another city being forced to sell crack. He was missing for more than a week and came back utterly traumatised from that. So you have some people that are absolutely forced, but I would say in general, it's that young people are targeted and they don't realise they're being groomed.

Another young person that I worked with had lost one parent to addiction and the other was still an active user whose flat was being cuckooed—used by a drug dealer to sell heroin and crack to other addicts. This boy was fourteen and he would get bought a meal from the chicken shop once a day and given a little bit of weed if he was out selling crack and heroin. He'd often do ten-hour shifts and get maybe twenty quid's worth of weed and a hot meal. So that was very much seeing an opportunity to exploit a young person because he had a need and getting him involved in selling drugs, which led on to other issues for this young person around conflict in his neighbourhood. But he thought these people were his friends, were looking after him, that they'd really got him on side. These were his people. He was never gonna snitch on them. They feed him. Because of the amount of neglect within his home life, it was a step up.

Then there are young people who seek out groups, or gangs for a number of reasons. There's obviously the perceived safety. If you live somewhere where there's a gang, if you're not part of it, you're probably scared, so if you can become part of it you feel safer in your own neighbourhood. You're not considering the conflict that might come with that from groups from different areas that have history with the gang.

There is some evidence that young people who are depressed, even suicidal, are drawn to gang membership (Watkins & Melde, 2016). Maybe they are looking for some spark to lift their depression, some action, even danger, to give them an adrenaline buzz ...[3]

Yes, it's a high, they want the kick. Maybe it's addictive. They want to be dressing up with the hoodies and the balaclavas and carrying knives and having a Gucci pouch. A few get tattooed with their postcodes. And there are also young people who definitely do it for kudos.

A lot of people from the inner city are known by their road name. A road name is like a nickname as opposed to their "government name". It's not always linked to crime but if it is then that is about anonymity, especially when it comes to the police. Another aspect is dissociation: "This is who I am when I'm on the road." Every young person out there who's involved is definitely hiding behind a persona. They are someone different at home.

Teenagers, and particularly those of colour or who are disenfranchised in various ways, crave respect. Adolescents are more aware of the wider world

[3] "[A]n audience of fellow youth heightens the rewards and excitement of deviant behaviour" (McGloin & Collins, 2015, p. 279).

and being a small fish in a very big pond. They feel unimportant and invisible so need to feel seen.

Yes, there are definitely young people who fit that category. "I'm in this gang, this is who I am. I'm gonna show up on social media, and now I'm the Big Bad."

Also, there comes a sense of belonging. We are social creatures with a need to belong. The groups we are part of express our identity.

Yes, but it's not just who you are but how other people view you. It's a myth that all gang members are Black. It's more to do with location than heritage; there's a more diverse demographic in the inner city which means the groups are also more diverse. We've had white British-born kids who have been involved and who've been murdered because of it, or have stabbed people. It's much more linked to poverty. But young Black boys are far more likely to have issues within the education system and be excluded from school. Exclusion makes them vulnerable. Exclusion leads to exploitation.

I guess if you've been excluded from school you have to display bravado, to tough it out rather than show any distress.[4]

I think one issue that goes unspoken is young people who are really searching for their identity. We find this often, specifically with mixed race or dual heritage young people. We know that knife crime and gangs is *not* a Black issue, it's a poverty issue, but we're looking at specific diasporas within that. Groups or gangs where the majority is made up of people with Caribbean descent, you might then have a young person who is dual heritage and the Caribbean side of the family is not involved in their lives. So they are growing up in a world where they don't know the Black side of their identity, but they know their white side, and what they're fed in the media is very much that Black is attitude, aggression, Black is gangs, Black is knife crime. They're told all of these stereotypical

[4] "Just over half [of young men in a Home Office study of gun crime] had been excluded from school and so were disconnected from the positive influence of peers and teachers. Such disconnected young men may be highly fearful, or highly fearless—both states of mind that are a defence against negative affects like shame, humiliation, anger, and distress" (Adshead, Fonagy, & Sarkar, 2007, p. 837).

things, and then when they hit teenage years, especially the boys, I think they go out looking for their identity.

Because all they've ever been told about Black culture or Caribbean culture is the negative stereotypes perpetuated by the media, they go and look for that; they wanna be down, they wanna be part of something that represents them. I think that young men with identity crises really get drawn into gang situations because they want to be "Black" but they've not been given a positive sense of Black African or Caribbean culture to identify with.

I think there is a difference between a dual heritage person raised by a single, white British parent and one raised by a Black Caribbean parent, because the environment that you grow up in is what your culture is and what you know. So if you grow up in a Black household, if at least one of your parents in the house is Black, the household is a Black household. If your mum is of Jamaican heritage, you're going to have the Dutch pot, you are likely going to have soup on a Saturday and when you hear that reggae music playing early in the morning, you know it will be a day for cleaning and tidying. You are going to have things that fit in with Jamaican culture, and you're going to grow up in that, so you're going to have a really good understanding of what "Black" is.

But if you grow up in a white household and the Black parent is absent, then you're missing that role model both personally and culturally, so I think you're then looking to fill that gap. Also, if you grow up with a single Black, say, Caribbean mother and possibly in an extended Caribbean family, you're still growing up in Britain, which is at least nominally white, so you're familiar with that culture as well. You're getting that from wider society, but if it's the other way around, then you're really missing parts of your identity. And it's not just young dual heritage boys I see it in. I see it with girls too who have a real misconception of what "Black" is, regardless of the fact that they are dual heritage. That is one avenue that ends up with young people getting recruited into gangs.

Looking for what has been missing is also a communication, perhaps a protest both to the family that is there and to the absent one. "Why have you kept this from me?" and "Where have you been?"

One of the main gangs I worked with in Bristol started as a group of friends that grew up in St Paul's. A lot of them had struggles in their own lives, single-parent households, abject poverty, absent mothers or fathers, all kinds of things. They were all similar age, all went to the adventure playground together as kids and once they hit teenage years, they started doing music videos and began to dabble in minor criminal things. Then they became labelled as a gang by the police because they were a group of young Black boys of just eleven, twelve, thirteen, and once they realised that's how they were being viewed they started to identify as a gang. They thought they had kudos now.

We set up a young men's project working with this group before they became a gang. Every Monday we'd have about twenty young people turning up. We just emulated the family environment. We'd cook and eat together and have debates and conversations around the table. It was really impactful. We did a lot of really positive work. It's just a shame that the funding was cut when it was. They were just kids in the community dabbling here and there with some stuff that was not quite legal, but they were not selling crack and heroin in an organised manner or having beef with other groups. It was once they were labelled they took on that identity and became the biggest gang in Bristol over the last ten years.

So others joined?

Yes. Once they hit fifteen or sixteen there were then younger kids, their younger brothers or cousins or kids in the area who knew them, that wanted to be part of it. They looked up to the older boys and emulated what they saw their slightly older peers do.

They were just a group of friends who hung out together but ended up going down a path that created this gang mentality and attitude, and sadly it led to some of the biggest conflict that Bristol has seen ever in youth violence. They were a group we worked with when they were eleven or twelve years old. We saw them every week, but then our funding got cut. A few years later we saw them again, but at our specialist services. Out of the fifteen or twenty young people that attended, five of the young men are now either dead or in prison for murder as a result of knife crime and conflict due to being linked to that group. That is the most challenging part of my job as these are young men from my community that we are losing.

You wanted to say something about exploitation?

Yes, there's a really important distinction to make around exploitation and helping out. It's about understanding culture.

So, if I'm growing up and my mum is a single parent and she's struggling, and my older cousin was involved in some illegal stuff and he's gone off to prison, his friends would probably look out for me. Their way of looking out for me would be, "Look, we can support you, we can make sure you're making money, we'll look after you, we'll protect you." And their intent is not to groom or exploit but to look after because you are part of the family, part of the community. They end up doing very much the same things that groomers would do, but the intent is different. While there are people who specifically look for a vulnerable young person to groom and will exploit them and do whatever to make money off of them, there are also lots of people in the community that will do what they deem as "hooking up", or helping out, a younger person who they see struggling. But the only way they know to do that is to say, "Hey, look, I'll get you some crack. You can sell it. You can pay me back when you made the sales. I'll get you started. We're gonna make sure we teach you right so you're not putting yourself at risk." It's a weird kind of attachment. But if a young person is looking up to someone older who's just trying to help them out, we need to have a different approach. It's not the same, you don't have the same push–pulls as where a young person has been groomed and then ends up fearful of their exploiter. It doesn't make it OK but just means we need to think about it differently.

That means if somebody goes to jail, then you need to look at their family?

Yes, and think who might become more vulnerable now because presumably the person in jail has been bringing money into the family. Around the country now there are violence reduction units. Every area has a VRU [Violence Reduction Unit] specifically focused on reducing serious youth violence, normally made up of police, social care, education, with a senior youth worker. They work in a joined up, multi-agency, holistic way. One task is to create lists of vulnerable young people and they have a red, amber, green system to identify who is most at risk of getting involved in violent crime.

That's not necessarily a problem if the list is handled professionally, recognising that biases exist. The problem is that we still have unconscious bias and institutional racism. If you're young and Black, you're more likely to end up on this list than if you're young and white, even if your family is involved in crime. If a parent finds out their son's name was on the list and they've never been involved in anything, it's just they're young, they're Black, and they know someone older who's involved in criminal activity, they see it as profiling: "Why are you doing this to my son? Why is my son on the list for gangs?"

Schools are notoriously behind on their education around child criminal exploitation, serious youth violence, and gangs. I've seen schools find excuses to exclude a young person whose name is on a VRU list because it's assumed they are gang affiliated. So rather than that young person being protected, they are punished.

Poverty and racism fuel the raging fires of gang violence.

Absolutely. Then, because these things happen, we have a lot of young men, Black, white, brown, whoever, living in these areas who are scared to go outside and pick up a knife for protection with no intent to use it. But statistically, if you're Black and you're young, you're more likely to be stopped by the police. If you get caught with a knife, you're looking at up to five years in prison, potentially. You don't feel safe walking to the shops. You're not in any way gang affiliated, but you're stereotyped, stopped and searched, and you end up with a criminal record which affects everything. I'm not saying all gang members are Black, but it's the Black kids who are most likely to get police attention.

Danger

Dealing drugs is the main way young people in gangs make money, and with that comes danger. We've seen addicts pull knives out on young people who are selling them drugs because they don't want to pay, especially if the young person who is selling some crack and heroin is new to the lifestyle and isn't confident. Then, as soon as you're making money there are people who are interested in taking that from you, so you're at risk of being robbed of your money or your drugs.

When young people are being exploited, an aim is to get them into what's called a debt bond. For instance, you might start by giving the young person an ounce of weed, which is worth £120 or £150, and you say, "Right, you're gonna go and break this down. You're gonna sell it for me." But then somebody else is sent to steal the ounce of weed, and now that young person owes money to the exploiter who says, "You owe me money, you need to sort it out. The quickest way for you to do this is go on a county line, go to this trap house, work for me for the week, and then you'll be paid off." But it's a never-ending cycle. There's always something else. The debt is never cleared.

This is like modern-day slavery with debt bonding.

Yes, the child trafficking aspect falls under the modern-day slavery definition. A common misconception is that a young person has to be going to places outside of their own city for it to be considered trafficking. You can be trafficked between two addresses in the same area but lots of professionals don't recognise this, meaning that safeguarding concerns are not always escalated appropriately.

Another danger is conflict with other gangs. A while back there were twenty-seven reported stabbings and a number that were unreported over an eighteen-month period between two groups within a small area of Bristol. And that's where we get to things like the points system. The points system spread to Bristol through drill music. I'm not here to blame drill music, I think art imitates life and life imitates art. It was perpetuated in certain drill songs where they talk about their points. You get points for stabbing somebody, different points depending on where you stab them. For a leg or an arm, you get fewer points than a body shot. And then if you get an attempted murder or a murder, that's more points. That became a thing here, where our young people were boasting on social media, "I got three points this weekend." It was this perceived kind of kudos, being feared, or what they deem as gaining respect. They will then rap about it in their songs.

According to Minne and Kassman, "The community where gangs are born has now got the ingredients similar to a war zone—angry young people, filled with energetic rage, the source of that rage being located in the rivals (or the mirror) and not towards the real source, the segregation of the poor still present in society" (2018, p. 189).

Yes. After the first young person died in one of the gangs, their rivals released a song with a line stating: "All of our team's still alive and we can't say the same about yours." What teenager is not going to react to that provocation? This was fairly early on in the conflict and really escalated the aggression. Over following years, there was a series of back-and-forth stabbings between them, ultimately leading to a young man being murdered for being in the wrong place at the wrong time. He wasn't even affiliated, just childhood friends with one of the groups and he lost his life tragically due to the ongoing conflict.

Earlier we touched on identity. Part of that is who you are not; you're not a member of the other crew. That means you see them as not just a potential threat to your income or your standing but as Other. You would need to somehow dehumanise someone if you intended stabbing them. That may be easier to do if you are already traumatised. And traumatised people are also likely to be hypervigilant and more reactive.

We all talk about post-traumatic stress but for our young people it isn't "post", it's current. Every day they're living in trauma. If you're worried for your life every time you step outside the house you're always on edge in fight-or-flight mode. There's trauma throughout. A well-rounded, well-supported young person is not likely to end up in a situation where they're deep-rooted in gang culture, knife crime, violence, and exploitation. A lot of the young people we work with have been through the care system or had multiple adverse childhood experiences at home and unresolved issues.

You know, young Black boys are some of the highest achieving in primary school and some of the lowest achieving at the end of secondary school, so something happens over their teenage years that makes them feel disenfranchised and disengaged from the British education system and Britain as a culture. They become more aware of the racism, getting told to go back to where you came from. All the Black, dual heritage, and mixed-heritage young people I've worked with have had some experience of being targeted specifically because of their race, and they could be just ten or eleven years old. Being in a gang isn't always about being safe from other young men. It can be feeling protected from wider society.

Experiencing racism is deeply shaming. It's not about anything you've done but about who you are fundamentally, what you can't change, how you are perceived, and that gets internalised. As a consequence, there's the need for a tough façade and trouble if the person feels disrespected. Those with multiple adverse childhood experiences may have a more fragile sense of self, be prone to feeling shame, so more inclined to retaliate. How easily violence can escalate.

Another source of danger may be going along with your exploiters. One young man was in some kind of debt to exploiters and selling crack and heroin for them. Aged sixteen, he was told to get in a car that had been sent for him and go where it took him by his exploiters, ten years his senior. He didn't feel able to say no and ended up being charged, through joint enterprise, with murder. He is now serving a minimum of seventeen years, even though he did not stab anyone. He was in an impossible position—refusing the command would have potentially put his life at risk.

What about crime families?

It's rare here for a parent who is involved in gangs wanting their kids to get involved, though it does sometimes happen. There are certain families with "names" in Bristol; and if you're part of that family, everyone knows that's what your family does so there's a pressure on you from a young age to be part of it, to be this person they expect you to be. You've got something to live up to, and then the cycle repeats. But personally, I haven't seen a parent who wants their son to get involved and sell drugs. They know what comes with it, they know the dangers, though they might be happy to exploit other people's children. When I look at the older people who ran the original gangs, the Aggie crew, which was really notorious in Bristol, and the Urban crew, their sons are involved in playing football now or they're doing other things. It hasn't carried on in general. They've tried to keep their sons out of it.

But if your dad is involved with gangs and crime and he's in and out of prison, that is more adverse experiences for their kids. They get numb to it. They don't see that they're passing trauma on, they just see it as this is life, so "We're gonna protect the people we care about, and this is how we know how to do it."

The East End of London is on my doorstep and it seems to be a more common phenomenon there, a tradition of being an organised crime family that is respected and feared, and it's understood that if you get involved as a woman with that family, any children you have will become the next generation of the gangster dynasty.

I'm painting with really broad brushstrokes here, but I do see it a bit more in the white working-class areas where it's expected that the boys will carry on the tradition, that someone will be selling crack for their uncle, but they're all working together as a family. Everybody knows it's a criminal family and what's going on, and that's just what they do.

We've talked about knife crime but what about guns? In my East London neighbourhood there have been numerous shootings over many years related to gangland activity. Going back to the 1960s, notorious gangsters the Kray twins lived in my road. They, and other members of their gang, the Firm, were responsible for a number of shootings and murders in the area. Not so long ago, turf wars involving firearms led to another local street being named "murder mile". Many of the more recent incidents seem connected to Turkish drugs rings. Earlier this year, a nine-year-old girl was seriously wounded and three men injured in a drive-by shooting in broad daylight nearby.

Thankfully we haven't seen much of firearms here yet.

A lot of gun crime in London seems to be drive-by shootings between rival gangs. Perhaps those involved tend to be older than the young people you work with?

Maybe, and perhaps it's more the organised criminal gangs using firearms, not the young street kids who do the selling. It could be the people who get the crack into the country and distribute it, and they have no direct contact or dealings with the runners who are the lowest in the system. But whatever's going on in London, we know that in a few years it's going to come to Bristol. It is a concern.

Prison

Can we talk about prison experience? I imagine that life on the street gets unbearable; there is too much stress, maybe too many drugs, too much threat and violence. I wonder whether there is an unconscious longing for prison as a place of safety; a benign authority to put a stop to all the trauma. A prison or young offender's sentence could be an opportunity to make changes in life and reinvent yourself, but it seems that it is just as often another dangerous environment.

I don't think young people tend to take prison that seriously until they've been there, and then, depending on their experience, it can really impact on whether or not they are worried about going back. They usually get a sentence for possession with intent, so they've been caught with class A drugs a number of times and are given a short time in prison. Some see it as a badge of honour to have done time. But young offenders' places and prisons are full of gang members. It's a roulette game who you're in there with; if it's your own crew you have a safety net around you but if it's your rivals you're in trouble.

There's a story about tattoo tears, that you get that for murdering someone. But one person I spoke to, an older guy, said that what used to happen if you were in prison and you were assaulted, if you were raped, they would tattoo a tear on you to let everybody know that had happened. That was a real humiliation so when people came out of prison with tattoo tears and everyone was asking what that's about, they created this story of it being because they had killed somebody.[5]

I've worked with young people who've been attacked in prison over things that have happened in the community. On more than one occasion, a young person has ended up in a young offenders' institution or prison with people from opposing groups or gangs. This has led to young people being forced to strip on camera to humiliate them, or beaten up. Sometimes they've been forced to say things on camera that put their own friends down or admit to things that are not true. This can lead to a

[5] Galeotti reports a similar practice among the Russian mafia who were imprisoned in the gulags. Inmates who had been sexually assaulted by other prisoners "were deemed 'debased' in the macho *vor* culture, considered to have been victims of their own weakness … [and] forcibly tattooed with eyes over the groin and the word 'slave' on their face" (Galeotti, 2018, p. 71).

deep need to retaliate to regain their pride, either in prison or once they have been released, continuing the cycle of violence.

If the court sends them to jail they do look at where to place them and think about conflict with other groups, but then they may get sent further away, which means it's harder for family to visit. Sometimes they might be around these other young offenders who are facing a life sentence for murder when they are just there for possession with intent to sell.

I just want to say one more thing about danger in the lives of these young men; that is, the damage done to their psyches from this way of life. Minne and Kassman write about the need to develop a "protective psychopathy" then "the young person is ... in daily training not to care" (2018, p. 192). Dehumanising others also dehumanises oneself.

Yes. If his crew has beef with another one and he gets stabbed or someone is killed, it's just life, you know, they've lost another friend, it happens.

Turning points

Once young people hit their early twenties and they find a girlfriend and maybe they've got a kid on the way, they usually want to step away. It's definitely possible because when you see your friend doing well and getting a job you support that, but it's not always easy. What often keeps them there is fear from the conflicts that already happened with opposing gangs retaliating and needing someone to watch your back.

One young man had been attempting to leave that way of life and managed to get an apprenticeship in the building trade. He had a job in an area that was not safe for him due to his previous affiliations, and was stabbed while working on a house there. Although he survived that attack and continued to distance himself from his previous lifestyle, sadly he was murdered a few years after this incident.

With the more organised, exploitative side of organised crime gangs where young people are being groomed and threatened by older people, there is a feeling that they can't leave because they owe money. Or, if an exploiter can see that this young person has no protection around them, it's very easy to control with fear and say, "I'll do this to your mum. You won't be safe walking down the street. I'll tell everyone you did this or you did that." They maintain fear by making sure everyone knows they are prepared to do what they threaten. It's coercive control.

And people get hurt to prove that these are not empty threats?

Yes. The person being exploited can't leave. But it could be that the police are onto this young person and they're always being tracked and stopped. When the exploiter feels the risk is too high, once it gets too hot, there's no more use for that young person and they'll move on to the next one.

So, either you're scared for your own safety from the people exploiting you or you're scared from the beef that's been created over the years with other gangs and now you're on your own. There are people who've got away but a lot of them are still looking over their shoulder.

Here in Bristol we don't tend to see the practice of getting jumped in to a gang and having to get jumped out. That is an initiation where you had to rob someone, or beat them up, or stab them to be allowed into the gang. And then there are certain rituals to jump out, like taking a beating so you'd earn your right to leave. It's a kind of warning about what will happen to you if you snitch. That was very much more the American gang culture that spilled over to England a long time ago, but we don't really have that here anymore.

You've mentioned that becoming a father can be a turning point for some young men that motivates them to look beyond hanging out with their gang mates, dealing drugs, risking violence and arrest. I know you were involved in a project encouraging young dads to be involved in their children's lives. Can you tell me about that?

That was Dadcast, set up in 2017 by myself and my friends Kinney and Jason. We're all fathers. I'm white British, Kinney is Black British-born, but Jamaican heritage, And Jace is dual heritage, so his mum's Jamaican heritage and his dad's white. We all grew up around the same area. We all worked together and were sick of the narrative around young dads, especially young Black dads, the stereotype of the absent dad, and we wanted to encourage fatherhood and challenge the culturally negative perceptions. I grew up in a single parent household and I've got Black friends who had both parents at home. So Dadcast was a platform for fathers on YouTube with us sitting and chatting, and then it grew. We were on local radio every week for about a year and got funding to do something called Dadcraft at a local arts venue on the first Saturday of every month where dads could bring their children and we made all kinds of things. But then I started fostering, Jason was doing his master's, Kenny had changed jobs. We all work full time and we're fathers, and we just couldn't keep it up.

Projects like Dadcast could support young men who are gang-affiliated by encouraging them to be actively involved in their children's lives. It also occurs to me that, when they become fathers, they may identify with their young children, see how vulnerable they are and how harsh their own lives have become.

Yes, they want to be better role models and we supported that. You need to bring the money in to support the family, but also you need to protect them. We wanted to set up a fatherhood group where young dads could come along and we'd have older dads there as well. Just a weekly meeting with cups of tea and biscuits and conversation, but leading to doing residentials with fathers, going away and doing team building and confidence building. I was really keen to work with young dads in prison too. We had so many things we wanted to do to encourage that but just didn't have the capacity.

While becoming a parent is a positive turning point, I imagine sometimes the last straw for many who are involved in gangs and knife crime is experiencing extreme violence, being attacked, witnessing it happening, or even committing violent acts themselves.

I was working one-to-one with a young person who'd been away at a young offenders for about nine months. During that time, his friend had been killed. It was an accident. But this young person told me, "I wanna be angry at somebody but I don't know who to be angry at because they're saying it was an accident." He had a real reputation on the road. He'd been stabbed. He'd stabbed somebody. Everybody was scared of him, and he was there saying I don't know what to do with my feelings.

There is a lot of grief. I grew up in an inner-city community and, working with young people, I need clinical supervision and therapy for the work I do. When I lose a young person, it's hard, it's painful, and it's sad. A young person was murdered last year, and the whole community was grieving. No one's been caught for the murder, so there's no closure.

Maybe this is the opportunity for me to ask you about being a white youth worker in a mixed community but with a significant Black population. How are you viewed?

I don't have any problems because I think it's about authenticity. I'm from the community, I can speak on behalf of my community. As soon as they know I know their older cousin or their uncle or I went to school with their mum or whatever, they know I'm not just some guy who's come in. They see me down the corner shop and getting food from the local Caribbean place. But for sure we talk about the fact that young Black people experience racism and discrimination more than their white friends, that there's white privilege.

Most young people walk away from gang activities by their early twenties, but do some stay involved?

Yes. There are people who have lived their whole lives in and out of prison. This is all they really know, or they've got too many hurdles in their way to be able to move on. I've worked with many people who want to get out of it as an adult but what holds them back is finding work. They're young, they're Black, they've got a criminal record, they're from St Paul's or Easton, which are notorious areas locally, and employers are not going to give them a chance. They apply for jobs and they've got a child to feed, so what can they do? So many of them go back to selling crack and heroin rather than being on Universal Credit; they don't see that as a viable choice.

So there's a poverty trap that gets in the way of starting a new life?

Absolutely. And there's so much unresolved grief, ongoing trauma. Every day they wake up, they've got to be worried about who's driving past them, where are their friends, where's their safety. You put somebody like that in regular work, and then there's a conflict, and all of a sudden they go into fight or flight.

But some do enjoy that way of life. The older they get, the more they become the Big Boss and everybody knows who they are. There are definitely older people who have just always lived that life and are notorious in the area. They are often the ones grooming other young people and running the show.

I'm curious to hear what your answer would be to that? What help do people need to see that they've grown up with trauma and to stop it being passed on to the next generation? Even if counselling or psychotherapy could be made available to all families with multiple adverse experiences and disadvantages, I guess it could not begin to address the underlying systemic problems.

From my experience, inner city culture in general is quite anti talking to professionals like counsellors and therapists. We youth workers do therapeutic work with young people, and they don't realise that when we mentor them it's very similar to therapy.

But I think that we really need to look at the root causes of things and, where possible, prevention. There is plenty of evidence that knife crime and serious youth violence is higher in areas of abject poverty. We know that young people who have had multiple ACEs, adverse childhood experiences, are more likely to be involved, young people in the care system or who've been excluded from school. We need to invest in education, youth services, social care, mental health services, health, police. Here in Bristol we have suffered statutory youth spending cuts of 78 per cent over the years. You have to look at the problem holistically.

For instance, Mum's got mental health issues, all of a sudden there's no adult mental health support. Mum's on her own, so her son's going off hanging out with his friends and doing what he's doing, getting into trouble.

Then funding has been cut in education so there are fewer learning support assistants. Often within inner city schools, the lowest paid staff members are the most diverse, the people who look like you or your family, who can understand when you're doing something that's a cultural thing it's not simply bad behaviour, but they're the first people to get their jobs cut to save money.

We need a lot more funding for youth services and community groups like adventure playgrounds and youth clubs so young people have activities where they can achieve in things like sports and music, and have role models to look up to.

I can see that if your gang crew are your attachment figures, especially if your parents are vulnerable or absent, then it's really tough to make a new life outside that without another community to belong to.

Youth clubs saved my generation. We had a lower crime rate in our generation. Most of my friends have gone on to be successful, but we had the most funding back in the late nineties. I had strong male role models there from my community, I had all these things that I craved as a young man or a boy, but, you know, most of those clubs have shut down now. The police used to come and kick football with us, they'd come in plain clothes and they'd have a play around with us but they don't have time to do that anymore so there's a bigger divide between the police and the community. That's not the police's fault. Ultimately the only way that you can change it is through investment in services and fundamentally looking at supporting children in poverty because we know that poverty is the trigger.

If they're being exploited, it might be that you get an NRM in place, which is the national referral mechanism, which protects them from criminal charges, not against violent crime but things like selling drugs. If a fourteen-year-old gets caught in another city with five grand's worth of crack, you can safely guess they're being exploited, and if they have an NRM in place, they can't get charged with possession with intent to supply. An NRM highlights them and makes them a bit more "hot" so they're going to get stopped by the police when they're seen. Not a stop-and-search necessarily but, "Are you alright? Just checking." If exploiters see the police taking an interest they get edgy and might let the young person go.

Also, everybody whose work is public facing needs education about unconscious biases, that we all have them, and we can talk about them and recognise that there is such a thing as white privilege. These biases affect everyone. If you're telling a teenage Black boy that everyone who looks like him carries knives and he's going out every morning in an area where everyone looks like him, he's going to be wary. If he gets into a situation where he needs to go to the police, there's no trust there if he's been on the receiving end of being stopped and searched just because he's a young Black boy. There is such a distrust for the police among young, especially Black and mixed-race children.

In the right environment, a prison sentence could also provide an opportunity to help gang members find ways to move away from their old lives once they are released. Education and skills training would help, I imagine. One pilot project I'm aware of was called Changing the Game, a group for gang members in Grendon, a therapeutically run prison. It provided a safe space where group members could talk about their experiences, tell their stories, and be heard, not judged. It seems that many who took part were able to let their hard-man masks drop and show their vulnerability, grieve, and feel remorse. At the end of the pilot programme, almost all who had taken part were keen to become "regular" members of society, be called by their "government names", and be better role models to their children. They wanted to be involved in helping others in the same situation they had been in. For those young men, prison gave them an opportunity to create a different life for themselves (Minne & Kassman, 2018).

You mentioned the extent of grief in communities over all the lives lost, and anger about things like institutional racism. I know of numerous church- or religion-based voluntary projects that try to provide guidance and opportunities to give up knives and follow a different path but the unprocessed trauma and allegiances remain. What about community healing?

There's a big need for that. Communities do come together—there'll be meetings called when something terrible has happened, a young person has been murdered. There are organisations that support the parents of murdered children but nothing seems very organised in Bristol. We should have community development officers whose job is to facilitate bringing communities together, listen to their experiences, and give them a platform. Then they can produce a community action plan to address specific needs.

I think, too, of the importance of rituals, and that the arts can be useful in expressing deep emotions and memorialising events. For instance, in the United States, textile artist Maria-Theresa Fernandes' Social Justice installation documents the lives lost to gun crime and police brutality, and she was commissioned to create a work, *The Innocent* (2023), with images of children killed in school shootings at Robb Elementary School and Sandy Hook.

Yes, creative projects are really valuable. One that I'm really proud of is "Unjust Stop". Working with the Creative Power Town community arts hub (2024), I brought a group of young people together with the aim of empowering them and giving them a voice to talk about what they felt was important to them around stop and searches. Come the end of this project, they had created a video that highlights how it feels to be targeted by the police due to the colour of your skin. This film demonstrates the mistrust from young people towards the police within our community, something that has far-reaching repercussions. The video is available on YouTube.

Of course, one of the most profound forms of healing comes with being useful, sharing your own experience with others in order to help them. Whether it is an ex-gang member or a community traumatised by knife or gun crime, being valued by, and valuable to, others is triumph over trauma.

I agree. People with lived experience make an invaluable contribution and impact on the next generation but they can't do it on their own. There needs to be a huge focus and funding put in to providing professional support and training. Experts by experience need to understand things like safeguarding, how to navigate situations where the police and social care may be involved, situations they may not naturally be comfortable in. Then, if you have lived experience *and* professional expertise, that is truly a force to be reckoned with!

References

Adshead, G., Fonagy, P., & Sarkar, S. P. (2007). Violence and gun crime. [Editorial comment.] *British Medical Journal, 335*(7625): 837. https://doi.org/10.1136/bmj.39365.683877.BE

Boswell, G. (2013). Trauma experiences in the backgrounds of violent young offenders. Lecture notes: University of East Anglia.

Centre for Social Justice Report (August 2018). It Can Be Stopped: A proven blueprint to stop violence and tackle gang and related offending in London and beyond.

Coleman, S. (2025). *Life and Hope Out of Darkness*. London: Karnac.

Creative Power Town (2024). *Unjust Stop*. https://youtube.com/watch?v=4Z2cDtfDWfI (last accessed 28 October 2024).

Fernandes, M.-T. (2023) *The Innocent*, 2012–2022. [Textile and mixed media art.] https://bakerartist.org/portfolios/wwwbakerartistorgportfoliomaria-theresafernandes (last accessed 15 January 2025).

Galeotti, M. (2018). *The Vory: Russia's Super Mafia*. New Haven, CT: Yale University Press.

Home Office (2024, 16 December). County Lines Programme data. https://gov.uk/government/publications/home-offices-county-lines-programme-data/county-lines-programme-data (last accessed 15 January 2025).

McGloin, J. M., & Collins, M. E. (2015). Micro-level processes of the gang. In: S. H. Decker & D. C. Pyrooz (Eds.), *The Handbook of Gangs* (pp. 276–293). Chichester, UK: Wiley.

Minne, C. (2023). From gangs (ideal ego) to groups (ego ideal). In: A. Cordioli & P. Fonda (Eds.), *The Knot Garden: War* (pp. 135–152). *Journal of Centro Veneto di Psicoanalisi, 2*.

Minne, C., & Kassman, P. (2018). Working with gangs and within gang culture. In: B. Kahr (Ed.), *New Horizons in Forensic Psychotherapy*. London: Karnac.

Sergi, A. (2018). Widening the Antimafia net: Child protection and the socio-cultural transmission of Mafia behaviours in Calabria. *Youth Justice, 18*(2): 149–168. https://doi.org/10.1177/1473225418791420_(last accessed 12 October 2024).

Watkins, A. M., & Melde, C. (2016). Bad medicine: The relationship between gang membership, depression, self-esteem, and suicidal behavior. *Criminal Justice and Behavior, 43*(8): 1107–1126. https://doi.org/10.1177/0093854816631797

CHAPTER 8

When a South Korean therapist meets a North Korean client: Meaning-making and miracles

Hyun Suk Lee

As far as we can discern, the sole purpose of human existence is to kindle a light of meaning in the darkness of mere being.
—Jung, 1995, p. 326

... both religion and psychotherapy form part of the cultural repertoire our species has devised to facilitate and enhance [...] mind-healing processes.
—Holmes, 2024, p. 61

Introduction

Psychotherapy, like art and religion, is an enterprise of engaging with meaning, and all can be characterised by their enquiry into human experiences on the nebulous boundaries between the internal and external. This is not to say that psychotherapy is religion or art, but they share something indispensable for being human, namely, a meaning-making process.

Meaning-making is also a matrix where an attachment develops. In psychotherapy, not only are we making a link among thoughts and feelings, but also we are building a therapeutic relationship in the hope that its benign and reparative qualities can be transferred outside. Any religious practice also intrinsically aims to build and sustain a community—with a deity at the centre—from which an individual's resilience cannot be separated.

A Jungian concept, the collective unconscious, accentuates the communal aspect of our psyche, a source of strength and creative energy. The collective unconscious counter-argues Freud's position, where he sees the unconscious mainly as a depository of a repressed personal desire and memory. Attachment theory emphasises our fundamental need to reach out for a connection, where a caregiver and the attached become a basic building block that needs to be sustained within and for a community.

Where Jung's approach to religion is "top down", or spiritually empirical, attachment theory's approach is "bottom up", or scientifically empirical. Jung encourages us to tap into the wealth of religious traditions in order to clarify what psychotherapy is. Attachment theory is helpful for us to understand religion from a perspective of psychological needs and functions, drawn on from evolutionary perspectives. My view is that their different approaches are both enriching and they seem to meet somewhere in the middle to reaffirm human resilience and an imperative for connection as the fundamental necessity for human existence.

I will explore a case with the help of Jungian concepts as well as attachment theory. They are instrumental: not to impose my agenda onto my religious client, Eunhye, but to open a space for us to reaffirm her meaning-making journey, one that involves miracles.

Case study: Eunhye[1]

Initial contact

Our first meeting happened in November 2022. Eunhye was a single mother in her late thirties with two young children (five- and seven-year-old girls). In her earlier sessions, she disclosed a history of post-natal depression but she had refused the antidepressant medication or talking therapy offered on the NHS. Instead, she got through the period of depression by relying on alcohol, which she later confessed was an

[1] For confidentiality, some of her personal details including her name were changed. *Eunhye* 은혜 (恩惠) means grace in Sino-Korean.

ongoing issue despite having much improved since. She was concerned about her difficulty giving attention to her children but was now seeking help as she had suicidal feelings, instigated by shaming attacks on her by opponents from a North Korean community conflict she was involved in.

There had been factions in this community, but the recent conflict escalated out of control, sparked by a leadership election. According to her, the opposition group organised and ran an election process in such a way that there could be no other candidates to compete with theirs, and in the end their only candidate was elected. When Eunhye and her cohort challenged the process and outcome, she and the other challengers began to receive disturbing messages from an unknown sender on social media, many of which were body-shaming. For instance, her private part was named, described in a graphic way, and mocked. Understandably, from the beginning, she voiced her explosive anger, which could be described as a murderous rage, as well as overwhelming shame to a point she could not look at herself in the mirror and became afraid of going out with a fear of bumping into someone who might have read those vicious messages. For about a year she always wore a baseball cap to hide her face to come to her sessions.

Context

Eunhye was one of several hundreds of North Korean escapees who had settled in the UK, and most of them made London their home alongside their outnumbering South Korean counterparts.

To talk about Eunhye, I also need to talk about North Korea. My short writing here won't do justice to the complexity, but it is important to draw our attention to an important aspect, that North Korea has become a perfect container for the bad (oppressive, inhumane, and deprived), while South Korea represents the good (free, democratic, and prosperous). In my view, this simplified version of narrative is still very powerful and dominant in the media and public opinion, often underplaying South Korea's own dark history and ongoing problems, such as civilian massacres in the name of an anti-communism campaign, numerous human rights violations during the military dictatorship era, and many current sociopolitical issues. For instance,

South Korea has one of the highest suicide rates in the world[2] and sits at the bottom of a gender equality table among OECD countries,[3] which some analysts link with the alarmingly low birth rate. The South Korean government has spent more than $200 billion to boost the population over the past sixteen years, but financial initiatives have so far failed to reverse the trend.[4] The recent political turmoil, after the now-impeached president declared martial law, reflects the fragility of democracy as well as the resilience of people, who have gone through many forms of human rights violations under the authoritarian rules, scorched in their collective memory. While the South has achieved remarkable economic growth and become a cultural powerhouse on the world stage, the country has also the shadow of cut-throat competition in every sphere, and a growing number of lonely deaths, both of which can be seen as symptoms of the breakdown of the community spirit that has underpinned traditional Korean society (the North and South combined).

North Korean escapees have further contributed to the narrative of the good South and the bad North. The implication in the therapy room is that when a South Korean therapist meets a North Korean client, this stark polarising and splitting is a backdrop that has to be worked through to make a connection. An implicit or sometimes rather explicit power dynamic where the South is the "goody" and the North is the "baddy" is likely to be entangled with the therapist's assumed authority in therapy sessions. In this sense, our meeting is not just a psychotherapy session but a politically charged event where, potentially, a symbolic war could break out. This is a way of framing that I have made use of in trying to understand the rather too many ruptures (in comparison to other client groups) between myself as a therapist and some of my North Korean clients. I have learnt from those ruptures that, in order to make a connection, I need to name and work on these challenges and differences.

In terms of the therapeutic relationship between Eunhye and myself, there were challenges that needed to be faced from the beginning.

---

[2] https://worldpopulationreview.com/contry-rankings/suicide-rate-by-country

[3] https://oecd.org/en/topics/gender-equality.html

[4] https://cnn.com/2024/05/09/asia/south-korea-government-population-birth-rate-intl-hnk/index.html

We spoke Korean, our mother tongue, but the countries we grew up in couldn't have been more different in some important senses. Certainly, we were not free from the conflicts inflicted on our two countries over seventy years, including the Korean War with an estimated two to three million casualties. I had to be upfront about our potential misunderstandings due to the subtle language and culture gaps, widened by the separated history and polarising politics. Our internalised othering of each other had to be named in order to take a journey of trust building.

Eunhye's history: Attachment, dangers, and survival

There was a terrible famine in North Korea in the 1990s, after its staunch ally and supporter, the Soviet Union, collapsed, and during which up to three million people were estimated to have died.[5] The regime called it "Arduous March 고난의 행군" to mobilise its population under the grandiose political banner, but the regime started to lose its firm grip on people and the cracks on the national distribution system began to appear. Black markets were set up and South Korean products sneaked in through China. South Korean soap opera DVDs became one of the biggest threats to the regime as North Koreans could be exposed to the outside world, including the wealthier South, and make comparisons with their own harsh reality. Many North Korean escapees would testify that they became disillusioned with the North after watching South Korean soap operas, which instigated their decision to defect. The late 1990s were when North Korean people started to defect in their hundreds to the South. The number peaked at up to three thousand per year in the 2000s, then declined, mainly due to the strengthened border controls and crackdowns, to less than a hundred in 2022.[6]

In general, North Koreans tend to be smaller and shorter than South Koreans due to malnutrition. Eunhye's memory of experiencing hunger was still vivid. She said that not knowing when it would end was more terrifying than the hunger itself. Her family was very poor and Eunhye couldn't have a carefree childhood as she had to work to survive, carrying heavy goods and selling South Korean drama DVDs

[5] https://bbc.com/news/world-asia-65881803

[6] https://unikorea.go.kr/unikorea/business/NKDefectorsPolicy/status/lately/

on the black markets, risking her life. If caught, she could be tried and given a harsh punishment, even executed for a crime of spreading propaganda of the enemy state, the South. Her home, however, couldn't provide much warmth, either. Her father was another component of her harsh reality. He became disabled through an accident while serving his military duty in the North. He drank to forget or fuel his grievances[7] and became violent towards her mother at first, and then started to target Eunhye and her younger sister when they became adolescents. She remembered his abusive words, directed at her, as early as at the age of five. However, when he was sober, he was capable of displaying his affection and guilt.

Eunhye recalled an occasion when, as a child, she drank some alcohol from the bottle which she had been sent to fetch for her father on her way home. This was partly out of curiosity, to discover how it could change him so dramatically, and partly to reduce the amount he could consume in the hope that he would become less violent. Here one may glimpse a seed of her resilience in this tragic situation. Eunhye as a child did not stay passively as a victim but was trying to respond to her adverse situation. She hoped to change her emotionally confusing and unreliable parent, and to understand him with empathy, however misguided. I hope to show that this seed has germinated and grown strong to become a thriving tree.

One of the important events involving her father happened when Eunhye was fifteen years old. He was drunk and became threatening, but this time she strongly felt that she had to protect herself, her younger sister, and mother, even at the cost of her life. She couldn't cope with his violence any longer. As he was about to lash out, she pushed him to the ground and picked up a kitchen knife, threatening him with it. She shouted at the top of her voice that if he ever touched any of them, she would kill him. He never raised his hands after that incident, but became withdrawn and crestfallen.

The seed of her resilience started to germinate in the many arduous adversities—famine, political oppression, emotional and physical abuses at home, to name a few. According to her, she had suicidal feelings even before her teenage years as she felt trapped and hopeless. Her dream of

---

[7] One may say she was contextualising her father's issue here.

finding a new life away from the North started to grow. Her first attempt was to cross a river (*Aprokgang* 압록강) between China and North Korea when she was sixteen with a group of other teenagers. It was not well planned but carried out from desperation and on a whim. None of them managed to succeed as the current was too fast and strong and she almost drowned but survived. (In one of her sessions, she wondered out loud if it was also a miracle that she didn't die then.)

Two years later, she made another attempt to escape from the North to China. This time, she tried to be better prepared. One of her grandfathers was a Chinese foot soldier, who had fought for the North during the Korean War, and he stayed behind and married a North Korean after the war. She had a letter from her uncle in China, addressed to the grandfather, to show it to a border guard as proof that she was travelling to China to visit him, in case she was caught. However, even before she made an attempt to walk across a frozen river, she was caught by patrolling border guards and eventually sent to prison.

The following episode reflects the dire situation in the North in the 1990s and how people were treated by the regime. After her second failed attempt to flee the country, Eunhye was detained in a prison run by State Security (보위부), where tortures and executions occurred. "Miraculously" (in her word), she was not tortured or beaten like others, which she still couldn't fully understand, but strongly felt that one of the guards must have taken a liking to her. She also understood that her uncle's letter might have been favourable to her, but still it could not explain the benign treatment she received in the notorious prison. She recalled that she had been forced to give away her own food, supplied by her family, which was the powder of various grains (misutgaru 미숫가루), for two captured soldiers' last meal before their execution. She learnt that they had been caught having stolen a cow and run away to a mountain to kill it to eat for about a month between them. Since then, she has not been able to eat any food made from misutgaru. A few months later, she was set free with a warning, but her desire to escape became even stronger than before and she started to save money to hire a broker, who could take her to China, and had to take more risks to do so.

An overwhelming majority of North Korean escapees' ultimate destination for freedom and prosperity is the South. However, they have to take multiple risks to avoid the Chinese authorities and take treacherous routes to reach a country like Thailand, which has a stable diplomatic tie with the South and, unlike China, will not deport them back to the North. I have become aware through some of my clients that North Koreans in London have organised regular protests against this policy in front of the Chinese embassy. In extremely rare cases, a few defectors managed to cross the DMZ (demilitarised zone) on foot but ironically (despite its name) it is a heavily militarised (the most in the world) strip of land running across the Korean peninsula,[8] or by boat via the seas (West and East) on either side of the mainland. These "short" routes are deemed to be impossible and whenever one succeeds, it becomes national news as it is so rare.

Eunhye finally managed to flee the North at her third attempt, aided by "miracles" (this will be discussed in more detail later), and settled in South Korea. There, she went to university but dropped out, as her study and campus life felt too removed from the reality she had experienced. Then, she ran a few retail businesses, which were quite successful, and she indulged in "the dazzling and lavish nightlife" with hard drinking and clubbing, in which she felt she was experiencing a "free and luxurious life" she had never had in the North. She recalled how hard she had played after a hard day's work and often ended up drinking to oblivion day after day. Now she could see how much her guilt at having left her family behind and grievances towards her own life must have played a part in that lifestyle. In the end, Eunhye managed to take out her mother and younger sister to South Korea by using a broker, whom she had sent money to. Now her mother lives with her in London.

Then, she married a South Korean man and tried to settle. However, she and her husband faced an unexpected difficulty as she became suspected of being a spy by the South Korean intelligence and her husband, who had a rank in the army, was pressured to divorce her. All North Korean defectors go through a settlement programme as well as an in-depth vetting process in a special facility for months as soon as they arrive in the South. So potentially they are all subjected to suspicion.

[8] Another ironic fate is that the DMZ has become a natural haven for many plants and animals because of almost no human interference for seven decades.

The polarising politics of the bygone cold war era is still very much alive in the Korean peninsula, impacting individual lives whether in the North or South. It is telling that South Korea's martial law is still constitutionally justified on the grounds of the North's threat. When the now-impeached president declared emergency martial law in December 2024, he said it was "to safeguard a liberal South Korea from the threats posed by North Korea's communist forces and to eliminate anti-state elements". The analysis of many political commentators is that he abused his presidential power in order to defeat his political opponents by framing them with the North. His paranoia may be laughable to many of us, but its political force is no laughing matter.

Eunhye fell foul of this kind of paranoia. She and her husband decided to leave South Korea and resettled themselves as asylum seekers in the UK. Their application was granted and they had two daughters in their new home, but eventually divorced.

Therapeutic work

Eunhye's father died many years ago, after she had settled in South Korea. In her later therapy sessions she showed her capacity to mentalize, and her empathetic understanding of him, his victimhood with no proper rehabilitation or compensation from the state, and his suspected difficult childhood. This was not to justify his violence, but more to modify her murderous rage, by mourning a father she had never had. Exploring these memories in sessions also enabled her to link them with her current murderous feelings towards her opponents, and this realisation opened up a thinking space for her to have some emotional distance from her own shame and rage. As she felt her father's alcohol-fuelled violence might have been a result of his victimhood, she wondered if her opponents might also have been "unwell", "not knowing what they were doing".

Exploring her murderous rage towards her father and linking it with current opponents enabled her to humanise them. What they had done to her was monstrous and "evil", but there was a realisation that ultimately we can't really know what made them do such things, while she tried to conjecture with her empathy that their own adversities had made them "unwell": "physically, they left the North but mentally, brought it with them."

This exploring and linking also demands that she tries to see him, and them, in wider contexts.[9] It made her think that she could also behave like them in certain circumstances. At least, she could see alcohol dependency as her and her father's common defence against psychological pains and its associated potential "evil", her father's violence and her neglectfulness at times. The more we explored, the more we had to admit not knowing; not knowing the true and full story of her father and her opponents. This opened up a space where her empathy could emerge. In this sense, not knowing is embedded in meaning-making and empathy.

Eunhye also started to voice some of the feelings she found difficult to accept, such as an envy towards her children as well as anger towards her mother, seeing that her mother was looking after her children so affectionately in contrast to her own experience of her mother, not so caring and too weak to protect her from her father's violence. Sometimes, she felt her first daughter was "greedy and selfish" when she started to compare herself as a deprived child with the daughter, who was fighting over a toy with the younger sister. Voicing these unpalatable feelings was important in order for her to be able to offer a secure attachment to her children, by owning rather than denying them. This acceptance of her own psychic reality has been instrumental for her to gain more confidence and to acknowledge her children's complex needs for her as their more containing mother. Eunhye also recognised a vicious circle she and her mother created between them by triggering verbal attacks on each other. One day, she mourned a mother she had never had by talking about her "poorer" childhood friend's mother, who was so kind and warm to Eunhye. Eunhye recalled that she had desperately wanted her friend's mother to be her own. The tears felt so painful and important. I think this exploring helped Eunhye to become more appreciative of her own mother. Voicing unpalatable feelings is an integral part of her accepting and exploring something beyond what she thought she had known about herself and others.

[9] Cundy discussed the importance of contextualising individual experiences, "[I]n order to 'earn' security, the [...] client needs to turn his thoughts to that bigger picture in order to define himself within his own relational, social, cultural and historical context. This is the arena of storytelling, or at least of story creating. I encourage patients to think about their family origins and, if possible, discover more. Social and historical events create ripples through the generations and give every family a unique identity" (Cundy, 2016, p. 19).

Three miracles

This therapeutic work was the backdrop of her starting to confess her faith. She said she had experienced three "miracles", without which she would not have been able to be with me here and now. All these miracles involved clouds. The following is a gist of her accounts across multiple sessions.

Two of the miracles happened during her third and final attempt to flee the North. She and a few more people were led by a broker to cross the border with China on a night with a bright moon, and they climbed into the back of a lorry at a prearranged meeting point. They were supposed to pass one checkpoint, and they planned to get off to go through the woods in the mountain beforehand and get back on board after the lorry passed the checkpoint. However, somehow the lorry driver got lost and strayed from the planned route, and they ended up passing three checkpoints instead of one. Moreover, they couldn't get off the lorry ahead of the two unexpected checkpoints as they were in clear view of the border guards. If they had been caught, they would have been imprisoned or even executed. Eunhye started to pray for her life. Then, dark clouds appeared, and the skies opened with torrential rain. From the back of the lorry, she could hear the soldiers, who would have usually checked any vehicle thoroughly, grumbling, reluctantly letting the queuing vehicles pass. As soon as the lorry passed the checkpoint, the rain stopped as if nothing had happened. Then, another miracle happened at the next checkpoint, but this time with hail instead of rain. Still, clouds appeared as if intended to protect her in response to her prayer.

Life in China was not what she had anticipated. She was sold to a family as a housemaid and became a modern slave, which happens to many North Korean escapees in China. At that time, she "cried days and nights" and her owner let her be friends with another North Korean escapee, a woman in her early twenties, similar to Eunhye's age then. The new friend had a young baby, and had saved some money over several years of captivity. They became close and started to dream together about a life they never had. Eunhye suggested they run away together, and made a plan to do so on a night in December. But when the time came, there was a full moon, too bright for them to escape without being caught. Again, she started to pray. As her owner had an outdoor toilet, she knew she could have a ten-minute window of time when her absence would not raise suspicion. As she went out near the arranged time, she could witness a big cloud approaching to cover the full moon, and it became pitch dark so she could run away safely with her friend.

Initially, she thought these were "all coincidences". Even when she prayed to "God", she had hardly any knowledge of religion. There is no freedom of religion in the North as the communist regime sees this as reactionary to socialist progress, and organising any religious group is seen as a threat to its control over the population. When she encountered Christianity later in the South, these events became understood as miracles, "God's interventions". For her, the fact that she prayed for her life in those life-and-death situations bears a meaning, itself a miracle. I cannot help wondering if any religion, any notion of God, she encountered would have provided a therapeutic frame to understand her miraculous experiences beyond rational comprehension.

It is interesting to see that clouds have become symbols for her faith as they did for Jews in the Bible. If we look at a few passages in the Bible,[10] we can see that clouds were connecting Jews with God like a "transitional object", borrowing Winnicott's concept (1953), through which they could sense His presence. The Old Testament could be read as a faith confession in which God heard their prayer to save Jews from slavery and deliver them to the promised land, and clouds represented His presence throughout the journey, a sign of guiding and protecting them. The Bible can be read as a story of trauma becoming triumph through miracles. God is the archetypal caregiver. When something is to become a miracle, for the modern mind, it focuses on its being supernatural and beyond scientific explanations, whereas, for the faithful, it is more about their experience of God, feeling connected to Him. When Jews declared they were God's chosen people, psychologically speaking, it was their way of saying they were survivors through the grace of God, not victims, despite all the hardship they had gone through as slaves and adverse journeys as refugees. Eunhye said to me many times that she felt she was chosen by God, and for me, it didn't feel far-fetched to link her faith to that of Jews in the Old Testament.

[10] Genesis 9:13; Exodus 2:16, 16:10, 19:9, 34:5, 40: 38, Numbers 10:34; Nehemiah 9:19; and Psalms 78:14.

What do we do, as psychotherapists, when a client brings their religious faith and experiences into the room? How do we work with them when they may not be in line with our own views? Eunhye's faith was beyond my understanding but, as her therapist, it felt important to be with, to stay with the not-knowing. This attitude created a demand on me to be curious about religiosity, and religions, the enormous wealth of traditions that have held humanity for millennia, and still now do so for billions of people.

What is a miracle? Could it be a moment of experiencing being with God, yearning for safety and security in the midst of adversity, of going through a life-and-death situation? Our narrow-minded rationality, armed with a modern scientific approach, may wish to explain it away with only hard evidence, which often disregards it as delusional or fantastical. But here, my interest and scope as her therapist was in my client's experiences, what they meant to her in her life and us in the room. It does not mean I need to validate any of my clients' faith or experience, no matter what, but to suspend my own judgement. Respecting the not-knowing seems therapeutically imperative to open up a space for exploration. For me, her passion for supporting the senior members of the community was born out of, or at least aided by, our therapeutic exploration, and it seems enough as an indication that her sense of reality is not of a delusional nature.

Eunhye's experiences of the miracles were the important foundations for her faith, from which a new coherent narrative unfolded. Traumatising adversities in her life gained meanings, through which they started to integrate into her life story: she has become who she is, not in spite of them but *because* of her traumatic experiences. The transformation itself can be seen as a miracle. When she said God wanted her to understand her own and others' suffering, and use her to help them in some way, I could see her faith as a miracle in the sea of traumatising adversities, demanding respect from me.

Therapy sessions became a secure base and safe haven in an emotional sense for her. She is well-known as a "feisty fighter" within the community. No one knows she can be emotional, depressive, or suicidal, according to her. She often said she was determined not to cry in sessions with me, but often failed. Since her arrival in South Korea, she had never cried in front of people except in church. In fact, she had stopped attending services because, once she was in church, she could not stop crying in "God's presence", overwhelmed by feeling grateful and safe. But she could not get over others' gaze, and what they might think of her. However, a therapy room became a safe container where she could anchor herself, feeling safe and secure, which enabled her to think. Its ritualistic elements and boundaries enabled her to deeply engage with her inner world, full of the unknown and yet of developing new narratives. The therapy sessions became a sacred space, where a secure attachment and strong bonding could be felt.

In fact, our sessions were held at the vestry at a local Anglican church with their generosity (no room hire fees), expressing their wish to contribute towards the North Korean community-building. I wonder how much religiosity, manifested in their generosity and encapsulated in religious symbols in the room, has been channelled to our meetings as well. In religion, a deity is the centre of community and meaning-making, and meaning is only created when linking is made. No word stands alone as no individual exists without any connection. I am grateful that the church has become part of our therapeutic endeavour, forming a link within the network for her resilience.

Not rejecting her miracle experiences in the name of rational and scientific sensibility was therapeutic. Again, not-knowing played a crucial role here, and it enabled me to meet her on her own terrain, where her own life story was unfolding. It required me to take a leap of faith in her experiences. She asked me on a few occasions if I could believe in her when she talked about the miracles. On the first occasion I held back my judgemental, or at best suspicious feelings, and replied along the lines of a need for further exploration. Then, later, I was able to acknowledge that she was expressing her faith and genuine experiences, and I could believe in them as hers. I think that voicing my validation in her faith and experiences has created a space where she feels safe enough to explore.

Inner resources

Her paternal grandmother is a very important figure in Eunhye's life, who seemed to have been an emotionally safe haven for her. Eunhye remembers her grandmother as someone who really cared for, took interest in, and listened to her. She often volunteered to do errands to be with her grandmother. Her identification with her grandmother, who "could not turn a blind eye to injustice", for instance, has become a defining foundation for her identity. She recalled that, having heard the news of her grandmother's death, she had become suicidal. At that time, Eunhye was in South Korea, in the process of taking her family out from North Korea through a broker. She felt overwhelmed by crushing guilt that she had not saved her grandmother. Again, she drank to oblivion for many months, leaving herself vulnerable on many occasions. The guilt was so intense that she had to destroy cassette tapes of her grandmother's voice and photos of her grandmother that she had treasured for many years. However, Eunhye confessed that she could still feel her grandmother's presence like an angelic figure that generates feelings of security and meaning in her life. Moreover, the pain of the loss of her grandmother has become instrumental in her passion to serve the elderly in the North Korean community in London.

Therapy sessions seemed to have helped her develop her community-minded ideas. One day she aired an idea of organising singing group sessions for the elderly in the community. She described a group of people who gather at a local coffee shop for hours almost every day. Many of them are living by themselves, with no English skills to engage with activities available to local residents. When we explored her passion for the idea, it became clear to us that they were a reminder of her grandmother, and supporting these elders was her way of remembering and honouring her grandmother. There were also other changes. She reported that now alcohol tasted bitter for her, that she strongly felt she needed to stay away from it in order to serve the community as well as to look after herself and her children better.

Around this time, she also suggested not leaving a window open, contrary to what she had requested from her first session. Since her childhood, she could not stay in a room if a door or at least a window was not open, even in the winter. Now she said she wanted to move on from the "fear". For me as her therapist, these changes are like "miracles", in a sense that I cannot fully understand and explain how the transformations could have happened.[11] Religion may explain it as God's grace, or a psychological theory might hold that she is

[11] I think Jung's idea of "transcendent function" is to explore and understand these transformations, which occur through integrating the conscious and the unconscious. Again, our primary need for connection and relatedness is the foundation for any change and development.

more conscious of what previously was her unconscious defence, enabling her to take more responsibility. Whatever has brought it about, I cannot help feeling in awe of the transformations she managed to bring to her life.

Here, it is worthwhile pausing to consider that the therapy project of making the unconscious conscious could make us arrogant in a sense that we become a "knower". With years of personal therapy and ongoing training, an experienced therapist can still fall into that pitfall, feeling that they are equipped with experiences and many complicated techniques with which their patient's unconscious mind can be analysed and understood. How we love to make an interpretation often readily validated by our countertransference, which itself can become our gospel for getting to know our client's unconscious mind. I would argue that the point of a therapy project is for us to experience being in awe of the vastness of the unconscious and to understand that what is made conscious is only a speck in the universe of the unconscious.

Attachment theory investigates the functions of religious faith and proposes two different angles, where the relationship with God either "corresponds to" or "compensates for" their attachment style (Granqvist & Kirkpatrick, 2016). In Eunhye's case, it can be seen that her insecure attachment to her parents was compensated by, and her secure attachment to her grandmother corresponded with, her faith in God. Still, we may wonder, without her grandmother, may her faith in God have happened in such an empowering way?[12] Perhaps the secure, loving relationship she provided enabled Eunhye to find a benign, loving God? Her grandmother can be also seen as someone who helped Eunhye to experience God within. Then, her religious faith, kindled by the miracles, has re-framed her life in a way she can be more in touch with an internalised secure attachment. This has also manifested in her grandmother's angelic presence.

Eunhye's story of becoming a refugee is a survival story, requiring courage and resilience. For instance, as a child, she had to rummage

[12] "There is evidence that security in close relationships and experiences of sensitive/responsive caregiving are positively linked to loving God images … Also, coherent (secure) attachment discourse … predicted more benevolent God representations" (Cherniak et al., 2021, p. 127).

through a mound of imported waste from the West to fish out something worthy to sell. One day, she picked up an empty bottle of French perfume and smelt something amazing from it in the midst of the stench around her. She recalled it as one of many moments when she decided to flee her impoverished and deprived country. The discarded perfume bottle became a sign of hope only reachable outside North Korea. As I recall, she said a few times emphatically that "I survived only by risking my life." I believe the expression represents her inner strength, with which she hardly portrayed herself as a victim from the beginning of our meetings.

Discussion

Etymologically, the term "therapy" originated from the Greek word *therapeia*, which means "healing", or "service" of the gods.[13] For Jung, "religious undertaking and the religious object are not only potentially meaningful, but necessary if man is to survive" (Kelsey, 1984, p. 190). Eliade suggests, "[L]ife is not possible without an opening toward the transcendent; in other words, human beings cannot live in chaos. Once contact with the transcendent is lost, existence in the world ceases to be possible ..." (Eliade, 1957, p. 34).

Attachment-based therapy is concerned with helping clients unlearn an ill-fitted attachment style by a psychotherapist becoming a secure base in a therapeutic space. This implies that an innate template, or archetype, can be reactivated through a therapeutic relationship to grow and better fit current reality. If a secure attachment figure is a guiding presence for openness and exploring beyond oneself, can God be seen as a symbol for a secure attachment, and can establishing a secure attachment style be described as being in touch with the Self or God image, in Jungian terms?[14] While attachment theory recognises the importance of having an internalised secure base, "[I]n Jung's perspective the unconscious is not just a container for repressed wishes but it contains

[13] "Within Greek mythology, the gods themselves were often associated with therapeutic practices." Stoicism as Therapeia (θεραπεία)—Plato's Academy Centre (platosacademy.org)

[14] "Jung's approach assumes the presence of an a priori God image in the psyche, which he referred to as the Self. The Self is an intrapsychic ordering principle that depicts itself by means of imagery that arises from the unconscious" (Corbett, 2013, p. 148).

a supportive force which moves the personality toward one's potential wholeness" (Roesler & Reefschläger, 2022, p. 340).

It needs to be stated that God can be also experienced as punishing, distancing, judgemental, unreliable, and so on, perhaps in correspondence to insecure attachment styles. Here one may suggest God can be also a psychological receptacle for projection. Perhaps achieving secure attachment entails modifying one's "God" to be a reliable, protective, and encouraging deity? Following Jung's idea of archetype, therapeutic intervention can be more about supporting a client to be in touch with the innate template for development; to put it differently, their own inner resources or resilience, rather than introducing something completely alien to the client, wherein the therapist holds the exclusive knowledge of development.

Trauma and resilience are not mutually exclusive or contrasting opposites. We can easily agree that the more resilient you are, the less likely to be traumatised in the face of an adversity. However, without trauma, resilience may not be actualised or developed.[15] In this sense, trauma (or adversity, to be more precise) is an integral part of resilience. We may ask what makes one person more resilient than others. Why does the same adverse event leave some traumatised and others not?

It would be a mistake to think that individual therapy sessions should only focus on individual developmental issues or family dynamics. They are important aspects of understanding a person and their resilience, but they are not the whole picture, as a community and what it stands for, for instance, a country, culture, sociopolitical realm … etc., play an essential role in life, too. Despite all she has experienced, my client, Eunhye, finally sought therapy when a kind of war broke out in her North Korean community group in London, but her involvement with the elders' group has provided a new sense of purpose, belonging, and identity. Religions, which offer a model to think about resilience, also provide holding by community, where individuals are purposefully connected. One may conjecture that a community is formed as a fundamental way of human survival.

[15] Here, the term trauma is used in a loose sense, where it is almost interchangeable with adversity in the common parlance. However, it is important to state that psychologically speaking, trauma is not an external event but an internal experience.

As mentioned earlier, art is another meaning-making engagement that is on a par with religion and psychotherapy. I would like to briefly mention a unique singing tradition in Korea, called *pansori* (판소리)[16] as an example, in which a vocalist narrates and sings an epic story with their counterpart drummer, for the audience, who also actively take a part in a performance by shouting out encouraging filler words (*chuimsae* 추임새) in support of the performers. Wherever a pansori is performed becomes a stage regardless whether it is someone's garden or a market place. It is renowned also because a vocalist has to go through a rigorous training process to gain a desired hoarse voice. By constantly scarring (traumatising) their vocal cord by exerting various sounds with vigour during their arduous training, vocalists are able to voice any feelings evoked in adversity so that their performance can resonate with the audience. This whole process can be seen as a trauma-integrating and community building project, born organically for meaning-making. Again, the religiosity of connecting people and healing through trauma-integrating is very much alive in this artistic tradition.

Conclusion

Eunhye survived many dangers before settling in the UK. However, her journey did not end there. A miracle story does not end just with a survival. A miracle seems to keep churning out meanings for the experiencer to live in a way that guides their life. The essence of being therapeutic may not be so different from being religious, in the sense that they are about connecting and bonding what has been separated and broken.

Psychotherapy can be seen as a meaning-making process, as religions have been for millennia. Just as religious belief can create hope in the face of traumatising adversities and evils, the ability to be with not knowing, to contextualise, mentalize, and empathise that psychotherapy promotes can provide hope and resilience. Both religious faith and psychotherapy helped lift Eunhye from her suicidal despair.

[16] https://youtu.be/ufQUq_lJ_64—as a taster, watch the clip of a short passage in *Chun Hyang Ga* 춘향가 (an epic love story comparable to *Romeo and Juliet*) performed by a renowned pansori vocalist, Bang Ul Im (1904–1961).

Religiosity can be about being humble by acknowledging something beyond us. The more we know, the more we realise our ignorance. In other words, it is about recognising we are part of something beyond our understanding. In that regard, religiosity seems essential when Jung approximates the unconscious to the creative and supportive potentials within us.

Attachment theory also emphasises our innate relatedness and connection as essential for survival. Maybe there is a commonality with Jungian ideas in the sense that they both validate our fundamental need for linking with what is beyond us.

Acknowledgement

Eunhye's life story retold in sessions with me was so powerful and infectious it compelled me to write this article. I am grateful that Eunhye gave her informed consent for me to write and publish her story. I should add that her political views are different from mine and a symbolic war I mentioned earlier (p. 158) could have broken out: for instance, she expressed her support for the impeached president, suggesting the insidious North Korean regime's infiltration into the political left in the South is the reality. However, I find our interactions, where I shared my own views as questions, rather refreshing as we could still respect and hold our political differences without attacking each other. I think it was possible because we are more open to not knowing in the therapeutic space.

References

Cherniak, A. D., Mikulincer, M., Shaver, P. R., & Granqvist, P. (2021). Attachment theory and religion. *Current Opinion in Psychology, 40*: 126–130.

Corbett, L. (2013). Jung's approach to spirituality and religion. In: K. I. Pargament, A. Mahoney, & E. P. Shafranske (Eds.), *APA Handbook of Psychology, Religion, and Spirituality (Vol. 2): An Applied Psychology of Religion and Spirituality* (pp. 147–167). Washington, DC: American Psychological Association.

Cundy, L. (2016). *Anxiously Attached: Understanding and Working with Preoccupied Attachment*. London: Routledge.

Eliade, M. (1957). *The Sacred and the Profane: The Nature of Religion*. New York: Harper Torchbooks.

Granqvist, P., & Kirkpatrick, L. A. (2016). Attachment and religious representations and behavior. In: J. Cassidy & P. R. Shaver (Eds.), *Handbook of Attachment: Theory, Research, and Clinical Applications* (pp. 917–940). New York: Guilford.

Holmes, J. (2024). *The Spirit of Psychotherapy: A Hidden Dimension*. London: Karnac.

Jung, C. G. (1995). *Memories, Dreams, Reflections*. R. Winstons & C. Winstons (Trans.). London: Fontana.

Kelsey, M. T. (1984). *Jung as Philosopher and Theologian, Jung in Modern Perspective*. London: Wildwood House.

Roesler, C., & Reefschläger, G. I. (2022). Jungian psychotherapy, spirituality, and synchronicity: Theory, applications, and evidence base. *Psychotherapy*, *59*(3): 339–350.

Winnicott, D. W. (1953). Transitional objects and transitional phenomena. *International Journal of Psycho-Analysis*, *34*: 89–97.

CHAPTER 9

Leaving to live and learning to live with leaving: Experiences of people seeking refuge from persecution

Zibiah Alfred Loakthar

Introduction: Perspectives on departing a homeland due to fear of persecution

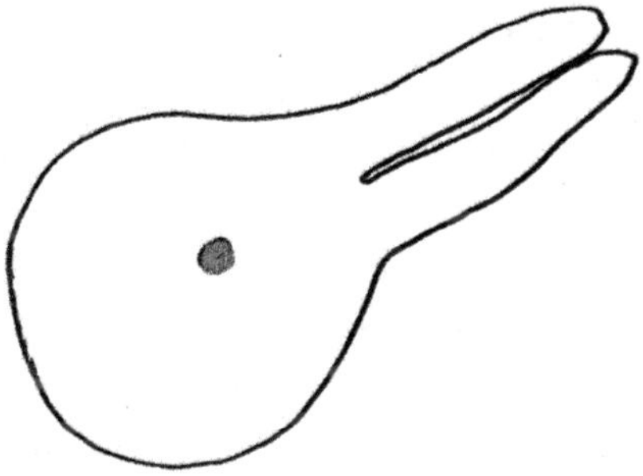

Figure 9.1 What do you see?

Look closely! What do you see? A duck? A rabbit? Or something else? A pair of scissors? Quarter of an octopus? Stand back and look again! What do you see? With further hindsight, what do you see? In discussion with others what do you see? What is permissible to say that you see and what is not?

The curiously ambiguous duck-rabbit image, made famous in Wittgenstein's "Philosophical investigations" (published posthumously in 1953) is useful for illustrating the idea that there may be multiple ways of viewing phenomena. While we might feel certain that we know what something is and how to name it, we often discover the possibility of alternative perspectives. Our viewpoints may be flexible, malleable, adaptable, dynamic rather than rigidly held. We may, for example, become aware that this image, that we might first perceive for instance as a duck can, arguably, also be viewed as a rabbit, or indeed as something else. Interestingly, while we may be able to recognise the shape of both a duck and of a rabbit in this image and see both in rapid alternating succession, it may seem impossible to perceive both rabbit and duck at the same time!

So too, we may find that there are different ways of viewing departure from a homeland in search of sanctuary. Is departing from one place for another always an act of leaving, or might it sometimes be considered as an act of arriving, or both, or neither? Can leaving and arriving be experienced at the same time, or is this as difficult as trying to hold in simultaneous view the duck and the rabbit? Indeed, what is to be understood by the term "leaving"? Is it always to be understood as a clear move from "there" to "here" or "here" to "there", or might it be something else, something in between?

This chapter considers different perspectives of "leaving" among people seeking refuge from danger of persecution, reflecting on the twisting stretch of twilight that may for some people exist between the state of leaving and the state of arriving. In considering how people seeking refuge may be urged to "leave" a former country for their own survival and expected to "arrive" psychologically in a new country, the idea of the "blues note" is introduced.

Arguably, "living" in a new land is not simply a matter of basic physical survival, of bodies continuing to breathe and hearts to pump, but of psychological thriving. We may thrive where our minds are also engaged in breathing, pumping, beating our feelings and thoughts into beautiful shapes, creating out of chaos new stories, new hopeful worlds in which we are happy to alight and rest and which align in harmonious ways with our lived experiences.

Thriving may be concerned more with arrival than departure. It may be facilitated by those seeking refuge adopting a frame of mind that enables openness to learning and new experiences and by spaces created for exercising agency. Thriving may be hindered, ironically, by well-meaning "helpers" and those in humanitarian work roles, attempting to offer support in ways that may perpetuate the "victim–helper–perpetrator" triangle (Karpmann, 1968; Papadopoulos, 2021). Support that continues to position people as "victims" may potentially cause harm, albeit unintentionally, impacting negatively on people's ability to exercise agency and upon their ability to move freely on to embrace new identities.

Reflections on the term "refugee"

"One person is forcibly displaced every 2 seconds—but not all displacements are the same" (Concern Worldwide, 2022).

Fear of persecution may drive people to seek safety in new locations. In common parlance, the term "refugee" may be used loosely to refer to such people. In legal terms, those who cross no international borders are termed "internally displaced persons" (IDPs) and those who do cross international borders may be termed "asylum seekers". Only people whose claims have been recognised and accepted by government officials in new lands are termed "refugees".

From a geographical perspective, becoming a "refugee" is connected with departure: the physical "leaving" of one land for another. Experiences of leaving may be diverse, complex, unique. Some people leave in haste, feeling there is no possibility to stay or that choices are being made for them by other people. Others may experience greater agency, acknowledging some degree of personal choice about whether, how, and when to leave. While some leaving their homeland to seek sanctuary elsewhere may feel hopeful of return, others may feel unable to contemplate return being possible or desirable.

This chapter explores the experiences of people who, in fear of persecution, have, at least in a physical way, left homelands for refuge in other lands, "leaving to live", to survive, to live free from fear. The chapter draws upon oral testimonies of those who have sought refuge in England and reflects upon people's emotional journeys of leaving. It is argued that leaving may be experienced not just at the point of physical departure from a homeland but in shudders. The chapter reflects upon how people may learn to live with leaving. Acceptance of refugee status may mark arrival and a new beginning but also be experienced as a form of leaving and loss.

The expression "people seeking refuge" is chosen over the terse term "refugees", with consideration for the feelings of people who find themselves in such circumstances. I have found, in working with refugee communities in London, that people often report feeling that their identity as persons may be removed and replaced deliberately, or inadvertently, by the "one-size-fits-all" label "refugee". The expression "people seeking refuge" is employed here to emphasise and respect personhood and humanity (Loakthar, 2023). The term "people seeking refuge" is also preferred to "refugees" as it can broadly accommodate not only those who have the legal status of refugee conferred upon them but also those seeking sanctuary who are still in the asylum system, and those who have come to the UK seeking safety, for instance from Ukraine, and other conflict-ridden countries, but who have not had an official "refugee" status conferred upon them (Esposito, 2022).

Types of persecution from which people may flee are wide-ranging. The 1951 UNHCR Convention specifically refers to persecution on the grounds of race, religion, nationality, and political belief (UNHCR, 2011). This Convention's reference also to "membership of a particular social group" has in recent years in the UK been argued to encompass other reasons, for instance fear of persecution because of belonging to a gender group at risk of genital mutilation and because of identification as lesbian, gay, or bisexual in a country where this may be outlawed, or punishable by imprisonment or death (UNHCR, 2023).

It is emphasised that while people who seek refuge may have experienced many different types, often multiple types, of adversity, it does not necessarily follow that they feel "traumatised" by their experiences (Papadopoulos, 2021). Too often assumptions are made that those who have sought refuge from fear of persecution have experienced adversity and therefore are "traumatised" and that "refugees" are "victims" in need of "sympathy" and "help" and in some way "broken". Instead, the view is taken here that people experiencing the kinds of circumstances that lead to seeking refuge can still be active agents in their own lives. While some may develop symptoms that over time could lead to diagnosis of post-traumatic stress disorder (as defined by the American Psychiatric Association *Diagnostic Manual*, 2013) and loss of agency and control, others find inner resilience to cope (Papadopoulos, 2021). Some people experience "adversity activated development" as a result of adversity, whereby they may find not only a well of inner resilience to draw upon, but also find themselves developing new strengths and skills and understanding they believe they did not have before (ibid.).

Uniqueness and complexity of individuals' experiences of departing a country to seek sanctuary elsewhere

People who find themselves fleeing one land for another in fear of persecution will have their own unique perspectives and recollections of such experiences. Memories may be dynamic, shimmering, shape-shifting, changing over the lifespan (Ofen & Shing, 2013). While some struggle to chase and hold onto elusive constellations of memories of seeking refuge, others may believe they have no memory clusters they can access, or clutch fragments of memories tightly in the hope that one day they will be in a position to unclench their grasp and try to piece fragments together in a way that might help make some kind of sense of their experiences. Yet others may be trying to cast sticky memories into the wind, or in vain be trying to escape from the shadows cast by haunting and vivid memories of adversities that might feel too unbearable to dwell upon, acknowledge, and name (Ripple et al., 2013).

Physical departure from one country for another may result in experiences of changes in external environment. These perceived changes, for instance in climate, food, surrounding language, and social cultural norms, ranging from negligible to dramatic may be embraced, but also may disorientate and create sometimes significant intrapsychic and interpersonal change. Papadopoulos (2021) has coined the terms "nostalgic disorientation" and "onto-ecological unsettledness" to help understand phenomena here.

Sometimes, people leave a country, entirely committed to arriving in a new land and making it their homeland. However, where people find that they do not feel wholly welcomed into this new land and are not offered a place of belonging, this may obstruct their wishes to enjoy the feeling that they have truly left behind their old land and fully "arrived" elsewhere. Kits (2005) for instance, comments on how refugee experience may feel "far from over upon arrival in a place of asylum", observing that in many ways,

> [The] struggle to create a new life has only begun. As refugees can attest to, the process of fully normalizing their lives—reuniting with family members, securing local education for themselves and their children, finding appropriate employment, and participating in the political life of their new countries—is one fraught with legal and procedural difficulties, a process that leaves many in "limbo" long after their new lives should be well under way. (Kits, 2005, p. 3)

At other times, people may understand they are being warmly welcomed into a new homeland. However, their own mindset may mean they may nevertheless falter between leaving a homeland and embracing a new one. People may, in reality, not wish to experience "arrival" where it signifies a sense of loss, a letting go of the hopes and dreams they once harboured and their loyalties to a land and a life and a family or social group they may have once lived within, or imagined they lived within.

Within the literature on exile and refugee care, much is made of the psychological experience many report of half-leaving, of leaving without arriving, of inhabiting a liminal world between "here" and "there", of being in limbo, of oscillating between two states of "here" and "there" and at an emotional level of never quite "leaving" while at the same time never really "arriving" (Alfred, 2010).

In conversations, in research studies, and through personal forms of self-expression and creative writing, people from diverse refugee backgrounds commonly report their encounter with a dilemma about whether to reconcile themselves to an existence "here" or "there". Refugee experience may prompt the unbalancing of identities and stir questions of commitment to being.

Feelings of being liminars, of being "neither here nor there", the experience not simply of "loss" but of being "lost", pervades the poetry of refugees from diverse cultural backgrounds. For instance, Bosnian writer Skorupan, in his poem "Neither Here Nor There", writes about the experience of dialling the number of his old home: "I heard an unknown voice saying that I wasn't there. I asked him if he knew what had happened to me, where I was, and he said that he had moved in recently and that he didn't know" (Skorupan, in Langer, 1997, p. 12).

In the same poem, Skorupan captures the confusing ambivalence of self, writing;

> I know perfectly well where I am, but I wondered whose
> head was on my pillow …
> And this is the way things are: I am not really here, and
> over there I am no more

Similarly, Kurdish poet Mirawdeli (2002) describes exile as an experience of being neither "here" in the country of refuge nor "there" in the country from which one lives in exile:

> You can only be here by being absent there. But the dreamflow of there ensures that for the most of your unconscious and even conscious time you are really somewhere/nowhere. In your real daily life practices you are absent: you can be absent-minded, away, thoughtful. There is always this unavoidable inner odyssey which makes sure that you have no real presence anywhere. (Mirawdeli, 2002, p. 110)

The ineffability of the "here-there" dilemma, the challenge to capture such a prevalent feeling in words, makes it a popular recurrent theme in poetry written in connection with experiences of leaving one land to seek sanctuary in another.

Numerous academic studies find people from refugee backgrounds remarking upon experiencing a tension between identifying with "here" and "there", a feeling of being metaphorically pulled in one direction towards their country of origin and in an opposing direction towards the country in which they now find themselves (Al-Rasheed, 1993; Camino & Krufeld, 1999; Shami; 2004; Chan, 2005). This pull between facing back to the past and out towards the future, the confusing ambivalent feelings towards "now" and "then", "here" and "there", may be disconcerting and disturbing, upsetting people's sense of self-identity and precipitating existential angst. This tension is rarely reported as an enjoyable, pleasurable feeling. However, as with sadness, some people show inclination to indulge, or succumb, to such a feeling.

Such uncomfortable psychic confusion, distinct from the pangs of nostalgic sorrow or trepidation and anxiety about what the immediate future holds, may be illuminated by the psychodynamic concept of ambivalence.

Ambivalence

Across different communities of people seeking refuge from different parts of the world, research studies have suggested that an "ambivalent relationship with their previous and current places and cultures" which may be maintained alongside an "intense desire" to return to their "homelands" is common (Naficy, 2001, p. 12).

The confusion for people seeking refuge is not simply about how to navigate legal systems and physical and emotional boundaries to return to "there" or arrive "here". Rather, there is a philosophical existential discomfort about where "there" and "here" may be. In the experience of persecution, boundaries shift; grounds once offering the illusion of security change to sand. While refugees may experience the pull of both "here" and "there" they may feel that they no longer can belong to either realm. They may find the "there" of homeland, family, and community, to which they may have once felt warm attachment and belonging, is unable to sustain and contain them safely. Elements within the realm of "there" have led to their experiences of being pushed away, forced out, expelled, and rejected. Just as ambivalent attitudes may now be sustained towards "there", so too may "here" excite ambivalent attitudes; the new place and people may offer safety and comfort, but also hostility and rejection, disempowering categorisation and restrictive stereotyping.

Oppositional discourse

The concept of oppositional discourse may be useful to draw upon when seeking to understand the complexity of "refugee identity".

Analysing the narratives of Bosnian refugee families in London to identify their core dilemmas within a systemic framework, Papadopoulos and Hildebrand (1997) found:

> a constant underlying tension between two polar opposite tendencies: on one hand, to privilege and remain loyal to the past … to honour the home culture and its belief systems … and the other hand, … to value the adjustment to their new life … to explore and benefit from the new life styles found in receiving country, and to look towards the future … (p. 217)

This observation underscores the complexity of attitudes towards "here" and "there". People from refugee backgrounds may not be neatly divided into those who privilege their past lives in previous lands, who never really "leave", and those who foreground their new lives in a present land, who are keen to "arrive" and belong in a new space. Rather, within a family system, different members may express apparently antithetical past and present orientations at different times. An individual might sometimes consider herself to be in a transitory position on a journey towards a future new life, and sometimes on a journey back to an old land to reclaim an old life, influenced by the assertions of others within her social network.

> [Refugee] families embrace both oppositional directions most of the time although, due to circumstantial factors, they temporarily may privilege one against the other ... what matters most is ... the ability of the families to contain the tension which is created by the presence of both oppositional tendencies. Families that find it difficult to hold this tension and choose one direction only, are likely to lose their vitality because both tendencies are psychologically and pragmatically indispensable. (Ibid., p. 232)

Inability to "leave" a homeland from where one has physically departed

In working with communities of people from refugee backgrounds on advocacy, arts and education, and oral history life story projects, I have encountered many who report that while they may have physically left a homeland, mentally, emotionally, spiritually they find they cannot leave. Some appear to idealise their former homeland (Jodeyr, 2003). Their dreams may be concerned with the homeland they have left and to which they yearn to return. The idea of settling and integrating in a new country may be difficult, indeed undesirable, to contemplate. Some people report feeling guilt at breaking a vow made to themselves and others that their heart will never leave their former land (Eisenbruch, 1991).

For instance, in an oral history interview Person A, comments:

> I thought I wanted to fit in, to find a way to feel at home in this new country, but I could not fit in and after a while I realised what was stopping me was myself, I felt guilty about trying to

> fit in, as if I was giving up on the country of my childhood … (Person A, 2023)

Rather like the "Hotel California" lyrics, "you can check out any time you like but you can never leave" (The Eagles, 1977), for some the possibility to leave behind on all levels a former homeland, however much they try, might be thinkable but nevertheless impossible.

Some people report relatively successfully moving on to make a new life for themselves, drawing a line under their past. However, protective amnesia from difficult experiences may not last forever. Interestingly, while sometimes memories of previous life may be triggered in predictable ways, for instance a noisy firework display in a new country reminding people of gunfire in a previous country, sometimes surprising things can catapult people back into vivid recall of their previous life. For instance, Person B reflects:

> It was the cat. It was seeing that cat that reminded me so much of a cat, a cat back home I used to love … I had tried so hard to forget everything but that cat, it brought me back. (Person B, 2023)

For some, feelings of unfairness, of being disrespected, of witnessing racism, of being excluded in the country in which refuge has been sought, can trigger recall of former experiences of persecution.

> I guess … I guess that experience highlighted to me that again I did not belong. I felt … felt shunned. rejected even and … and somehow this took me straight back to the time when I was looking to escape from my home country. The feeling of being rejected, unwanted, disrespected, disregarded … it felt the same, powerfully the same, overwhelming really. (Person C, 2023)

The drive to recreate the former homeland environment, for instance in the way a home is decorated or foods are cooked, is well documented in the literature (van Liempt & Staring, 2023).

Those forced to flee a homeland, disorientated in a new country, may grip tightly to old habits and customs. The way a person may decorate their new "home" to remind them of their former country, can exceed the way that they might have decorated their home had they remained in that country. Loyalty to a particular cuisine or room decoration scheme may sometimes have nothing to do with cultural pride, love of a former homeland, patriotism, or aesthetic taste, but everything to do with guilt and the fear of letting go of an old way of life and of becoming disconnected, the fear of loss, and of finding oneself to be lost.

People sometimes become much more assertive about their cultural identity than they might have been had they not faced exile. This is discussed especially in the literature on the experiences of second-generation refugees. Tension can sometimes arise where people within a family or community lean in different directions, on the one hand towards the traditions of the country left behind and on the other towards embracing new traditions of a country discovered.

As Person T, a daughter in the UK born to parents from refugee backgrounds, comments:

> I don't know why my mum she mostly plays that music. You know, she told me when she was growing up and my age she was never into it. But now ... she don't want to listen to anything else. (Person T, 2023)

Of course, where people flee in haste there may be limited or no opportunity to choose things to bring. The things that people arrive with, the shirt they wear on their journey of escape, the rucksack they bring, may later become precious objects to them forever, transitional objects that link them to the past and to the country they have left. People may choose to leave behind precious photographs and documents they yearned to carry out with them for fear of repercussions on family and friends left behind who may be identified and traced by persecutors. Others choose practical items—blanket, a cooking pot, warm socks—to assist their journey, or symbolic objects, overlooking the practicalities out of a strong desire to remember and remain connected to the life they are leaving; a jar of earth, a handful of seeds, a hefty typewriter. Precious possessions may sometimes be lost en route to, or after arrival within, a new country and the journey itself may change people's attitudes to the objects they sought to bring with them. What is a photograph, or a watch when it evokes memories of loved ones lost? Objects that have been sources of comfort can become sources of emotional torment and vice versa.

Not everyone will, even if they could access them, value "keepsakes or sentimental mementoes of home" (Marschall, 2019). For some, it is not traditional cooking pots or artwork that they seek for their homes; rather they may give place to specific "utilitarian objects", perhaps those received as gifts, which are turned into memory objects over time.

With the rise of the digital age, in recent years, people can often be found rebuilding cultural connection with a former homeland through digital tools. It is no longer necessary to possess a printed photograph of one's own to display on the wall of the shelter where one stays. For those with skills and access to the digital world, there is the possibility to scour digital photography banks and borrow imagery to paper the walls of the digital spaces in which one abides. The digital world offers the possibility to maintain connection with a former homeland in so many different ways. Talking with people from refugee backgrounds, some explain that the digital world seems sometimes to offer a shelter and place of refuge of sorts from the real world. Facing the reality of struggling to navigate the customs and codes of a new land, the digital world may sometimes be a welcome space for retreat even where harbouring in it may slow the process of adapting to and settling within the surroundings and communities of the new non-virtual environment.

Agency when leaving a homeland in search of sanctuary

Multiple push and pull factors may give rise to a person's decision to leave one country and seek refuge in another. The need for refuge may be a compelling, but not necessarily sole, factor prompting leaving (Van Hear, Bakewell, & Long, 2020).

Some people feel they have little personal agency over leaving a place where they fear persecution. Decisions may be made on their behalf by other family members or community leaders, or by humanitarian agencies offering the possibility of a route out of the country. For instance, Person J comments:

> I could have pushed back. But, but I did not feel that at the time. My uncle instructed me to leave that night. I had so little time to think. To be honest, I was glad! Glad that someone else was making the impossible decision for me. The decision to leave,

> perhaps it was one I would never have been able to make for myself. (Person J, 2023)

Others, however, feel varying degrees of agency over the decision to leave a place of persecution. A sense of personal agency may be accompanied by a wide range of emotions.

People struggle with the weight of responsibility for the decision. For instance, Person B remarks:

> It took me years to decide to leave, the situation became ever more impossible, I could not bring all our family out … my mother did not wish to leave at all so for a long time I did not do anything … I felt, I felt immobilised—I did not want the blame for leaving if things became better. But things did not become better. In fact they became worse and worse and finally I felt forced to leave … now I wish I had not hesitated for so long. I felt guilty about getting our family to leave and not having faith that things would get better. Now I feel guilty that I did not get our family out sooner and for all the losses on the way. I guess I have such regrets … (Person B, 2023)

People living through heightened stress and in fight or flight mode may lose the ability to recognise complexity in situations and instead begin to think in polar opposites (Papadopoulos, 2021). In a state of heightened anxiety, people may temporarily lose the ability to perceive the fine detail of a complex wider picture and convince themselves that fear of persecution has been the sole reason for a decision to flee. Yet later, in a calmer reflective space, people may come to observe other factors at play, such as curiosity to see the world, a desire to live nearer to friends and relatives, the need to seek opportunities to earn more money.

Person U comments:

> For a very long time, I … I could only think of moving away as far as possible from the situation in my homeland … long before such a difficult situation had arisen I was wanting to travel abroad, to visit Europe, to see more of the world … perhaps this made it easier to leave … at the back of my head I had this idea of moving, of experiencing a different part of the world, long before the necessity to leave my country arose … maybe this has helped me to embrace a new way of life in a new country. (Person U, 2023)

Speaking with people with diverse experiences of leaving to seek refuge in the UK, it is clear that at the point of physically leaving a country some people do not permit themselves to consider that they are leaving permanently, rather this realisation may be reached slowly. Realisation may initially splash, and later engulf people.

Person C observes:

> I still dream of going back, I know the river is flowing, if I go back things will not be as they were … still I dream of going back … I keep the shirt I arrived in to wear on my return … I do no, I do not like to think of how things will have changed … I cannot bring myself to look at Google maps. (Person C, 2023)

Waves of realisation

People have commented that in the process of fleeing one land for sanctuary in another, they may have been caught by surprise when they reflect on what this means for their own sense of identity and connection with homeland and when they realise that the label "refugee" applies, or is being applied by others, to themselves.

Recalling feelings upon receiving a phone call from the embassy to say that her family's application had been accepted and they could travel to sanctuary in England, my friend Luma reflects:

> It was a shock. I cried tears for going and tears for leaving. The knowledge that I would have to move further away from my land and my beloved family, made me feel so sad. On the other hand, the chance to leave was huge; at the time I was thinking only to be close to my other children. I was confused. I did not know if I was dreaming or if it would really be possible to hug my children and grandchildren. (Islami, 2007)

Luma goes on to describe her experience of flight to seek refuge in a new country, reflecting on her first confrontation with the idea of being a "refugee", on the plane to safety:

> The happiest passenger on the plane was my son. He was not bothered by the fact that he was being served by a steward who wore nylon gloves to protect himself from infection from us refugees.

> It was the first time that I faced the fact that we were being treated as refugees. (Islami, 2007)

Interviewee F in the Refugee Communities History Project (2006) shared how she felt she was "coming home" when, having sought sanctuary in the UK, she travelled out of England and upon return realised with a jolt of surprise that England now felt like "home". She realised that almost without noticing, the idea of being at home in a new country had crept up upon her. Realising she had "left" in her mind, her former country and arrived in another, almost without noticing, was a shock and experienced as a mixture of feelings including happiness, guilt, and grief, a confusingly welcome but also painfully upsetting feeling.

In my own thematic analysis of refugee community life story oral history interviews, I have identified an emerging theme of certainty, of being "this" not "that" (Alfred, 2010). People sharing their life stories often appear to find comfort in order, in defining their identities, in asserting who they were and where they have come from, and to where they might be going. A number assert unequivocal national identities. Those who do not feel tied to geographical land may still emphatically assert unequivocal cultural identity. For instance:

> Being a Gypsy? To me, I can't really say what it means. It's not a meaning—it's me, who I am, it's kind of the person that I am, where I come from. Because we don't actually come from a country, we say who we are. And we're Gypsies, we travel from country to country, that's what we've done in generations and centuries.
>
> So I think being a Gypsy really means, you know, saying that's me, that's the person I am, that's the person I'm always going to be, I've always been. That's the tradition I've been always holding up against, and the culture that I've always run with, you know. That's my life and that's who I am. (Interviewee P, 2006)

In becoming refugees, some people experience loss, at least momentarily, of certainty, of security, of feeling grounded. This loss may lead to an urgent compulsive reaching out to certainty.

> I am a refugee in my, in myself ... and you have been penalised so, for so long for being a refugee that finally you, you, you just kind of, like to be a refugee. (Interviewee M, 2005)

Arguably, outer identities can be thought of as offering a shelter for the self. People may hastily adopt new outer identities to aid survival in new social environments. Having lost former visible identities, for instance of social and professional roles formerly occupied in a home country, a person might shelter behind makeshift outer identities including those indicated to them by other people, for example "refugee". With time, an individual might outgrow these, or feel more confident to wander out to try out new identities. However, sometimes individuals may grow accustomed and comfortable within these makeshift identities and adopt them as their own.

In some life story interviews, I have observed a kind of phenomenon that might be described as "identity squatting". A person adopts a makeshift identity that may be vacant when they arrive in the UK, for instance "refugee". They may later claim this as their rightful identity, even where others point out that they might move on to occupy other identity shelters.

For instance, Interviewee M recalls an incident of being asked, "When exactly did you finish to being a refugee, I keep forgetting?" To this M recalls retorting, "I said 'Well well-done! I never stopped to be a refugee'." M reflects, "Officially I stopped being a refugee fifteen years ago, fifteen, sixteen years ago but nothing changed inside me" (Interviewee M, 2005).

The concept of ambivalence, of being neither "here" nor "there" appears to be a key theme in some life story interviews.

> I could not complete a picture of myself as a person, because of the inability to go home. And therefore this life, in a way, was split into these two parts containing two lives which lived, existed independently of one another: a life that had been once and a life that was now …
>
> I had led two parallel lives … They joined last year after I visited [name of city] for the first time in eleven years. And, somehow I found, on my own, this internal peace that I did not think I would find until I went home. (Interviewee N, 2006)

The "here–there" ambivalence occurs time and time again as a dominant theme across life story interviews with people from refugee backgrounds. People appear to conceive of their lives in sharply defined "here" and "there" categories which they readily bring up unprompted in life story interviews. For instance, to the question, "Have you ever done any work with artists or poets? Have you ever used your music to –?", Interviewee N (2005) replies "Here or there?" The questioner then responds, "Either", suggesting that reflection on any "here–there" dichotomy was not their intention here.

"Here" and "there": Double attraction, double repulsion

In some cases, people appear to feel strongly, often painfully, tugged like a rope between two conflicting loyalties. For instance:

> The second I arrive there I know that I belong there, that I come from there. But my life is here. I mean belonging, as it were, it is an emotional commitment that you have to a place … I went and spent that day on my own and cried my eyes out, because I felt that I was betraying myself, you know. Like, having decided that I wanted to go back to [name of country], that that was where I belonged, that is what everyone expected of me. And the natural conclusion of exile, that somehow you go back. And then of course I started missing England, my life here … And it was then that I felt, you know, "How can you be such a traitor to yourself?" … (Interviewee T, 2006)

Interviewees, like E, appear to identify strongly with "there". Asked to introduce himself, E responds boldly and unequivocally: "OK, my name is [name], I am an Ethiopian by nationality. I still remain an Ethiopian and I reside in London," asserting, "I love my country. I love my people so much" (Interviewee E, 2006).

However, this identification appears in sharp tension with E's passionate anger about the lack of freedom and poor human rights within his homeland, the circumstances within his country that resulted in the unjust killing of journalists and friends, and his bitterness about being forced to transform from a professional researcher into a "refugee".

Often people appear to have learnt to tolerate ambivalent relationships towards "there". Many describe how they have sought to maintain positive connection with "there" while developing connection with "here". For instance:

> I started writing songs in a way to, touch my country, that's the only way I could actually touch, be with my country, if I could

> actually write things about it [cough] so, so, I mean, so writing songs became a part of being there without being there, if you know what I mean. (Interviewee E, 2006)

It may be disquieting to listen to people expressing ambivalent tension by simultaneously identifying with and rejecting both "here" and "there". Perhaps partly to relieve their own discomfort, life story interviewers may urge people towards positioning themselves decisively either as "here" or as "there".

Sometimes people have declared uncertainty about conceiving of themselves, not as both "here" and "there", but as neither "here" nor "there". For instance, asked "Do you think London is your home?" S initially stalls; "That is a very tough question, my child." When nudged to answer, by the probe "somewhere to call home", S replies:

> No, I can't feel like home, I've never felt before and I never will, I never. This is my personal problem. I do not think other people think like me. I here, what you see here I know it as a house not a "home". Never, I do not know why that is but unfortunately and unfortunately I went to [name of country] and there was not my home, there also everyone is a stranger to me, the whole "system" is a, a stranger, everyone is in a different state. The only thing that I miss from [name of country] that I miss at the moment is its beautiful sun, which it truly has a sweet sun, no? And its weather and fruits and so. Its people have changed, the people I knew are not there. Actual fact all have left and there I did not find a home for myself and when I came back here, we have a saying your father knows, "kafe sare au" [bubbles in water], bubbles on water is where you leave a tap fully open, suddenly there are bubbles on the surface of the water, you know? And that is slowly, slowly being fades away. I, in this society, feel like a bubble in water, I think that I am here until I get old … (Interviewee S, 2005)

The image of "bubbles in water" conveys the fragile and whimsical nature of being. A person might feel herself drifting between "here" and "there", like frothy bubbles that are not still, like air that does not mix with water.

Ejected by, or repugnant of, homeland, or "there", and rejected by a new country, or "here", people may experience uneasy displacement.

This experience of double rejection from both the homeland and past from which one has fled and the country and future to which one might turn, could lead to feelings of being pushed away rather than of being drawn in, double repulsion rather than double attraction. Metaphorically speaking, a person may feel knocked out of kilter, sent spinning out of orbit. This might arouse feelings of anxiety at being not securely held anywhere. Alternatively, or simultaneously, this may also arouse feelings of exhilarating liberation.

People feeling the push of both "here" and "there" may hop up onto a new plane to avoid implosion. People from refugee backgrounds seem sometimes instead to conceive of themselves not as "here" or as "there" but on another level altogether as "global citizens" (e.g. Interviewee S, 2005).

Figure 9.2 shows two different ways of conceiving of a person's relationship to "here" and "there" which are represented as nebulous clouds. The upper diagram shows "here" and "there" as push forces, with arrows also indicating a person's rejection of "here" and "there" by pushing himself away. The lower diagram shows a more common way of conceiving of "here" and "there" as oppositional forces, pulling a person apart.

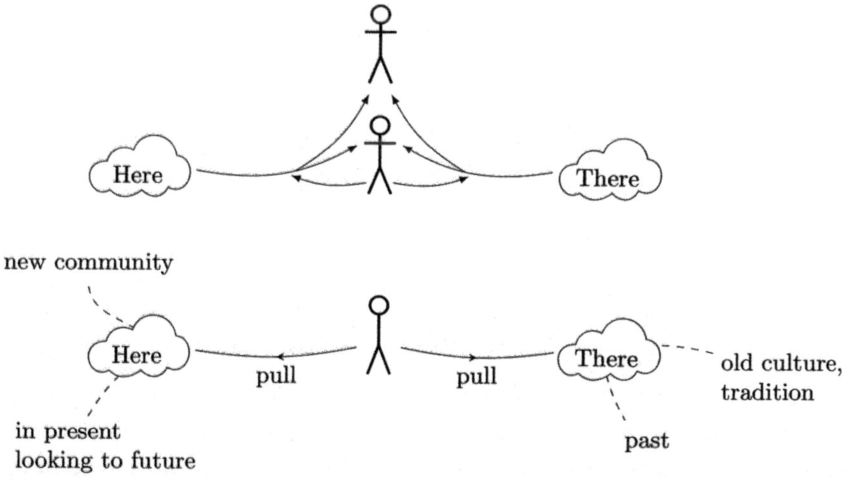

Figure 9.2 Attracting and repelling forces of "here" and "there"

The blues note: Intolerability of neither leaving nor arriving, of being neither here nor there

> 7th chords on the ukulele always go somewhere. The reason is this: 7th chords are unresolved chords. An unresolved chord is a chord that needs to be resolved. For example, within the key of C you are playing G7. You can play that G7 all day, but the song won't sound over until the G7 goes somewhere (usually to C). The only time you might hear a song ended on a 7th chord is in a blues song. Even then the 7th chord is the root. (Live Ukelele, 2010)

Interestingly, when narrating their stories of seeking refuge, some people will polish and smooth their stories and make them palatable for the listener, while others will share jagged edge stories, narratives that jar and that may have not been given neat resolution or happy-ever-after endings. Sometimes people narrating their stories are comfortable presenting life stories in this way, a way they may feel reflects their authentic experience. From my own observations and reflections with the Refugee Community History Project and other oral history encounters with people from refugee backgrounds, I have found that it is often listeners who may be alarmed by this. Human propensity often to categorise clearly, label and package neatly, can make it uncomfortable to hear stories where there are not clear and happy resolutions to narratives begun and where narrative threads are left hanging. This may be comparable with the experience of listening to blues music with an unresolved chord. While some people are passionate about blues music and can tolerate a seventh chord ending, others seek resolution of that chord.

Conclusion

In conclusion, people cannot be reduced to labels such as "refugee". Labelling may affect one's own sense of identity. Being perceived and labelled by others as "refugees" can obscure a broader identity as a human being. Leaving a homeland due to fear of persecution can become very much bound up in how one's personal identity is socially constructed; people may be seen, or indeed come to see themselves as those who have left, or at least those who are expected to have "left". People may present their life stories couching themselves as "leavers" according to the expectations they sense listeners have for the stories to be told in this way.

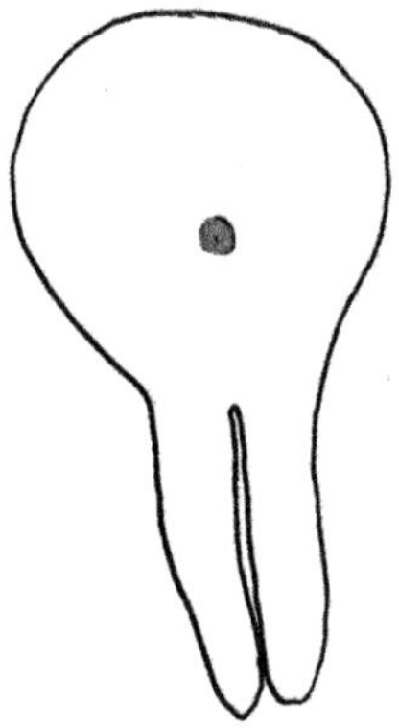

Figure 9.3 Key hole or key?

Among those who have sought refuge, a variety of factors may give rise to people thinking of themselves as "arrivees" rather than "departees". Constellations of such factors change over time and therefore people's feelings about whether they have "arrived" are dynamic and changing. It seems that feelings of "arrival" may be connected with the sense people have of establishing a sense of belonging in a new land and the power to make autonomous decisions and have some agency over their own lives. Confronting incidents of racism later down the line, can swing people's self-orientation needles from arrivees to departees or send the needle oscillating rapidly between the two. Experiences of being disrespected or rejected by others, for instance through feeling the target of racist behaviour, or discriminated against on other grounds, can stir up doubt that one really belongs and that one's arrival has been accepted by others.

However, rather than thinking in a binary polar way of either being in a state of leaving or arriving, we may be able to contemplate the complex idea of both leaving and arriving, and also of "hopping" into a new mental state of being where we are defined neither by leaving or arriving, of being neither "here" at home in a new land, or still "there" in a land we have physically left, but elsewhere entirely.

We can look through and past the experience of leaving to see something else. Tilted off axis, this image may be considered not simply a duck or a rabbit, but a keyhole, and perhaps also as a key!

Acknowledgements

Thank you to all who have generously shared stories and perspectives on "departing" a homeland and "arriving" in another land and to all who shared reflections and life stories within the Evelyn Oldfield Unit's Refugee Communities History Project (2004–2007) and beyond. People are anonymised here and designated by a code letter, but their contribution is significant.

Sharing stories helps everyone to understand a little more that people labelled "refugees" are individuals, with diverse experiences and different individual perspectives and ways of narrating and interpreting diverse experiences of seeking safety in a new land. It also helps each of us to see that the predicament of facing danger in a country one may have long considered one's own, can befall anyone. Where we understand that each of us might find ourselves in the future seeking refuge from persecution, in some cases not for the first time, we may find ways of showing greater tolerance and understanding for people currently facing such a predicament. This in turn may help us to find ways to challenge the injustices of government policy makers who, in 2024, may be found attempting to remove safe means of passage for those seeking sanctuary and sending those who do arrive into detention or offshore sites where their claims for asylum might be processed away from public sight.

References

Alfred, Z. T. (2010). *Constructing Refugee Narratives.* PhD thesis, University of Essex.

Al-Rasheed, M. (1993). Meaning of marriage and status in exile: The experience of Iraqi women. *Journal of Refugee Studies*, *6*(2): 89–104.

American Psychiatric Association (2013). *Diagnostic and Statistical Manual of Mental Disorders* (5th edn). Arlington, VA: American Psychiatric Association.

Camino, L. A., & Krufeld, R. (Eds.) (1999). *Reconstructing Lives, Recapturing Meaning: Refugee Identity, Gender and Culture Change.* London: Routledge.

Chan, B. (2005). Imagining the homeland: The internet and diasporic discourse of nationalism. *Journal of Communication Inquiry*, *29*(4): 336–368.

Concern Worldwide (2022, 4 May). Refugee, migrant, IDP: What's the difference? https://concern.org.uk/news/refugee-migrant-idp-whats-difference (last accessed 1 January 2026).

Eisenbruch, M. (1991). From post-traumatic stress disorder to cultural bereavement: Diagnosis of Southeast Asian refugees. *Social Science & Medicine, 33*(6): 673–680. ISSN 0277-9536. https://doi.org/10.1016/0277-9536(91)90021-4

Esposito, A. (2022). The limitations of humanity: Differential refugee treatment in the EU. *Harvard International Review*. https://hir.harvard.edu/the-limitations-of-humanity-differential-refugee-treatment-in-the-eu/ (last accessed 1 January 2026).

Evelyn Oldfield Unit (2004–2007). Refugee Communities History Project: Belonging: Voices of London's Refugees.

Interviewees H, M, & S (2005). Oral history life story interview conducted with fieldworker for the Evelyn Oldfield Unit and Museum of London's Refugee Communities History Project, London.

Interviewees E, F, N, P, & T (2006). Oral history life story interview conducted with fieldworker for the Evelyn Oldfield Unit and Museum of London's Refugee Communities History Project, London.

Islami, L. (2007). *Unwritten Diary True Story* shared by email with Z. Loakthar, London. [Unpublished autobiographical manuscript.]

Jodeyr, S. (2003). "Where do I belong?" The experience of second generation Iranian immigrants and refugees. *Psychodynamic Practice, 9(2)*: 205-5-214. https://doi.org/10.1080/1353333031000104820

Karpmann, S. (1968). Fairy tales and script drama analysis. *Transactional Analysis Bulletin, 26*: 39–43.

Kits, H. J. (2005). Betwixt and between: Refugees and stateless persons in limbo. *Refuge*, 22: 3.

Langer, J. (1997). *The Bend in The Road: Refugees Writing*. Nottingham, UK: Five Leaves.

Live Ukulele (2010). Resolving 7th chords [online]. http://liveukulele.com/chords/resolving-7th-chords/ (last accessed 1 May 2024).

Loakthar, Z. A. (2023). Good practice around inclusion of people from refugee backgrounds in universities in the UK. In: S. T. Saeed & Z. Min (Eds.), *Global Perspectives on the Difficulties and Opportunities Faced by Migrant and Refugee Students in Higher Education* (pp. 219–252). Information Science Reference. https://igi-global.com/gateway/chapter/324879 (last accessed 5 January 2026).

Marschall, S. (2019). "Memory objects": Material objects and memories of home in the context of intra-African mobility. *Journal of Material Culture, 24*(3): 253–269. https://doi.org/10.1177/1359183519832630

Mirawdeli, K. (2002). *Passage to Dawn*. London: Millennium Awards.

Naficy, H. (2001). *An Accented Cinema: Exilic and Diasporic Filmmaking*. Princeton, NJ: Princeton University Press.

Ofen, N., & Shing, L. I. (2013). From perception to memory: Changes in memory systems across the lifespan. *Neuroscience & Biobehavioral Reviews, 37*(9), Part B, November: 2258–2267. https://sciencedirect.com/science/article/abs/pii/S0149763413001024 (last accessed 1 May 2024).

Papadopoulos, R. K. (2021). *Involuntary Dislocation: Home, Trauma, Resilience and Adversity-Activated Development*. London: Routledge.

Papadopoulos, R. K., & Hildebrand, J. (1997). Is home where the heart is? Narratives of oppositional discourses in refugee families. In: R. K. Papadopoulos & J. Byng-Hall (Eds.), *Multiple Voices: Narrative in Systemic Family Psychotherapy* (pp. 206–236). London: Duckworth.

Persons A, B, C, J, S, T, & U (2023). Oral history life story interview conducted in English with Z. Loakthar and transcribed verbatim. London. [Unpublished oral history interview.]

Ripple, G., Schweighauser, P., Kirss, T., Sutrop, M., & Steffen T. (Eds.) (2013). *Haunted Narrative: Life Writing in an Age of Trauma*. Toronto, Canada: University of Toronto Press.

Shami, S. (2004). New approaches to migration? Transnational communities and the transformation. *Journal of Refugee Studies, 17*: 246–248.

The Eagles (1977). Hotel California. *Hotel California*, Track 1. Asylum Records.

UNHCR (2011). The 1951 refugee convention relating to the status of refugees and its 1967 protocol [online]. https://unhcr.org/uk/3b66c2aa10 (last accessed 1 May 2024).

UNHCR (2023). LGBTIQ+ persons. https://unhcr.org/what-we-do/how-we-work/safeguarding-individuals/lgbtiq-persons (last accessed 1 May 2024).

Van Hear, N., Bakewell, O., & Long, K. (2020). Push-pull plus: Reconsidering the drivers of migration. In: *Aspiration, Desire and the Drivers of Migration* (pp. 19–36). London: Routledge.

van Liempt, I., & Staring, R. (2023). Homemaking and places of restoration: Belonging within and beyond places assigned to Syrian refugees in the Netherlands. In: F. Hillmann & M. Samers (Eds.), *Cities, Migration, and Governance Beyond Scales and Levels* (pp. 142–160). London: Routledge.

Wittgenstein, L. (1953). Philosophical investigations. G. E. M. Anscombe (Trans.). *Philosophy, 30*(113): 173–179.

CHAPTER 10

Dangerous liaisons: Picking up the pieces

Linda Cundy

Packing for America
— my father in Tabriz, 1960

He can't take his mother in the suitcase,
the smell of khoresht in the air, her spice box
too tall to fit. Nor will it close when he folds
her sajadah into its corners. He can't bring
the way she rose and blew out the candles
at supper's end, rolled the oilcloth up, marked
the laying out of beds, the beginning of night.
He knows the slap of her sandals across
the tiles will fade. He tosses photographs
into the case, though not one shows her eyes;
instead, she covers her mouth with her hand
as taught, looks away. He considers strapping
the samovar to his back like a child's bag;
a lifetime measured in tea from its belly.
Finally, he takes her tulip glass, winds
a chador around its body, leaves the gold rim
peeking out like a mouth that might
tell him where to go, what is coming next.

—Marjorie Lotfi, 2023

(By kind permission of the poet and Bloodaxe Books, www.bloodaxebooks.com)

Introduction

Lotfi's enigmatic poem captures with eloquence and economy of words the push–pull dilemma so many people have experienced at the point of departure. In this scenario, the poet's Iranian father appears deeply attached to his home and his mother yet he is packing to leave that life behind. It is clear that this is no holiday he's preparing for. Maybe he's moving abroad to study or work, to take up new opportunities and he plans to return in time. So why does he take just one suitcase? And why the farewells to so many mementos of his mother? Perhaps she is no longer living and her home holds more than memories, it houses her spirit. Or maybe he has already moved away but returned after her death to find some keepsakes?

As I read the poem I sense urgency as this man "tosses photographs into the case". He may simply have a plane to catch—or possibly there is another reason for his haste. In my imagination I conjure the story of a man driven to hurriedly abandon the home of his family and childhood, fleeing far away to a world where his language, customs, and way of life are alien, and the people uncomprehending of everything he has needed to abandon. Other than escape, he has no clear plan for the future. All he has for guidance is the memory of his mother evoked by her precious tulip glass wrapped in her shawl, as he, perhaps, was wrapped in infancy.

It is possible that these associations are evoked by experiences closer to home in my family.

When to go?

It is 20 July 2024. At 8.20 in the morning sirens ring out. Fifty years ago to the hour, Turkey invaded northern Cyprus and days later my mother-in-law's family fled their home in Varosha leaving almost all their possessions behind. The house, like everything else in that area of Famagusta, has lain abandoned ever since, a territory held as a bargaining chip in negotiations between Turkey and the Cypriot Turks in the north, and the Greeks south of the island. The situation remains unresolved half a century later as the most glamorous resort of its time in the Mediterranean has crumbled and rusted. Like every building in this ghost town, the Christophe home lies looted and decaying, off limits to all as the occupying soldiers patrol. But a couple of years ago, perhaps as a goodwill gesture in attempts to find a political solution, it became possible to visit Varosha and walk along its main roads during daylight hours. One family member took the risk to slip through and film the property, a house where she and my husband spent a great deal of their early lives.

I try to imagine the atmosphere in 1974. There had been decades of conflict, first between Cypriots and the occupying British; then, following independence in 1960, between the two major ethnic communities with many Greek Cypriots fighting for *enosis*, union with Greece. On 15 July, a coup d'état backed by Greece overthrew the government, threatening the safety and rights of Turkish Cypriots and triggering the invasion by Turkey days later. The woman who became my mother-in-law had already settled in London but her family remained back home. While she anxiously watched events unfold from a distance, they followed news of the fighting as the battle front came closer and closer, until they could see the Turkish planes and parachutes overhead, hear machine gun fire and explosions. I imagine a combination of terror and disbelief, of cognitive dissonance, would paralyse people in that situation. I wonder who finally spoke up and said it's time to go. I picture the urgency with which most treasured possessions were grabbed, panic as whole neighbourhoods crammed into vehicles that joined barely-moving queues of traffic on the roads out of town, and the battle noises grew louder. Did they know where to go next? Had anyone, or anything, been forgotten in the desperate rush to escape? Certainly pets and other animals were left behind to fend for themselves. I look around my home—what would I grab if I had to leave NOW?

Thirty-nine thousand residents of Varosha fled in just a few days. I am sure that none thought for one moment they could never return. Ultimately, almost half the population of the island was displaced, with Greek Cypriots moving south and Turkish Cypriots heading north. But for many from both communities, resettlement followed years living under canvas in refugee camps in areas still held by the British as overseas territories.

Despite the displacement, most families stayed together, except for those who chose to join the fighting. Thousands were killed on both sides, with more than two thousand still missing half a century later. A Missing People's Forest has been planted in their memory, and efforts continue to locate their bodies, identify them, and enable families to properly lay loved ones to rest.

Although my family connection is to the Cypriot Greek experience, I feel equal grief for the Cypriot Turks. In the 1980s I worked at a mental health day centre and there met a young woman with classic hysterical symptoms—a kind of physiological dissociative split between the left side of her body and the right. She identified one side as Turkish and Muslim, the other as British and Christian, and suffered occasional hemiplegic paralyses with no organic cause. We tried to understand her unusual presentation in the light of what we knew about her childhood, with a violent father and her arranged marriage to another cruel man. However, she had arrived in the UK with her family as asylum seekers from Cyprus, a traumatically divided island, and I believe this to be expressed through the form her distress took.

Previous chapters in this book highlight the value of specialist knowledge, and possibly specialist training, when working therapeutically with certain groups such as cult survivors, asylum seekers and refugees, people trying to exit gangs, and those with dissociative identity disorder resulting from organised child abuse. Various approaches for processing trauma are helpful across the spectrum of clients who have lived in violent and unpredictable environments. This concluding chapter aims to identify some of the themes that run through the book and highlight core therapeutic features that contribute to resolution, recovery, and creating a new life, whether trauma is present or not. I will outline an attachment-informed model of psychotherapy that, I hope, will be useful to those practitioners who do not specialise in a particular client group but may encounter survivors of danger in their general therapy practice. In this category of people who have experienced life-threatening situations I include those recovering from anorexia, where the "attachment" to self-denial continues to pose a significant risk.

Who and what we are attached to

While caregivers are essential for an infant's survival, we hope they also supply the essential nutrients for thriving—love, affection, enjoyment, encouragement. They need to provide fair, consistent boundaries to protect children, but also help them acquire the skills to recognise danger and ultimately keep themselves safe. Whether they are capable of this or not, most parents do keep children alive. Our attachment figures, in infancy and throughout our lives, may not always be sensitively responsive but they are our anchors. We are important to them. They are part of us, and we are part of them. We exist in their minds—they *know* us.

Attachment concerns survival but encompasses two other important aspects—belonging and identity. Belonging relates to "a person's membership of, and acceptance by, a group or society" (*OED*). That could include a family, a gang, a cult, a religious or spiritual group, or even a loose affiliation of people who use and supply street drugs. As members of a social species, a sense of belonging helps to define us; likewise, one's country and culture, even for those who experience themselves as misfits. Others who recognise and share many of our cultural references and features of our experience are a kind of tribe.

Each of us comes into the world with our genetic inheritance and remarkable capacity to adapt to the family set-up, community, and culture we are raised in; we are shaped in response to that early environment. We learn language, culturally required behaviours, roles, values, and expectations. This is the core of identity. Later, life experiences and choices may take us on a different trajectory, to membership of other groups. Each of us has a dynamic Venn diagram of groups we belong to and identify with that is the basis of our unique identity. Sometimes, membership of a particular group (or couple) becomes so all-consuming that other sources of belonging and sense of self are banished or forgotten. This is a red flag, suggesting the possibility of coercive control. Eating disorders specialist, Julia Buckroyd, describes the danger when a cohort of anorexic inpatients develops a group identity based on their illness, where mutual support can morph into something competitive and life-endangering (Julia Buckroyd, personal communication). One client of mine, despite years of recovery from her eating disorder, heard news that a woman she met during her treatment had recently died. She described feeling a kind of shame about her own well-being, that she has not been a "good enough anorexic" to starve herself to death.

Abandoning our place of belonging, whether a partner, faith group, cult, gang, life of addiction, or homeland, entails a myriad of losses:

features of our day-to-day lives that we have taken for granted, our routines and rituals, dress codes, gender roles, what and when we eat, our familiar environment, possessions, shared references, and memories … Perhaps also language, work, sources of income, relationships, status and place in the world—exiting a threatening situation may require putting aside much of how we know and define ourselves. This highlights the significance of belonging, of an attachment matrix that each of us is shaped to fit into and where we are recognised. Even when features of this matrix are toxic or dangerous, it is tough to abandon so much of who we are without a familiar hand reaching out, or the hope of finding comfort and acceptance provided by strangers, a new community to belong to. How can we be sure that the world *out there* is not equally hostile? Or that our persecutors will not track us down? While the idea of a fresh start with new possibilities may beckon, it is hardly surprising that decisions to leave are often fraught with ambivalence.

That decision is often more straightforward when escape is undertaken with others, or to protect or rejoin loved ones. Perhaps it is more difficult when prolonged entrapment and fear create a psychobiological freeze response and submission, when abuse has eroded one's spirit.

Attachment and detachment

Not everyone who gets drawn into abusive situations has a history of trauma. A natural desire for companionship, social values, a wish to be useful to others or to lead a spiritual life can also be perverted by those who deceive and manipulate for their own ends.

While home and family may not provide the optimal environment to feel safe and secure, we all develop strategies to get the best out of our circumstances. We adapt to fit a very specific niche in a familiar environment. How we perceive *out there*—the wider world—will depend on our core pattern of attachment. Those who have had the benefit of a secure attachment, which provides a fertile environment for epistemic trust to flourish, can venture out and explore an enticing world filled with people perceived to be basically welcoming and trustworthy. The secure base is internalised in the form of benign, supportive "internal objects" that continue to provide nurture and encouragement. This, in turn, shapes self-perception, self-worth, healthy narcissism. Ironically, it seems that secure attachment does not always promote survival in high-risk situations. A securely attached person is not necessarily well equipped to detect and avoid danger; epistemic trust and a tendency to give the benefit of doubt is not always appropriate and greater wariness is called for on occasions. When it does become clear that all is not as it seemed, these individuals may be more inclined to stay and try to repair relationships, to bring about positive change rather than abandon all. Ultimately, survival may depend on the capacity to *detach* and to give up hope. Some research suggests that protecting family and loved ones can delay action in dangerous situations, yet their cooperative approach and organisational skills can be invaluable once action is mobilised (Ein-Dor, 2014).

For individuals with *dismissing* defences, early relational experiences have frequently been rejecting of attachment needs: pain, longing, and vulnerability must be repressed. Getting close risks further hurt and rejection. Therefore, the unknown world is no more or less risky than the familiar, and self-protective strategies evolve to keep others at a safe distance. Competence can provide self-esteem, as well as respect from other people. Sometimes contempt for others, especially those viewed as vulnerable, is an exporting of contempt felt for one's own vulnerability. It may seem unlikely that such a person would be drawn into a violent relationship, abusive cult or gang, or be prepared to stay when threatened. However, the attachment instinct is not extinguished in those who develop avoidant strategies and, in certain circumstances, the sense of belonging, feeling valued and respected, meets important needs. While some adopt a solitary life, others find the companionship of community without the intimacy of one-to-one relating feeds that hunger. I suggest that some narcissistic leaders are able to manipulate this character trait to keep people trapped in abusive situations, appearing to value them and give them status within the group or community while using them for their own purposes.

Meanwhile, people who are more *preoccupied* in their attachment style have often experienced unpredictable caregiving. Attention is then focused on the availability of the attachment figure to the detriment of developing agency. These individuals may view the world as fraught with dangers, and perceive themselves as lacking personal resources to cope alone. The effective strategy, to stay close to identified attachment figures, can inhibit self-protective action and is especially problematic if the nominated attachment figure is a source of danger. Again, I will suggest that highly manipulative people can instil and exacerbate such anxious attachment for their own purposes.

In his paper on social defence theory, Ein-Dor proposes that "Some people ... detect threats quicker and more accurately than others," while those who are "compulsively self-reliant ... tend to employ self-protective actions more rapidly and effectively" once alerted to danger. Meanwhile, another group of individuals is "better at massing collective efforts and leading group actions because they are more relationship-oriented". These three responses to potential danger echo the *preoccupied*, *avoidant/ dismissing*, and *secure-autonomous* patterns of attachment.

Ein-Dor suggests that there may be an evolutionary advantage to a distribution of attachment patterns in social groups, in particular noting that those with a preoccupied pattern who are hyperalert to both abandonment and danger, are better equipped to read signs of interpersonal risk. However, preoccupied attachment, going hand-in-hand with an impaired sense of agency and fear of separation, can inhibit decision-making in terms of taking steps to escape, especially if there is no one to take the initiative or escape to.

The stress of danger is likely to inhibit flexibility of thought and incline individuals to respond according to their default core strategies. For those anxiously attached preoccupied individuals, this may incline them to cling to the very people who are responsible for the threat. Research suggests that "people high on attachment anxiety were ... better at detecting cues of interpersonal deceit" (Ein-Dor & Perry, 2014). This relates to mentalizing, the capacity to read the other person's intentions. However, in my clinical experience, this hypervigilance to signs of deception is potentially inaccurate; threat is sometimes perceived where none exists, with accusations of lying, cheating, and infidelity being levelled against partners and others sometimes without grounds. Rather than ending "duplicitous" relationships, attempts often follow to control the "offending" partner and keep him or her close. There is an addictive quality to these relationships that mitigates against abandoning them.

The last straw

These chapters narrate stories of people who are driven to prioritise survival over attachment. Sometimes the danger is environmental, such as natural disaster or climate-related crises, yet frequently, as we have heard in previous chapters, the person we turn to for protection is the source of abuse. Like the young boy I described in the preface, people caught up in these relationships are frequently both loyal towards and protective of the abuser—they are "attached to bad objects".

Kerry was one of the younger children in a large working-class family. Her parents were not cruel but, with so many mouths to feed, they had no time to pay her attention and she was raised by siblings who themselves had little life experience or inner resources to pass on. In her teens, she met Mike. He was some years older than her and had a reputation locally as a trouble-maker but he was good-looking, fun—and he noticed her. He was protective of her, as it seemed then. Later, in therapy, she began to wonder of he was possessive rather than protective. She had not learned to keep herself safe and her hunger for attention and a bigger life than she grew up with made him irresistible. Initially at least, her self-esteem blossomed.

Mike liked sex. Kerry was petite and he seemed to enjoy overpowering her. He refused to use condoms or let her take contraceptive pills. Kerry felt desired and believed he wanted her to have his child. She moved in with him. However, once she became pregnant he changed. He was often angry and shouted at her. He demanded money that he spent drinking, then came home to fight with her. This always ended with sex, after which he was loving, gentle, and apologetic. She feared for the baby inside her and considered leaving him, returning to her parents' home but knew that would burden her family, and Mike's distress after these episodes felt genuine. She worried that he would do harm to himself if she left him. She also later confessed that she feared what he might do to her if she tried. The pattern that developed in their relationship followed closely that described in Walker's classic study of battered women (Walker, 1980).

As the pregnancy progressed, the violence and control escalated. Sometimes Mike would beat Kerry then leave her bruised and shaken, locking her in their flat while he went drinking. He told her she had trapped him into the relationship but, once trapped, he found her disgusting, especially her pregnant body. Kerry's fear of him, love for him, and shame, made it impossible to take self-protective action but, when her son arrived, she was determined that Mike would not harm him. She began to hatch an escape plan, should that day ever come. And it did.

Kerry had needed hospital treatment on several occasions with cuts and concussion. Her bruises were witnessed. She was questioned about this and urged to notify the authorities or contact a domestic abuse organisation but Kerry had always refused. However, this was her way out and one day she took it after Mike, drunk and aggressive, had handled the baby roughly. She stood in his way, taking a beating and knew this would be the last. Once he left, slamming the door, she gathered up her son and a few clothes then headed for the hospital. When I began working with her several years later, Mike was serving a prison sentence for violently assaulting a gambling partner, and Kerry was rebuilding her life and identity as a young mother with ambitions to have a career. She had been involved with several charities that provide support to victims of crime and domestic violence, and discovered feminist politics, an eye-opener for the woman who left school without qualifications and was a mother by the age of nineteen. With the little one now attending school, she enrolled at college and was studying for GCSEs.

Chaotic or calculated

Mike was impulsive, addicted to alcohol, gambling, and possibly sex. He could not hold down a job and this created serious financial problems. Ultimately, he was sentenced to a prison term for violent behaviour. In Kerry's therapy we did not explore Mike's early life but all evidence indicates multiple ACEs (adverse childhood experiences). His chaotic lifestyle no doubt expressed a chaotic inner world. His unpredictability and intense rages may also suggest dissociated self-states during which he had no access to empathy or resources to modify his violent outbursts. His behaviour shows many narcissistic features; he could be charming but had a grandiose sense of self-importance and entitlement, his needs mattered and Kerry's did not, any opposition would not be tolerated, and his rage was extreme when he felt disrespected, for instance when Kerry refused to hand over the money she was keeping for food and rent. He appeared to experience her financial worries as personal accusations, her preoccupation with her pregnancy as a kind of infidelity, and her loss of enthusiasm for sex during the pregnancy as defiant withholding. He was at serious risk of a life of addiction and imprisonment without help to break away.

Mike's impulsivity, possessiveness, apparent rivalry with the unborn baby for Kerry's attention, his hypervigilance to being left by her, and intense emotional outbursts are suggestive of a combination of a preoccupied pattern of attachment alongside unresolved trauma. He alternately drew Kerry to him, almost attempting to merge with her, then violently rejected her. His hypersensitivity to perceived insults indicate a core of intense and unbearable shame. The powerful waves of affect precluded mental space for reality testing, for making and carrying through plans, for building a satisfying life. This mix of preoccupied attachment with unresolved trauma is a recipe for emotionally unstable personality disorder.

In cases of domestic abuse, cognitive dissonance created by alternately praising then humiliating sets the scene for a kind of relational addiction, with all attention focused on the manipulator, afraid of rousing his or her wrath and contempt, craving another "fix" of affection and approval. Erschak (1984) explores the dynamics that are played out in a violent assault and states, "They are addicted to each other and to abuse. The system, the interaction, the relation takes hold; the individuals are as powerless as junkies" (p. 249).

For both parties, the intense emotional and physiological arousal of violent episodes stimulates the production of painkilling endorphins. Once the attack is over and immediate danger has passed, these opioids can leave a pleasurable high that gradually wears off, with symptoms that are similar to withdrawal from other opiates. As physiological tensions build again, the stress hormone cortisol builds up leading to craving for another "hit" (sometimes, literally, another attack) of endorphins. This is not to say that victims of violence "ask" to be hurt again; putting themselves in risky situations, with adrenaline and cortisol pumping, and *not* being harmed can also create a high. This trauma cycle may also feature in the narratives of cult or street gang members.

Hypervigilance, always scanning the environment for signs of the other's mood and imminent attack, precludes any introspection or agency. Peter Fonagy and Mary Target suggest that children whose attachment figures are traumatising are "hypervigilant of the caregiver's behaviour, they use all cues available and may be acutely sensitized to intentional states, and thus may be more ready to construct a mentalized account of the caregiver's behaviour", but "they may be poor readers of their own mental states, out of touch with their own internal world" (Fonagy & Target, 1998, pp. 20–21). In adults, too, this hyperfocus on the other at the expense of one's own agency strengthens the perverse bond between "follower" of whatever age and manipulative "attachment figure". Van der Kolk (1989) points out that many who experience violent attacks dissociate and, therefore, these episodes feel somewhat unreal, further contributing to their difficulty taking action to escape further danger.

While Mike's narcissistic traits were part of a chaotic and impulsive personality, there are other manipulators who are far more calculated in meeting their own needs. Researching domestic violence, Johnson (2004) differentiates between "typical batterers" who act impulsively and feel regret, and "patriarchal terrorists", who are coercively controlling, perpetrate emotional abuse and extreme violence, and feel no remorse. ("Patriarchal terrorism" describes a certain brand of misogyny but, as Kelly describes in Chapter 2, not all perpetrators of coercive control and violence are men.) In this latter case, psychopathy and narcissism feature.

Malignant narcissism

This is not a book, or even a chapter, specifically about narcissism, yet an attempt to understand the roots of "malignant self-love" (Vaknin, 1999) may help in appreciating the dynamic that is created when a person with these traits engages with others. We all have the potential for healthy narcissism—in fact, I consider it to be an outcome of effective psychotherapy. Yet, for some, this appears to be perverted into a very different manifestation, a disorder of the self. What kind of early relational environment might we find in the narratives of cult leaders, coercive controllers, grandiose and dangerous political figures, and so on? Might the characteristics of a narcissistic personality disorder—an inflated sense of self-importance, need for attention and adulation (narcissistic supplies), either simmering or dissociated narcissistic rage—represent brittle and extreme defences against unbearable humiliation? Has healthy narcissism been corrupted by early relational trauma?

It is a common perception that narcissists, or people with narcissistic personality disorder, lack empathy and cannot mentalize, yet these individuals demonstrate a sophisticated cognitive appreciation of the attachment dynamic, reading the needs and longings of others in order to manipulate them, creating dependency and relational addiction by alternately bestowing special attention or affection then ignoring, ridiculing, shaming, or rejecting, as described by Davies, Kelly, and Smith in their chapters. These are the quintessential features of trauma bonding (Dutton & Painter, 1993). The vital skill of reading the mind of a frightening caregiver (referenced by Fonagy and Target, above) enables some abused individuals to use this ability in order to control others. Perhaps their capacity to mentalize is distorted by their own trauma and, rather than developing epistemic trust, they perceive everyone as a potential threat to be dominated.

A cult leader's interference in child-rearing, preventing parents from taking their role as primary caregivers to their own children, demanding that *they*, not the child, receive attention, also suggests a degree of awareness of the innate attachment-caregiving system. Despite attempts to undermine members' bond with their children, the prospect of leaving them behind in the "care" of the cult is a further hurdle to leaving for parents. Something similar may also happen in families where coercive control features.

Infants exposed to overwhelming fear develop a disorganised attachment relationship with the parent who is the source of their trauma. Initially the infant cannot access coherent strategies to safely express attachment needs. However, Liotti (1992) suggests that, over time, a child in a dangerous environment is likely to develop survival techniques that help minimise the threat and give some control. He described three possible developmental routes: a "seductive" approach, an "agonistic" or aggressive position, or a compulsive caregiving/controlling strategy.

Many narcissistic characters appear to exhibit all of these, switching between self-states according to the situation.

In cultish groups and abusive relationships, people are deliberately cut off from other relationships. Many cult leaders choose geographically isolated locations from which to operate, such as remote regions of Colombia, New Zealand, Canada, and Guatemala, and limit access to communication with the outside world. Likewise, manipulative partners and parents control contact with family and friends, alienating them. Paranoia is stoked, drip-feeding the message that everyone outside is a threat or, at the very least, that anyone "other" is less than, not one of the chosen people, and not to be trusted. All other attachments are actively polluted and authorities demonised. One young woman, born into a Christian cult, said, "I knew the outside existed but I didn't know the extent of the outside." The Children of God practised regular "persecution drills" to prepare for invasion by "Systemite authorities" who, they believed, would kill the children (Mestyanek Young, 2022). Katy Morgan-Davies, born into a "communist cult" in London, was told that neighbours were fascist agents who practised satanic rituals involving cannibalism (Morgan-Davies, 2018). In these situations, however awful the reality of life, the abusive leader or attachment figure presents him- or herself as the rescuer. A similar dynamic is at play in states ruled by fear, where citizens are deterred from defecting by a narrative that presents the world beyond its borders as hostile, primitive, politically or morally corrupt.

Narcissists seem to intuit that one of the most efficient ways to control others is to make them hate themselves; coercing them to take part in degrading acts, or perpetrate cruelty towards others, or be complicit bystanders to such events. This violates their moral code and is a highly effective use of power. Having bound a person to them, creating an anxious, preoccupied type of attachment, the narcissist further controls the other by eroding their self-respect. Mary Kelly describes just such a situation in the cult she was drawn into, and Ruthie Smith also acknowledges the impact of hearing testimonies of abuse within the spiritual community she was part of. In some situations, an illegal or immoral act is demanded to "earn" entry to a group: Joe Secrett describes the initiation rite of "jumping in" to a gang by committing a mugging, a beating, or a stabbing.

For the gaslighter, outsourcing their sadism further binds followers to them; how can they leave, carrying that burden of guilt, perhaps fearing that their crimes are tattooed across their foreheads? Whether viewing themselves as powerless victims or as shameful, culpable actors, the abused parties are trapped in stasis.

For those who do break away, there are further trials ahead. In his paper, "Extreme migratory mourning (the Ulysses syndrome)", Achotegui (2019) points out an additional challenge to grieving for one's country and previous life: the homeland still exists but the migrant is exiled from it. Should he ever return, it will have changed. The land of his childhood is just a memory. Also, he will have been altered by his subsequent experiences and become alien to family and friends who stayed. He may no longer belong there. One person who escaped threats in her country and settled in Britain described her grief at the thought of being forgotten. The same is true of all the situations described in this collection; the one-time partner, spiritual or faith group, cult, gang, addictive substance of choice, and abuse group still exist and can appear at any time. Not just reminders of the past but messages from the present are deeply unsettling. A man who came to the UK seeking political asylum and was granted leave to remain compulsively followed news stories about politics and conflict in his "motherland" and was tormented by the thought that he could not be present at his parents' funerals or buried beside them when his time came. For the recovering addict, encounters with social groups associated with use of substances or behaviours exerts a powerful pull, and a strong new community is needed to redefine one's identity.

My mother-in-law had made a new life for herself in Britain before the invasion and occupation of her home town. She could visit Cyprus, stay with family and friends, but could not return to the town she grew up in or to her family home. This haunted her. It is possible that she would have chosen to be laid to rest there when she died. I visited Varosha recently, walked along the crumbling main street and stood at the entrance to the road leading to her childhood home, as close as the occupying army permits. I found some stones under the rampant vegetation and brought them back to London to place on her grave.

Therapy

My own client group is diverse. I do not specialise in cult survivors, people with addictions, or refugees, but in almost forty years of mental health work I have heard many stories of surviving danger; survival but rarely thriving. As the previous chapters in this book attest, there are some common themes. Based on attachment theory and research, object relations and clinical experience, I have developed a model of psychotherapy to guide the work: the A-IM (attachment-informed model), intended to help clients thrive by developing secure attachment.

I propose that each individual client is likely to benefit from focusing over time on seven dimensions of experience:

1. Staying safe and finding healthy ways to manage emotions
2. Creating an intergenerational narrative
3. Having a better understanding of mentalizing, the impact of their own inner world on thoughts, feelings, and behaviour, and the capacity for a more nuanced and plausible understanding of other peoples' motivations
4. A process of mourning losses, recognising and grieving for what was needed but not available
5. Developing a stronger sense of self and identity, a better relationship with the self
6. Building rewarding relationships with others, and a sense of belonging
7. Internalising a strong new "secure object"—an inner presence that supports, protects, encourages, enjoys, and challenges the self.

This is not a structured, step-by-step approach: each individual client will need a different balance of these ingredients, moving between and revisiting these themes over time. But what is the relevance for those who have endured long periods of fear and escaped danger of any kind?

Affect regulation: Chronic danger sets the nervous system to hypervigilance and reactivity, and day-to-day stresses become magnified. Survivors need to find safety, from people who harm them and from themselves. They need to detox from the addictive traumatic bond that has contributed to keeping them trapped. Attempts to manage hyperarousal often include forms of self-medicating—alcohol, street drugs, putting oneself in situations that lead to traumatic re-enactment. They need to know what safety feels like in their bodies, and their nervous systems need to be down-regulated using any resource that works for the individual: yoga, breathing techniques, exercise, music, horticultural or equine-assisted therapy, cooking, or just stroking the cat. According to van der Kolk, "The only reason to uncover the trauma is to gain conscious control over the unbidden re-experience or re-enactments" (van der Kolk, 1989, p. 413). Potential triggers also need to be identified and, if possible, sidestepped, or managed in ways that minimise distress. Having a trusted companion at these times can be transformative.

Creating an intergenerational narrative entails ordering experiences as a timeline from birth to the present, with rich detail of significant people and events, both good and bad. Family dynamics can be explored, as well as the social context—historical, cultural, economic, religious, political, and so on—that will have shaped the relational environment the client was born into and grew up in. This was most helpful to Kerry and is beautifully illustrated in Charles Brown's chapter. Further, the life story does not begin with birth but needs to include the parents' experiences, what informed the people they became, the way they parented. This puts the addiction, domestic violence, membership of an abusive cult, eating disorder, or, perhaps, acquisition of political views that subsequently endangered life into a bigger picture, and often it is a story with a before and after. By including and reviving memories of people who cared and were helpful, entirely negative perceptions of the world can be modified. Becoming a "storied self" (Holmes, 2001) with a coherent narrative defines the outline of one's identity. One further benefit is that this may enable clients to let go of the self-blame many describe feeling due to decisions they made.

The capacity to mentalize is one feature of secure attachment, but when attention has needed to be focused on scanning the environment for danger, familiarity with one's inner world is a luxury. Self-awareness comes from developing an "observing self" that stands back and notices how events and interactions are experienced, the impact on the body, the thoughts that accompany these physiological responses, and one's behavioural impulses. Connections are made and unconscious motives may become clearer.

Appreciating that actions are determined by obscure inner motives enables us to reflect on the behaviour of other people too. Understandably, it may be very painful to consider what motivated someone to do harm, bully, or degrade. While much energy may have been required to predict the mood and actions of an abuser, reflecting on *why* requires a safe place from which to imagine. Making sense of the other's inner world does not demand forgiveness, but can highlight that his or her history played a significant part in the traumatic relationship that evolved. Again, this can free survivors from a deeply held belief that they themselves were to blame, and help to create separation in what may have been a highly merged, mutually addictive bond.

With the therapist encouraging mentalizing, a client's misconstruing of other people's communications can also be questioned. For instance, my client Ruby firmly held the belief that she was held in contempt by everyone in her life. I questioned this often, and eventually she conceded that it was unlikely; in fact, *she* had behaved in a hostile fashion towards anyone who approached her, and they merely reacted to her unfriendly attitude. The danger for Ruby was not current but in the past. She was encouraged to think about her parents' lives before she was conceived and she spoke of her father who had been imprisoned and tortured in his home country for opposing the regime. His trauma played out in her parents' marriage. Violence was commonplace in that household and Ruby believed that all relationships were cruel and perverse. I suggested, as gently as possible, that her perception that everybody despised her had an air of defensive grandiosity, that perhaps she was not such an important character in the minds of others. She agreed to consider this a possibility. Hers was a case of intergenerational trauma; although her parents had finally escaped oppression and persecution, they carried much of their history unprocessed into their new life.

Mourning: Just as with a close bereavement, escaping from a life of fear entails innumerable losses. While leaving some experiences and people behind may bring relief and hope, much of the familiar fabric of life must be abandoned too. For those seeking refuge in other countries, that may include the mother tongue; a new life with a new language can leave all of one's previous existence in a bubble, one's previous identity dissociated, traumas unprocessed. "Certain people, by speaking in a second language learnt in adulthood, are able to construct a safety barrier against primitive emotions, sensations and affects in which the mother tongue is deeply rooted and embedded" (Mehler, 2022, p. 175). However, this safety barrier prevents mourning, integrating, and moving on. Therapeutic support may not be available in native languages but feeling safe, regulated, and respected by a therapist can provide an environment where grief is permitted. I met a number of refugees and asylum seekers during my years working for a bereavement service. For them, news from family or events back home in the news crumbled those defences and led to them seeking help.

Letting go of the past and redefining oneself for the future requires an emotional engagement with grieving for all the good, important people and meaningful experiences no longer present in one's life. Anger and sadness cannot be avoided when reflecting on lost time, missed opportunities, good things spoiled. However frightening and distressing it may have been to live in a dangerous environment, there will have been aspects of that life that were valuable. Judy Davies (Chapter 1) writes about the excitement, intellectual stimulation, and creativity shared with her husband, not just at the start of their relationship but between his violent and controlling episodes. Mary Kelly (Chapter 2) acknowledges the values she held dear that were practised in the cultish group she became trapped in. For her, in finally breaking away, she had to leave her children behind. The pain, not only of leaving them, but also of being prevented from parenting them as she believed they needed, further complicated her grief. Both Davies and Kelly recognise what, in their own histories, made them vulnerable to manipulation and abuse; the absence of an essential sense of safety needed to be mourned.

While acknowledging loss is vital, brooding on painful experiences keeps them alive, still exercising power. Ultimately, reconnecting with life requires letting go. John Bowlby (1980) described "relocating the lost object"—relegating that relationship, those years and experiences to a small side chamber of our inner world rather than occupying the main stage. That phase of life may have left scars but it is in the past.

Relationship with oneself: "Some traumatized people remain preoccupied with the trauma at the expense of other life experiences and continue to re-create it in some form for themselves or for others" (van der Kolk, 1989, p. 408). Trauma has become an identifying feature of their self-experience with their identity coalesced around a traumatised core. Escaping a dangerous environment is not necessarily the beginning of a new life. There are ghosts that continue to haunt, restricting the ability to adapt to a new, safer reality, to thrive. One of the most pernicious of toxic relationships is one we may have with ourselves. Here, an alien "bad object" takes up residence in the psyche and, rather than attempting to evict or challenge it, we become bonded to it. This internal oppressor keeps the self crushed, refusing to allow good experiences in, undermining opportunities for healing and development of a new identity. This is perhaps the greatest therapeutic challenge, to help someone who *will not* feel compassion for themselves, a kind of relational anorexia, depriving themselves of inner resources and nourishment offered by others. Despite escaping from the original oppression, breaking free from this particular dangerous liaison feels impossible, keeping a person bonded to an abuser.

Yet an inner dialogue of self-hatred, however cruel, may be a protective strategy: "I am contemptible, pathetic, damaged. Other people would be horrified if they knew what I have done, what I am." Such messages prevent opening up to relationship and therefore becoming vulnerable and, thus protecting against further potential hurt. But they also contain a whisper of prosocial values, a notion of what it is to be a good person. What *kind* of person do you want to be? And how can you go about creating a life of value? One man, Leon, had suffered the most awful childhood cruelty, abuse, and neglect that created dissociative splits in his sense of self. He had a long history of addiction and violence—rather like Mike mentioned earlier in this chapter. Leon also spent time in prison but very much wanted to escape from his past and turn his life around. He committed to attending 12-step groups and worked out at a gym every day. He needed structure and boundaries and, with therapeutic help, was able to put these in place. He found employment and learned to keep himself safe in social situations. He arranged to meet his ex-partner to apologise to her for the distress he had caused, and reconnected with a foster mother who had been supportive to him during his troubled adolescence. He was earning self-respect. I noticed in him a strong moral code by which he judged himself and which drove him, yet he was often cruelly harsh in his attitude to himself, an echo of his violent stepfather's emotional abuse. I challenged him; rather than a lifetime sentence of self-imposed punishment, is it possible to be worthy of a pardon for mistakes or "crimes" committed? This may involve some kind of restitution or commitment to community service. Leon began to imagine a future for himself where he might work to support young men in the criminal justice system, helping them reinvent their own lives, reimagine their futures.

There is dignity in transforming personal trauma to become a valuable member of society. Many chapters in this book attest to this; self-respect can be earned through helping others who may be struggling to free themselves from similar toxic situations.

Relationships with others: Where relationships have featured invasion of boundaries, violation of trust, coercion, and manipulation, it would not be surprising if a survivor becomes wary of everybody's intentions and, feeling paranoid like Ruby, reacts with self-protective aggression; or, continuing to muddle attachment and abuse, is drawn into further dangers. Therapeutic work entails helping clients who have escaped such situations learn to recognise signs of genuine danger but also identify people who do not pose a threat and risk opening up to them. With a newfound sense of agency, boundaries can be set in place at the start of a relationship. It may be possible to repair old relationships, perhaps making amends in some way for any harm caused. Such old friendships connect with a past that may predate the trauma of entrapment, holding memories of a time when life could have taken a different path, a reminder that, although experiences change us, old dreams may still call. Old hopes and ambitions can be revived, new interests explored. As outlined earlier, the groups we belong to and identify with contribute to identity and sense of self. For some survivors, relating to individuals remains stressful while a community provides containment and, often, purpose.

Establishing a strong, supportive internal presence: An internal secure base is constructed from introjecting experiences of being loved, protected, enjoyed, and encouraged. For those with a history of control or domination, any such memories fade and need to be sparked back into life; loving family relationships, old friends, kind teachers who saw and nurtured potential … For Leon, his foster mother was his significant "good object". For Hyun Suk Lee's client, Eunhye, her grandmother was an important attachment figure in her inner world who provided the foundation stone for a secure base, and Joe Secrett had internalised the protective function of his youth worker with whom he then identified.

The presence of good internal objects provides resources, enabling us to build resilience to cope with challenges, assures us that life is worth fighting for, and reminds us that there is goodness in the world. Even when there has been abuse, there may have been occasions of feeling loved and cared for that can be rediscovered. Current relationships also provide good source material for a "secure attachment object", an inner companion that keeps us safe, delights in our achievements, reminds us to think before saying "yes" or "no", accepts our failings philosophically, encourages us to try and to not give up, to take in and be nourished by good experiences. I often ask clients to describe or draw a portrait gallery of these important figures in their lives. One aim of psychotherapy is for the therapist, too, to be internalised, enabling the client to conjure us up at any time to provide the needed care.

One client who had struggled to separate from an addictive relationship that kept her trapped for many years told me that recently she has been enjoying chatting with strangers at bus stops, accepting assistance when offered, and even asking for help when needed. I stopped her for a moment and commented: "Hang on—you're beginning to sound like someone securely attached! Whatever has happened to the avoidant, self-sufficient woman I know?!" She acknowledged that, when she approaches others with openness, she is frequently rewarded with a surprising warmth and helpfulness that is challenging her perceptions of the world. Her response: "I may have to blame you for that!"

References

Achotegui, J. (2019). Migrants living in very hard situations: Extreme migratory mourning (the Ulysses syndrome). *Psychoanalytic Dialogues*, 3: 252–268.

Bowlby, J. (1980). *Attachment and Loss. Vol. 3. Loss: Sadness and Depression.* London: Hogarth.

Dutton, D. G., & Painter, S. (1993). *Emotional Attachments in Abusive Relationships: A Test of Traumatic Bonding Theory.* https://researchgate.net/publication/15006319_Emotional_Attachments_in_Abusive_Relationships_A_Test_of_Traumatic_Bonding_Theory (last accessed 5 February 2025).

Ein-Dor, T. (2014, 10 December). Facing danger: How do people behave in times of need? The case of adult attachment styles. *Frontiers in Psychology. Cognitive Science Section, 5.* https://doi.org/10.3389/fpsyg.2014.01452

Ein-Dor, T., & Perry, A. (2014). Full house of fears: Evidence that people high in attachment anxiety are more accurate in detecting deceit. *Journal of Personality, 82*: 83–92. https://doi.org/10.1111/jopy.12035

Erschak, G. M. (1984). The escalation and maintenance of spouse abuse: A cybernetic model. *Victimology, 9*: 247–253.

Fonagy, P., & Target, M. (1998). An interpersonal view of the infant. In: A. Hurry (Ed.), *Psychoanalysis and Developmental Therapy* (pp. 3–31). London: Karnac.

Holmes, J. (2001). *The Search for the Secure Base: Attachment Theory and Psychotherapy.* Hove, UK: Brunner-Routledge.

Johnson, M. P. (2004). Patriarchal terrorism and common couple violence: Two forms of violence against women. In: H. T. Reis & C. E. Rusbult (Eds.), *Close Relationships: Key Readings* (pp. 471–482). London: Taylor & Francis.

Liotti, G. (1992). Disorganized/disoriented attachment in the etiology of the dissociative disorders. *Dissociation, 5*(4): 196–204.

Lotfi, M. (2023). *The Wrong Person to Ask.* Hexham, UK: Bloodaxe.

Mehler, J. A. (2022). Immigration, loss and memory. In: J. Szekacs-Weisz & W. Ward (Eds.), *Lost Childhood and the Language of Exile* (pp. 168–181). Bicester, UK: Phoenix.

Mestyanek Young, D. (2022). *Uncultured: A Memoir.* New York: St. Martin's.

Morgan-Davies, K. (2018). *Caged Bird: A Memoir.* London: Bantam.

Vaknin, S. (1999). *Malignant Self Love: Narcissism Revisited.* Czech Republic: Narcissus.

van der Kolk, B. (1989). The compulsion to repeat the trauma: Re-enactment, revictimization and masochism. *Psychiatric Clinics of North America, 12*(2): 389–411.

Walker, L. (1980). *The Battered Woman.* New York: Harper and Row.

Index